D0725146

Praise for **TRANSFORMATIONAL ENCOUNTERS**

"*Transformational Encounters* is a smart, thoughtful, and pace-setting collection of essays that will help us reimagine student affairs praxis. The beautiful narratives of the thought leaders in this volume provide extraordinary road maps for the next generation of leaders who seek positive transformation in the world."

—AJAY NAIR, President, Arcadia University

"*Transformational Encounters* is an excellent resource for institutions that espouse a commitment to hiring racially and ethnically diverse leaders yet fail to enact this goal. The narratives and vital information contained in this book are instructive, honest, and can significantly contribute to the continued increase of senior higher education and student affairs professionals who can and will facilitate greater equity, diversity, and inclusion on college campuses across the country."

—LORI PATTON DAVIS, Professor of Higher Education and Student Affairs, Indiana University

"This book teaches us what other leadership books often ignore: lessons learned from the experiences of people of color who rise against adversity to become among the nation's most exceptional leaders. These 10 highly respected higher education leaders provide an inspirational, thought-provoking account of leadership shaped by lessons from early upbringing, vigorous work ethic, mentoring, resilience, family support, social justice consciousness, and spiritual nobility. If you seek to join the ranks of the next generation of higher education leaders, look no further than these uplifting stories from extraordinary individuals to become your inspiration and to transform your own views of leadership itself."

—LAURA I. RENDÓN, Author of *Sentipensante Pedagogy: Educating for Wholeness, Social Justice and Liberation*

"This unique and highly readable book blends personal storytelling with professional analysis, making it a very useful guide for leadership development. The stories are not only engaging and inspirational, but also insightful and instructive. What is most impressive is these stories are being told by people of diverse backgrounds who are in or have been in high-level leadership positions, rather than by consultants or scholars who have never served in such positions."

—BOB H. SUZUKI, President Emeritus,
California State Polytechnic University, Pomona

"*Transformational Encounters* is a thoroughly engaging and creative approach to the topic of leadership and leadership development. The book contains compelling narratives by 10 former or current senior leaders in student affairs about their journeys to their roles, along with the roles that mentors have played. Significantly, each chapter also includes brief commentary by the person who hired them. This book makes an important contribution to the literature on leadership and to leadership development efforts across the country."

—DARYL G. SMITH, Senior Research Fellow and Professor
Emerita of Education and Psychology, School of
Educational Studies, Claremont Graduate University

TRANSFORMATIONAL ENCOUNTERS

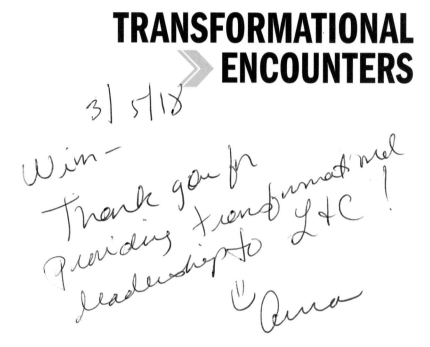

3| 5/18

Win —
Thank you for
Providing transformational
leadership to L+C !
♡ Ama

100 YEARS
1919 2019
NASPA®
Student Affairs
Administrators in
Higher Education

TRANSFORMATIONAL
ENCOUNTERS

Shaping Diverse College and University Leaders

EDITORS

**Anna K. Gonzalez, Doris M. Ching,
Lori S. White, and Robert D. Kelly**

Foreword by Kevin Kruger

100 YEARS
1919 2019
NASPA®
Student Affairs
Administrators in
Higher Education

NASPA®
Student Affairs
Administrators in
Higher Education

Copyright © 2018 by the National Association of Student Personnel Administrators (NASPA), Inc. All rights reserved.

Published by
NASPA–Student Affairs Administrators in Higher Education
111 K Street, NE
10th Floor
Washington, DC 20002
www.naspa.org

No part of this publication may be reproduced, stored in a retrieval system, or transmitted in any form or by any means, now known or hereafter invented, including electronic, mechanical, photocopying, recording, scanning, information storage and retrieval, or otherwise, except as permitted under Section 107 of the 1976 United States Copyright Act, without the prior written permission of the Publisher.

Additional copies may be purchased by contacting the NASPA publications department at 202-265-7500 or visiting http://bookstore.naspa.org.

NASPA does not discriminate on the basis of race, color, national origin, religion, sex, age, gender identity, gender expression, affectional or sexual orientation, or disability in any of its policies, programs, and services.

Library of Congress Cataloging-in-Publication Data

Names: Gonzalez, Anna K. editor.
Title: Transformational encounters : shaping diverse college and university
  leaders / Anna K. Gonzalez, Doris M. Ching, Lori White, and Robert Kelly, editors.
Description: First edition. | Washington, DC : NASPA-Student Affairs
  Administrators in Higher Education, [2018] | Includes index. | Description based on
  print version record and CIP data provided by publisher; resource not viewed.
Identifiers: LCCN 2017052159 (print) | LCCN 2018003722 (ebook) | ISBN
  9781948213004 (eBook) | ISBN 9780931654671 (pbk.) | ISBN 9781948213028 (hbk.)
Subjects: LCSH: Student affairs services--United States. | Student affairs
  administrators--United States--Anecdotes. | Educational leadership--United
  States. | Education, Higher--Aims and objectives--United States.
Classification: LCC LB2342.9 (ebook) | LCC LB2342.9 .T73 2018 (print) | DDC
  378.1/97--dc23
LC record available at https://lccn.loc.gov/2017052159

Printed and bound in the United States of America

FIRST EDITION

The editors wish to give special thanks to Kirsten R. Fix, who served as project manager for this book project.

Contents

Foreword

Kevin Kruger

I n 2011, for the first time in U.S. history, the percentage of babies born who were non-White topped 50% (U.S. Census Bureau, 2012). In fact today, children under the age of 18 who are non-White account for 48% of the total U.S. population (Colby and Ortman, 2015). For today's youth, the United States is nearly a minority-majority country, and these young people under the age of 18 will be our future college students. Today, we are already seeing annual increases in racial and ethnic diversity among college students: 42% of college students between 18 and 24 years old are not White (U.S. Department of Education, National Center for Education Statistics, 2016).

We will not have to wait another 15 to 18 years for the issues around racial and ethnic diversity to become significant ones for our students. While the 2015 University of Missouri protests will be remembered as the start of a new wave of activism around race and equity, in fact

Kevin Kruger draws on more than 30 years of experience in higher education. He joined NASPA–Student Affairs Administrators in Higher Education as associate executive director in 1994 and became its first executive-level president in 2012. He represents NASPA in national forums such as the Washington Higher Education Secretariat, which includes the leaders of approximately 50 higher education associations. He has published and presented nationally on leadership development, the use of technology in student affairs administration, international education, change management, and trends in higher education.

the anger and frustration of college students have been increasing over the past several years. Students have found their voice with regard to these issues. They are challenging colleges and universities on a wide range of issues related to equity, inclusion, diversity, power, and privilege. Students are asking for their colleges to address issues of systemic racism and racial injustice and to provide resources and staffing that support the wide range of racial and ethnic identities represented at their institutions. They are demanding that their faculty and institutional leaders reflect the diversity of the student body itself. Many of the demands from student activists across the country relate to increasing the number of faculty of color.

The sad truth is that the representation of faculty of color at most colleges is well below the diversity represented in the student body. On most campuses, the percentage of Black faculty is between 2% and 4%, and as recently as 2015, "no state's 'flagship' public university campus had a black faculty population approaching [10 percent]" (Thompson & Walsh, 2015, para. 2). Similar findings exist when we examine the data on college presidents. Historically, the percentages of college presidents of color nationally do not reflect the racial and ethnic diversity of today's college student body. In the most recent American College Presidents Study, only 17% of respondents were presidents of color (Gagliardi, Espinosa, Turk, & Taylor, 2017). At U.S. independent colleges, presidents of color actually declined from 8% in 2006 to 6% in 2011 (Song & Hartley, 2012).

It has been a slightly different story for student affairs leadership over the past decade. NASPA's 2015 Vice President for Student Affairs Census found that 20% of VPSAs identified as either Black or Hispanic. At public four-year institutions, 27% of VPSAs were either Black or Hispanic (NASPA, 2015). Although there are no national data on the racial and ethnic breakdown of student affairs professionals, data from The Placement Exchange (TPE) events in 2015 and 2016 suggest that student affairs professionals are more diverse than other sectors in higher education. Sixty-one percent of candidates looking for a job at TPE in 2015 identified as White. Sixty-nine percent identified as White in TPE 2016. The fact that between 31% and 39% of candidates (most of whom are graduate students or young professionals) are non-White attests that student affairs has become a more racially and ethnically diverse profession, and this is why this book is so important for the future of student affairs and the role senior leaders in student affairs play in shaping equity and diversity policy and programs for colleges and universities.

The authors here reflect the best of student affairs. They represent a range of trailblazers who have provided critical leadership around issues of social justice. They have challenged racial injustice and policies at their own institutions to make their campuses models of inclusive excellence. Perhaps more important, they have served as mentors, coaches, and role models for young and mid-level professionals who aspire to college and university leadership. In their writing and presentations they represent a moral compass for student affairs—a lived example of what student affairs should be when at its best.

Students benefit from senior-level role models who reflect their own racial and ethnic and gender identities. More important, "having leaders from a wide range of backgrounds and experiences enriches the intellectual and cultural climate in which students learn. And exposure to and experience working with people from different cultural backgrounds better prepares students for the real-world working environment of their futures" (Azziz, 2014, para. 8). This is the power represented in the 10 stories contained in this book. They are stories worth reading.

References

Azziz, R. (2014, April 24). Back to the future: Why is the diversity of university leadership stuck in the '80s? *Huffington Post*. Retrieved from http://www.huffingtonpost.com/dr-ricardo-azziz/back-to-the-future-college-presidents_b_5200573.html

Colby, S. L., & Ortman, J. M. (2015, March). *Projections of the size and composition of the U.S. population: 2014 to 2060* (Publication No. P25-1143). Retrieved from U.S. Census Bureau website: https://www.census.gov/content/dam/Census/library/publications/2015/demo/p25-1143.pdf

Gagliardi, J., Espinosa, L., Turk, J., & Taylor, M. (2017). *The American College President Study: Key findings and takeaways*. Retrieved from American Council on Education website: http://www.acenet.edu/news-room/Pages/American-College-President-Study.aspx

NASPA–Student Affairs Administrators in Higher Education. (2015). *NASPA vice president for student affairs census*. Retrieved from http://census.naspa.org

Song, W., & Hartley, H. V., III. (2012). *A study of presidents of independent colleges and universities*. Retrieved from The Council of Independent Colleges website: https://www.cic.edu/r/r/Documents/CIC_PresSurvey2012.pdf

Thompson, C., & Walsh, G. M. (2015, November 15). Missouri would likely be alone with 10 percent black faculty. *Associated Press Big Story*. Retrieved from http://bigstory.ap.org/article/f8c454994227483fae71796bcfd4b6fe/missouri-would-likely-be-alone-10-percent-black-faculty

U.S. Census Bureau. (2012, May 17). Most children younger than age 1 are minorities, Census Bureau reports. Retrieved from http://www.census.gov/newsroom/releases/archives/population/cb12-90.html

U.S. Department of Education, National Center for Education Statistics. (2016). *Digest of education statistics: 2015*. Retrieved from https://nces.ed.gov/programs/digest/d15/ch_3.asp

Introduction

Anna K. Gonzalez

I n March 2015, Lori White, Rob Kelly, and I were part of a panel of vice presidents for student affairs (VPSAs) at the NASPA Annual Conference. One by one, my colleagues and I shared our stories about how we became deans and vice presidents. As I listened, I thought of "The Danger of a Single Story," Chimamanda Ngozi Adichie's 2009 TED Talk. Adichie argued that if told enough times, a particular narrative becomes a single truth that defines entire groups of people. Over time, these narratives oversimplify the rich and complex history and sociopolitical reality of entire nation states and their citizenry, particularly those from subordinate communities. Adichie's message is not just about the danger of assuming one truth about a particular group; there is the other danger of a group starting to live up to that story, regardless of whether there is truth in the narrative.

When asked about our journeys within higher education and our journeys as executive leaders, all of us have had to avoid the trap of recounting *how* we came to be in our professions. Some of us didn't just fall into higher education by serendipity or accident: some of us were tapped for leadership roles. Others had mentors who helped them along the way. And still others found that pursuing this position, as a person of color, was about transforming the lives of those who come from disenfranchised communities. Although we all have many stories, what binds us together is that we all, at some point, have served within a division of student affairs *and* we identify as leaders from diverse backgrounds.

DIVERSITY IN ACADEME

A diverse faculty and staff reflect an important measure of success for an educational institution in a pluralistic society (Smith, 2009). Recent gains in diversifying higher education, as compared with 30 years ago, have become more evident as more individuals from racialized minority communities have assumed leadership positions—from VPSAs to presidents of colleges and universities (NASPA, 2004). Despite these gains, demographic data show that the number of individuals from underrepresented racial and ethnic backgrounds in executive, managerial, and administrative positions is still significantly lower than that of White individuals in similar roles.

A comparison of executive, administrative, and managerial categories by race and ethnicity in degree-granting institutions revealed the following: Whites, 80.0%; Blacks, 9.7%; Hispanics, 4.6%; Asian Americans/ Pacific Islanders, 2.9%; and American/Alaskan Natives, 0.6% (National Center for Education Statistics, 2010). Within student affairs, a survey of 7,762 members of NASPA–Student Affairs Administrators in Higher Education who work at U.S. institutions showed slightly higher gains made by individuals of color in that field, with 61% identified as White; 16%, African American; 8%, Hispanic; 4%, Asian American/ Pacific Islander; and 1%, American/Alaskan Native; the rest were multiracial or chose not to answer (Wang & Teranishi, 2012).

Recent calls for diversity among leadership within higher education—amid the growing population of professionals and students of color in academe—make this book a necessity. A 2017 study by the American Council on Education found that the demographic makeup of university presidents has not seen significant changes over the past 30 years (Gagliardi, Espinosa, Turk, & Taylor, 2017). One reason is that those from the senior administrative ranks of provosts and academic deans—from which presidents are often selected—are not diverse.

The narrowing racial gap in student affairs, as compared to that of other areas in higher education, provides an opportunity for highly qualified diverse individuals to be recruited for other positions in colleges and universities, such as the chief academic officer and even the president. Indeed, a 2015 *Chronicle of Higher Education* article posited that student affairs is an area from which colleges may select their next president because of the training and talent that make up the pool of individuals within that field (Gardner, 2015).

For instance, a 2014 report from NASPA, based on a comprehensive survey of VPSAs, revealed that Hispanic and Black VPSAs greatly outnumber their White counterparts in their aspirations to become college presidents (Wesaw & Sponsler, 2014). In fact, VPSAs are increasingly seen not only as members of the senior leadership but also as successful candidates for the presidency (Gardner, 2015). Because the authors here are clearly successful candidates for the presidency, this book offers instructive examples of how such institutional leadership has developed among people of color.

STUDENT AFFAIRS LEADERS AND TRANSFORMATIONAL ENCOUNTERS

Transformational Encounters: Shaping Diverse College and University Leaders is a collection of narratives and commentary from diverse individuals who are current or former VPSAs and from other higher education leaders who have worked in the area of student affairs. The authors discuss their successes and the barriers they faced in their careers, and they engage key concepts on achieving success as a professional, including the importance of collaboration, mentorship by White professionals and professionals of color, a clear concept of personal and institutional values, and a career map.

This book answers the following questions: How can the racial and ethnic gaps in leadership roles in higher education be addressed? What types of leadership development programs will provide individuals of color with the necessary skills and experiences to become prepared leaders in higher education? What educational, career, and other life choices did individual leaders grapple with as they pursued their administrative responsibilities? How did their racial identities help to shape their leadership development? In what ways did they provide transformational experiences for the students on their campuses? At the same time, how did they transform higher education to achieve inclusive excellence and equitable opportunities for groups and individuals?

The authors speak to their own leadership development as higher education professionals. They suggest possible answers to the question of how and why diverse administrators were selected for their executive positions. Narratives were invited not only from individuals who could respond to the problems raised by this volume, but also—perhaps just as important—from the executives who selected these diverse individuals for their positions to shed light on their reasons for doing so. Thus, this book is truly unique in staging conversations between the authors and their employers. Readers will benefit from discovering what presidents and board members look for when hiring a VPSA or president. Extending the uniqueness of the book further, a commentary in the form of an afterword by Gwendolyn Dungy, NASPA executive director emeritus, concludes each chapter.

This book plumbs the growing discourse related to racial discord in higher education. It responds to the dissonance that exists between the stated values of the institution and the ways in which colleges and universities act toward the students they are meant to serve. For instance, many college leaders insist that diversity is a core value, and yet, time and again, the flaws of their approach to its institutionalization have been demonstrated by the continuing underrepresentation of diverse officers among their ranks and by shortcomings in their curricular and cocurricular offerings. This book serves as a guide for student affairs professionals on how to balance their role as advocates for students without sacrificing their careers and limiting their institutions' ability to be effective in accomplishing the educational mission.

The personal narratives provide a window into understanding the unique and sometimes painful journey of leaders of color through higher education. The authors offer candid perspectives on the biopolitical processes that shape the existence of leaders of color, how the presence of these leaders in academe and their primary concerns are often reduced to *racial diversity* (i.e., as matters of demography, numerical representation, and racialized bodies)—even when the subject is furthest from their minds. Their stories illuminate the different reasons that led the authors to pursue their current positions and how their personal journeys have affected their leadership styles.

Finally, and perhaps the most compelling and imperative reason for this book, is the role of student affairs itself. Over the past decade, the VPSA role has become increasingly complex. VPSAs have had to deal with unprecedented governmental regulations, unfunded mandates, and demands to shrink their expenditures and increase revenue. Student affairs divisions are struggling to address the growing number of students who require more services for mental health issues and disabilities. In addition, student affairs leaders have had to raise their awareness of critical incidents, ranging from violence on campus to student protests, and develop procedures to respond to them. It is expected that tomorrow's students will ramp up their participation on various issues, such as criminal justice and environmental sustainability (Kueppers, 2016).

Student affairs has grown from its limited role of planning programs and events to developing institutional policies that address higher education's most critical issues. This book discloses the sense of purpose that enabled 10 leaders to successfully navigate the sometimes rough waters that accompany such transformations in higher education. It provides an intimate response to the two questions most often asked by students, junior professionals, and mid-level administrators when embarking on or persisting in a career in this field: Why student affairs? How do I succeed in this profession?

The inspiring stories that follow, which detail the careers and life choices of a wide array of higher education leaders, are intended to motivate and encourage readers. Most importantly, the commentaries shared by each author's mentor demonstrate the transformative power that people and events can exert on the individual journey.

References

Adichie, C. (2009). *The danger of a single story* [Video file]. Retrieved from https://www.ted.com/talks/chimamanda_adichie_the_danger_of_a_single_story

Gagliardi, J. S., Espinosa, L. L., Turk, J. M., & Taylor, M. (2017). *The American College President Study: Key findings and takeaways*. Retrieved from American Council of Education website: http://www.acenet.edu/news-room/Pages/Comprehensive-Demographic-Profile-of-American-College-Presidents-Shows-Slow-Progress-in-Diversifying-Leadership-Ranks.aspx

Gardner, L. (2015, March 26). New proving ground for the presidency: Student affairs. *The Chronicle of Higher Education*. Retrieved from http://www.chronicle.com/article/New-Proving-Ground-for-the/228907

Kueppers, C. (2016, February 11). Today's freshman class is the most likely to protest in half a century. *The Chronicle of Higher Education*. http://www.chronicle.com/article/Today-s-Freshman-Class-Is/235273

NASPA–Student Affairs Administrators in Higher Education. (2004). Ensuring a place at the table: Student affairs professionals of color share their perspectives. *Leadership Exchange, 2*(4), 5–9.

National Center for Education Statistics. (2010). *Digest of education statistics 2009* (NCES 2010-013). Retrieved from https://files.eric.ed.gov/fulltext/ED509883.pdf

Wesaw, A., & Sponsler, B. (2014). The chief student affairs officer: Responsibilities, opinions, and professional pathways of leaders in student affairs. Retrieved from https://www.naspa.org/images/uploads/main/CSAO_2014_FULLREPORT_DOWNLOAD.pdf

Smith, D. (2009). *Diversity's promise for higher education: Making it work*. Baltimore, MD: Johns Hopkins University Press.

Wang, H., & Teranishi, R. T. (2012). AAPI background and statistics: Perspectives on the representation and statistics of faculty, staff, and student affairs professionals. In D. Ching & A. Agbayani (Eds.), *Asian American and Pacific Islanders in higher education: Research and perspectives on identity, leadership, and success* (pp. 3–28). Washington, DC: NASPA–Student Affairs Administrators in Higher Education.

Richard Carvajal

Richard A. Carvajal is the 10th president of Valdosta State University. Prior to his appointment as interim president of Darton State College in 2015, Carvajal served as president of Bainbridge State College in Bainbridge, Georgia, from 2011 to 2015. Before joining the University System of Georgia, Carvajal was vice president for student success services at Cascadia Community College, dean of student services at Independence Community College, and associate dean of student services at Coker College. Carvajal holds a BS from East Central University, an MS from Southern Illinois University Carbondale, and a PhD from the University of South Carolina.

From Poverty to Purpose

Richard Carvajal

I n October 2011, after having just turned 40, I stood behind the podium and stared at an auditorium full of faculty, students, alumni, and other well-wishers, and I was scared to death. I wasn't frightened only by the thought of giving the biggest speech of my life; I was even more daunted by the task that lay before me—having to lead an institution, as I had recently been installed as president of a Southern college. In typical fashion, I began my inaugural remarks by acknowledging those in attendance as well as those who had played a role in my life and career, and while I was grateful to all of those whom I mentioned, I was particularly happy to be able to thank my long-time mentor, Gerald Williamson, who had traveled halfway across the country to be a part of the ceremony.

You see, it was tradition at my institution for someone from the new president's past to offer some reflections about the individual, and when I learned of this tradition, I knew that there was no one whom I wanted to be a part of that program more than Williamson. I obviously wanted him to see my big day, but I also knew that he would have a chance to tell my story to those assembled. I believe that you can learn a lot about someone by studying their past, and I wanted my audience, who did not yet know me that well, to get a better sense of who I was. As this chapter will clearly attest, few could hear my story without getting a pretty good understanding of what shaped me into someone who wanted to lead a college with the specific mission that ours fulfills.

IN THE BEGINNING

When I was growing up, my family was poor. No, I don't mean the living-paycheck-to-paycheck kind of poor. At my house, we grew up as card-carrying members of the I-wonder-if-the-lights-will-be-on-when-I-get-home socioeconomic club. Honestly, it wasn't always that way. I was born in Los Angeles to a father who was a successful furniture salesman and a mom who stayed at home with my older brother and me, and we were what most would describe as lower middle class—meaning, of course, that we didn't have a lot, but we had enough.

That changed, however, when I was 7 years old. My parents decided that the city was too dangerous a place to raise their two growing boys, and my dad accepted a transfer to a store in a rural community in northern California. It was a safe and beautiful place to call home, but what it didn't have was a lot of people who wanted to buy furniture. Soon my dad left that job, and after unsuccessfully trying a few other lines of work, he started a one-man janitorial business in an attempt to make ends meet. By *one-man*, I mean that the business wasn't large enough to support any other paid employees, but our entire family still had to help out. I can remember many a late night with my dad spent picking up trash, cleaning toilets, or waxing floors in one of the empty office buildings he cleaned after hours. We weren't rich, to be sure, but the single-wide trailer we lived in provided warm enough shelter, and I don't remember missing too many meals. If I'm being honest, I was pretty happy, as is evidenced by the fact that on my third-grade career day, I put on my best Sunday suit and proudly told my classmates that I, too, would someday be a janitor. I got some strange looks from my teacher and classmates, but I was proud of my dad and content in the life our family enjoyed.

That said, while I thought that my dad's new job brought in enough, the real truth was that paying the bills on time devolved into late or partial payments, before devolving further into no payments at all. Soon my parents got into trouble with the Internal Revenue Service, we lost our home, my dad had to sell his business, and we moved to faraway Oklahoma—which might as well have been a foreign county—on the promise of a good job that never materialized. The stress mounted, the fighting increased, and when I was 12 years old, my parents divorced.

While life as the son of a janitor may not have sounded like a lot of fun, it turned out that those years had clearly been the best of my childhood. Going forward, I learned what it meant to live in true poverty. Suddenly forced to be a single mom to my brother, me, and our two younger siblings, my mother kept a roof over our heads by doing one of the only jobs she was qualified to do: cleaning houses. We moved from one about-to-be-torn-down home that we could afford to another. In one case, my mom even spent an afternoon trying to convince my older brother and me that a house that had recently been condemned after being engulfed in fire was a great next spot; that one did not happen, but several others that were almost as bad did. When dinnertime rolled around, we ate with the help of food stamps, and I learned to love toasted sandwiches made with commodity cheese. We certainly did not have the benefit of air conditioning to survive the brutal Oklahoma summers. In fact, we often didn't even have lights, as it was embarrassingly common to come home to find, yet again, a disconnection notice on the front door.

One day in the late 1980s, when I was still in high school, things went from bad to much worse. My mother decided that she was no longer able to care for me, and after a short stint with my dad that similarly did not end well, I found myself living on my own in my old 1973 Ford Thunderbird. My bedroom became the back seat of my (frequently broken-down) vehicle, and a lonely streetlight in an otherwise dark public picnic area was my nightly address. While I honestly do not remember how long I stayed there, what I will never forget is the first night: I stared up at the dark sky and cried, wondering how things would ever get better.

Looking back, I realize that the chances of me finding any level of success were highly unlikely. After all, way too many people who grow up in such poverty never find their way out. But I had two big things going for me. (I will touch on one now; the second later on.) First, and miraculously, I continued to make school a priority. I could have dropped out, I guess, and some of my friends did. However, I liked school, and my own natural desire to compete led me not only to stay in school but also to make consistently good grades. At graduation, I was even named co-valedictorian. That honor came with a trophy and, more important, a scholarship, so off to college I went. My institution of choice—largely because it was the one I could afford—was a small regional public university where the tuition was only $35 per credit hour. My scholarship covered most of that amount, but student housing, at a cost of $88 per month, was not covered. That amount, plus the cost of food, had to be covered with the money I earned from a work-study job during the day and—no joke—an office-cleaning job in the evenings. After all, the skills I had picked up as a 10-year-old apprentice had to come in handy sometime, and in college, they allowed me to pay the bills and continue to progress term after term. I saw college as my opportunity for a better life, and I did my best to make the most of that chance.

In 1993, I earned my bachelor's degree but also gained something even more valuable. You see, during my first semester of college, I went to see a play staged by our college's theater department, and I saw someone on stage playing the role of a young woman looking for love, and I knew that I had to meet her. Thanks to a friend, I did, and for some reason, Cheryl actually said yes when I asked her out. What followed was a three-and-a-half-year courtship. Just a few weeks after walking across the stage to receive our bachelor's degrees, we walked down the aisle as husband and wife. Like so many of the things in my life, however, our union was not without its trials; to fully grasp the extent of our challenges, I have to go back a generation.

Long before my father was the successful furniture salesman I described earlier, he, too, grew up in tremendous poverty. A man of Mexican-American descent, my dad never knew his own father, who had chosen to run away from his young wife and new son when my dad was just a year old. While his mother ultimately remarried a working-class man who would, in so many ways, become my dad's true father and my beloved Grandpa Ray, none of that protected the family from financial hardship in what was still a largely segregated America. Despite the difficulties, my father—like his son would years later—stayed in school, and he worked his way out of the Los Angeles housing projects that had been his childhood home. While working as a cook at a local diner, he got to know a young White waitress, and the duo who would become my parents fell in love.

My mother, meanwhile, had grown up the oldest child of a sheriff. The family was middle class and had plenty; from all outward appearances, they were also seemingly happy. However, a closer look would have uncovered a violent father who regularly chose to discipline his children. He was also a racist, and his daughter falling for any person of color was unthinkable. It was that reality—coupled with a desire to do anything she could to show her dad that she could be her own person—that probably drew my mother to my father in the first place. Not too surprisingly, though, when she made the decision to marry my dad, her father responded by breaking off all contact with her and dis-owning her from the family.

Move ahead a generation, and once again a young man of Mexican-American descent chooses a White bride—this time, a blonde-haired young lady from a large Mormon family. The second oldest of seven children, Cheryl grew up very close to her parents and siblings. While she actually looks a good bit like my mother, the similarities of their childhood stop there. Cheryl's father was a large, stern man, but he never physically abused anyone, and he also taught his children ethnic tolerance from an early age. That said, the principles taught to a child can sometimes become much more difficult to live by when those same children grow into young adults and put those principles to the test. This unfortunately proved to be the case when Cheryl brought me home.

The parents who had always shown and taught love and acceptance had concerns that grew as our relationship became more serious. Ultimately, when Cheryl's parents realized that I wasn't just going to go away, the conflict came to a head. I asked for a meeting with her mom and dad to assure them that I loved and wanted the best for their daughter, but they responded by saying that they could not be sup-portive because they didn't like the way she acted around "someone like me." Shortly thereafter, I was asked to leave their home and not return, and Cheryl's parents broke off all ties with her when she failed to similarly cast me away. That's right, a generation later, when many would have at least hoped society had become more tolerant of such unions, history repeated itself, and my wife and our children have lived without the love and support of Cheryl's family ever since. Despite that, we have stayed together, and I have been the beneficiary of our union, having gained an amazing partner to aid me in my journey these past two-plus decades.

HELPING HANDS

I said earlier that my story happened largely as a result of two significant reasons. The first was clearly my persistent pursuit of education as a pathway to a better life. Whether it was staying in and finishing high school or, against all logic, continuing on to college to earn my undergraduate degree, I always saw education as an opportunity to become something more and to have a better life. That relentless push, coupled with an inherently competitive nature and a need for praise, meant that I did far more than just pass or get by; rather, I always worked hard to *excel*. I knew I was not the smartest student. My older brother is something of a genius, and compared to him, my mom called me her "well-rounded" child, mainly as a way to praise my other, nonacademic achievements, such as sports. However, when I had exhausted my limited talents on the playing field and began to focus all of my competitive energies inside the classroom, I worked my way to good grades and academic recognition, ultimately earning the award as my college's top graduate.

I did not achieve all this on my own, though. To fully understand my story, you must see the other significant reason I exceeded expectations. Along with the support of a loving partner over the years, I have also been extraordinarily lucky that so many people have helped me reach the point where I am today. Without their help—help of so many variations, given for so many different reasons—I would never have made it. Every time I took a major step back or stalled, someone took the time to reach out and lend me a helping hand. Much has been written over the years about the importance of having a good mentor, and if my story is anything, then it is clear proof that someone fortunate enough to have multiple mentors—people who become trusted supporters who invest some of themselves in a younger friend or colleague—can climb mountains they never would have been able to climb on their own.

The first extended hand of support came at a time when I needed it most. My home had become my car, in that lonely park I described before, and I was surviving on the little money I made washing dishes at a hotel restaurant. As you know, I was also still attending high school, and I had formed a close friendship with one of my classmates, James McKee. Through my parents' struggles, he offered words of support whenever he could; however, after I began living in my car, he decided to do more. McKee went to his parents and told them my story. As their son's new best friend, I had, of course, met them, but we weren't close. Nonetheless, when they heard where I was living, Jim and Shirley McKee reached out to me and asked if I'd consider staying with them. I could share a bedroom with my friend, have access to warm food and a shower, and stay as long as I needed. Looking back, their singular, generous offer undoubtedly changed my life. Yes, I gained a roof over my head, but I also gained so much more. I was reminded what it was like to live in a supportive family, and I began to hope that someday I, too, could have a close family of my own.

Skip ahead a few years. With the help and encouragement of my friend's family, along with countless others, I made it through my first year of college and returned for my sophomore year. I had just spent that summer working as a cook's helper in a less-than-glamorous state-run lodge, trying to earn enough money to support myself in the year ahead, and, truth be told, I still wasn't sure my education would lead to anything more than the restaurant or janitorial work that had supported me thus far. However, a life that had been full of challenge truly became one full of opportunity when a faculty member stopped me in the hallway and gave me a strange note.

To understand the significance of this next step, one needs to grasp the mindset I had at the time. I had overcome significant obstacles to finish high school, and although, in retrospect, tying with 3 others at the top of a graduating glass of just 28 people isn't really that big of an accomplishment, the fact is that I nonetheless had a valedictorian's trophy. Therefore, one would have assumed that I headed to college with a significant amount of self-confidence when it came to academics. Of course, anyone who would do so would be dead wrong. Instead, I understood all too well that I had graduated from a very poor high school. I had earned top honors despite setting my high school's record for most days missed in a single year (while still passing). In fact, I had not attended an entire class day once during my senior year—not once. Often, I was away from class to compete in an athletic event or to take part in some other school-related activity, but plenty of days were also spent hanging out at the lake with friends or sleeping in. One day, I did not even arrive at school until the start of basketball practice at 2 p.m., only to be pulled aside by my head coach—who also happened to be the principal—so that he could warn me that, in the future, if I was going to skip school, I needed to skip the entire day, because coming just for practice made him look bad. I agreed, and then he sent me back to my teammates to resume practice as if nothing had happened. At my school, this was not unusual; it was the norm. Given that the two previous valedictorians from my school had flunked out of college, one would assume that school leaders would recognize the need for change. Ultimately, they did, and the school is much better today. At the time, though, the norms were lax, and I took advantage of that freedom.

I knew, however, that much more would be required of me when I went to college, and I did not know if I could succeed under higher demands and expectations. I honestly assumed that it would just be a matter of time before someone at my college realized that I was not good enough, that I did not belong. As a result, when I arrived for my freshman year of college, I was terrified. My high school transcript said that I had been a stellar student, but I saw myself as nothing more than just the latest unprepared product of a bad school.

One day during my first semester, the head of the honors program reached out to me; after telling me that he had reviewed my very good high school record, he invited me to join the program. I replied with an answer he had likely never heard before. I said, "Honestly, sir, I'm just hoping I don't flunk out of this place," and I declined his offer. Staring back at me with a look of shock, he wished me well and allowed me to leave.

Full of that fear and knowing that college was my one and only possibility for a better life, I approached every class my first semester like it was my last chance. To my thinking, if I did not give a class everything I had, I would fail it and be sent home. Even after making a 4.0 GPA my first semester, I approached every class in my second semester with just as much fear. I know now that one does not go from the honor roll to the academic suspension list easily or quickly, but no one could have convinced me of that back then. So, when my professor handed me a note one day during the fall semester of my sophomore year, indicating that our institution's vice president for student services wanted to see me in his office, I truly thought someone had finally figured out that I was not good enough to be there; in my mind, I was about to be told to go home.

MEETING MY PROFESSIONAL FATHER

Note in hand, I gathered myself and made the long, thoughtful walk across campus to the administration building, where Gerald Williamson's office was located. I can't say that I was nervous as I entered his office; I was resolved to what was about to happen. I introduced myself to the serious-looking woman who served as the gatekeeper to the student services office, telling her about the note I had received. She asked me to have a seat, and I waited for my chance to meet with the most important man I had ever met. Minutes later, the gatekeeper walked me into that man's office.

Behind a large wooden desk sat a White man with salt-and-pepper hair and glasses, looking as serious as his administrative assistant. He asked me to have a seat and went right into why he had summoned me there. His reasons were not those I had expected. He told me that my name had been identified in a computer search of ethnic minority students who were doing well in the classroom; as such, he wanted to invite me to be the college's nominee for a national minority leaders internship and leadership development program in Washington, D.C., for the following summer. Only 65 students would be selected nationally, he told me, so there was certainly no guarantee I would be accepted, but he felt that I stood a good shot and should apply. If you assume I jumped out my chair with excitement and immediately said yes, you should reread the earlier parts of this story. Instead, every part of me wanted to tell him "no thanks" right then. I feared not getting the internship or—worse—being accepted into the program and then failing miserably. Thankfully, I did not turn him down right then; with his encouragement and the support of several others, including Cheryl, I ultimately accepted his invitation. I submitted my application later that fall, and in early spring, I received a congratulatory letter telling me that, come summer, I would be working in Washington, D.C.—not in yet another restaurant kitchen.

That summer, despite being surrounded by students from the Ivy League and other prestigious institutions, I did not fail. On the contrary, despite my fear of failure (or perhaps because of it), I did well in my internship and was even elected by my peers to serve as the program's main student representative.

But I certainly did not find such success there on my own. Williamson's influence had not stopped the day we sent off my application; instead, he had spent months coaching me for the big game that lay before me (he had once been a successful basketball coach). He gave me advice about what to expect, helped me find an internship that would provide real-world experience and open up new opportunities, and even arranged for me to meet an old friend of his who just happened to be the sitting head of one of the nation's two political parties. Williamson also arranged for an introduction to our local U.S. representative, a meeting that led to another fellowship in D.C. the following summer. What's more, after I had boarded my first-ever airplane ride and begun my program, he checked in on me regularly. Long before the days of e-mail, Williamson sent me several letters and called me on the phone. His support meant the world to me, and when I returned to campus the following fall, it continued. He arranged for me to be featured in several news reports about my experience, and he secured an invitation for me to speak to our state's higher education governing board about my experience. Then, midway through my junior year, he told me that he had another opportunity he wanted me to consider.

NASPA–Student Affairs Administrators in Higher Education had just launched a new pilot program in hopes of attracting more talented ethnic minority students into the profession. The new NASPA Undergraduate Fellows Program would pair a student interested in joining the student affairs field with a professional mentor whose job it would be to educate his or her protégé about such a career. Williamson told me that he thought I had the ability to help future students like me, students who needed encouragement and guidance to achieve their potential. I could pursue the kind of work Williamson did as a career of my own, and I was intrigued by that opportunity; I also very much wanted to continue working with him. So, I filled out the necessary application and was accepted into the introductory class of fellows for a national mentoring program that is now nearing its 25th anniversary and that has become one of the most successful of its kind in higher education. More important, I "officially" entered into what was supposed to be a yearlong mentoring relationship, but my work with Williamson evolved into a lifelong friendship—one of the most important connections in my life. As my primary mentor, he has had a hand in every professional move I have ever made, and he's been a source of advice for most of the significant personal moves I've made, too. I have said many times that everything I ever have been or ever will be, I owe to Gerald Williamson.

MORE MENTORS

As impactful as my relationship with Williamson has been, my path from a poor upbringing to a purposeful career was paved by others as well. I have been blessed by the support and guidance of more caring mentors throughout my career than anyone could possibly deserve.

Cheryl and I pursued our master's degrees at Southern Illinois University Carbondale (SIUC). She wanted an English literature program, and I wanted a degree in college student personnel administration, and SIUC had well-respected programs in both disciplines. However, the longtime head of the academic program I had chosen accepted another position and was replaced before my arrival, and I was unsure, at first, what faculty support I would find. James Wallace, an African American man with broad leadership experience, returned to his alma mater to teach and govern my academic program. Again, I was extremely fortunate, for Wallace quickly took a personal interest in me, and my next mentoring friendship developed.

Wallace challenged me in so many ways during my two years in the program. He had an amazing ability to see any issue from all sides, and he worked hard to make sure that his students developed the same skill. Wallace talked me into writing a thesis instead of taking comprehensive exams, despite my being dead set against the idea. It would be more difficult, but he knew the exercise would provide me with invaluable experience when I pursued a doctorate and needed to write a dissertation. Finally, he challenged me to lead, encouraging me to run for the presidency of our program's student organization midway through my first year of graduate study, and he then gave me significant responsibilities after I was elected, including helping him recruit new students and guide the incoming class after they arrived. Because Wallace held me up as a leader, the other students in our graduate program did so also, leaning on me regularly for advice and direction. In turn, I began to see, within myself, at least the potential to become a leader in my field.

That was particularly evident when Wallace, during my second year of graduate school, paired up with our university's vice president of student affairs to send me to a NASPA New Professionals Institute. There, I was challenged to think about my future by creating a career map that forecast where I would be in 3, 5, 10, and 20 years. I laid out an aggressive professional path that included being a director by my 20s, a dean by my 30s, and ultimately, a vice president. Like my mentors back home, the institute's faculty who helped me create that pathway encouraged me to believe that such a progression was realistic and obtainable. Only a few years after being sure someone would realize that I did not belong, I, too, began to believe that the path I had put down on paper was possible.

With my program nearing completion, I began to look for a job. After all, a written career map is all well and good, but everyone who has ever neared the completion of a student affairs graduate program has stressed over whether anyone would hire them. Like so many others, I went to a national conference, participating in its career center in hopes of someone giving me my next shot. Getting a job was not a given, as most of my experience was in student affairs areas where few entry-level jobs exist, and schools are usually looking for candidates with some level of prior full-time experience for the jobs they are trying to fill.

But I was lucky: One day, I found a handwritten note in my mailbox at the career center. The senior student affairs officer for a small private liberal arts college that just so happened to be the alma mater of former

U.S. President Ronald Reagan had sent me the note. Instead of inviting me to the brief 15-minute screening interview typical at these conferences, Dale Martin met me for lunch at the hotel restaurant. We talked for more than two hours about anything and everything other than his school, the job he had available, or my qualifications. Although I honestly don't remember much about what we did discuss, other than the challenges of coaching sixth graders on the basketball court (something we realized we both had done), I do remember that we laughed a lot, and it was a fun exchange.

At the end of the meal, as we were getting up to leave the restaurant, he told me that he was looking to hire a director of housing and asked me if I would be willing to come to his campus with my wife the next week for an extended interview. I told him that I did not have any experience in student housing, never having been as much as a resident assistant in my own college days. He said he knew that but still hoped we would visit. I agreed, and a week later, I was formally offered a job that included overseeing residence life at an institution where more than 90% of the students lived in on-campus housing and where I would be supervising a staff of several professional resident directors and student resident assistants. To say that my learning curve was huge would be the understatement of all time, but gradually I learned how to run a successful operation. The college's board chair even chose me to lead a new master planning committee, and our group ultimately completed the institution's first comprehensive facilities plan in more than 20 years.

While I will never know what led Martin to invite me to lunch, or what he saw in me that day we first met, what I do know is that the experience I gained during my time at that institution greatly accelerated my career progression. It also gave me confidence that I could take the kind of big leaps that are often required to move up to positions of greater responsibility: I knew I could hold my own while I learned the lessons necessary to do the job well.

LIFE AS A NUMBER TWO

Over the next few years, I moved into progressively more challenging administrative positions; gained valuable experience in front of
the classroom teaching communications; and, with the continued
help of my mentors, completed my doctoral degree. When those
same mentors told me it was time, I applied for and was ultimately
appointed to my first cabinet-level role. Over the next nearly eight
years, I would occupy two such positions, first at a small rural college
in Kansas, and then at a new suburban, nationally ranked college in
Washington state. Along the way, I reported directly to three presidents, and for some reason that I will never fully grasp, all three of
them took a personal interest in my learning and advancement, and
all three of them—like Williamson and Wallace before—played a
significant role in my accelerated career trajectory.

Judith Hansen was the first of these difference makers. A review of
my résumé will show that Hansen hired me to my first executive-level
position when she made me her senior student affairs officer in 2003.
What that résumé doesn't tell you is that, as lucky as I was to get that
kind of opportunity at just 32 years of age, she actually had to offer it
to me twice. When she initially offered me the position, I worried that
the college's challenges would be too much for me to handle. However,
two weeks after I declined her offer, Hansen did something that I have
never heard of elsewhere. She actually invited me back to campus for a
second look—no commitment needed, no strings attached. She feared
that I had not had a chance to see everything at the college, and she
said, this time, I could set my own agenda to explore the institution
and community in more detail. She also asked me to bring my wife for
this second visit, and when Cheryl made it clear following our time on
campus that she thought I was an idiot for turning the job down the
first time, I accepted Hansen's offer.

Once there, Hansen and I hit it off almost immediately, and she entrusted me with an unusual level of autonomy as I sought to make the necessary improvements. What's more, she confided in me often about the challenges she was facing as leader of the entire institution, regularly asked for my advice regarding such matters, and often challenged me to step out of my comfort zone and broaden my skill set by joining her in representing the college's interests in the community.

Hansen told me that I had the potential to someday follow in her footsteps as the president of a college, and she sought to mold me into such a leader. Ironically, from the beginning I went out of my way to tell her and anyone else who would listen that I never wanted to be a president. However, she continually encouraged me to consider the possibility, and one day she called me into her office to tell me that she had nominated me for a Future Presidents Institute and had reached out to the program's director to tell him about me. While acknowledging that she knew that I did not aspire to such a role, she said she hoped that I would someday change my mind. She wanted to make this learning opportunity possible for me while she still had the chance. As it turned out, Hansen soon thereafter accepted another presidency elsewhere, making me even more grateful today that she took that step when she did. The Future Presidents Institute was a game changer for me. On the first day of the institute, I was the only 1 of 35 participants to say I did not want to be a president, but by the end of the institute, I was not so sure. Institute director and longtime higher education leader Jeff Hockaday challenged our group to seek more leadership roles. If we had the *potential* to lead, said Hockaday, then we had the *responsibility* to do so.

Still, the career map I had created during graduate school did not include a presidency, and while the institute had gotten me thinking about the possibility, I was still a long way from actually pursuing the role. The main reasons were twofold. First, still just in my mid-30s, I obviously lacked the experience and wisdom that age and further growth would give me. Second, I had worked closely with several college presidents; I had seen the personal demands placed on those in this position, and I was not prepared for that level of commitment. Don't get me wrong: I worked extremely hard, and long hours were common. From my vantage point, however, it seemed that one had to put almost every other aspect of one's life on hold to be an effective president. The presidents I knew lived their lives with an almost singular focus on their work, and with a wife and young children at home, I knew that I never wanted my job to be so all-encompassing that I could not live a full life.

How grateful I am, therefore, that Terry Hetrick followed Hansen and became my new boss. While I have learned from every president and every position, Hetrick taught me the most important lesson. He was a highly effective and inspiring leader, and I saw him make those who worked for him believe that they could be better and that the college we led together could reach new heights. Of more lasting significance to me personally was that Hetrick did all this while making work just one part of a life extremely well lived. He worked with his senior leadership team to set a collective vision for where the institution should be headed and then fully empowered the members of that team to work toward that vision. He spent his time dramatically strengthening relationships in the community—something he clearly enjoyed doing—but he also started dating again, learned to play golf, spent time making and hanging out with new friends, and even took the occasional afternoon off just to take a nap when he was tired. He loved life as much as anyone I've ever known, and the effect was that all of us who worked with him were more relaxed, making the quality of our work better as a result.

One thing Hetrick did have in common with his predecessor was that he, too, took me under his wing. After suffering a heart attack, he regularly asked me to step in for him both on- and off-campus while he recovered, and we spent considerable time together when he was on campus, talking about various approaches to leading and living life to the fullest. When my stepfather passed away, Hetrick drove home the importance of life away from work, encouraging me to take a position closer to my just-widowed mother, who needed my help. Hetrick unfortunately passed away less than two years later, when his heart let him down one last time, but I will never forget the lessons taught to me by this amazing mentor and friend. Thanks to him, I saw that there was more than one way to be a successful college president, and I understood that I could do that and still have a full life away from work. For the first time, I accepted that once I had more experience—and if/when those I trusted told me I was ready—a college presidency might someday be in my future.

What I never could have expected was that my insanely good fortune would continue when I moved to suburban Seattle. In my new role as the vice president for student success at newly opened Cascadia College, I was a part of a once-in-a-lifetime opportunity to build a college from the ground up. It had been designed to be different, and those who worked there were challenged every day to pursue excellence in all that we did. That work led to an amazing learning environment that quickly earned national distinction. While being a part of such an experience was an amazing learning opportunity unto itself, my good fortune did not stop there. Yet again, I was able to learn from a highly effective leader and president. Bill Christopher gave me an outstanding lesson every day in what true collaborative leadership looks like. He gathered input, co-created a vision, garnered buy-in through what I began to refer to as "the art of the hallway conversation," and went out of his way to make people feel a part of the institution's growth.

Like so many before him, he also spent considerable time mentoring me. He let me have an insider's view into both the challenges and intrinsic rewards of serving as a college president. He expanded my job

duties to give me experience in academic affairs and community relations in order to ready me for myriad leadership areas and encouraged
me to accept a statewide leadership role to enhance my visibility. A few
years later, when several former mentors suggested that it was time for
me to consider making the big leap to a presidency, Christopher also
encouraged me to apply, and he began advising me on how to search
for a place that would be a good personal fit.

I was still anything but certain that I was ready, but throughout my
career, I had grown to trust my mentors to tell me when it was time for
me to consider the next big leap. Each time they had, a similar exchange
took place. I was sure I wasn't ready—I was too young, too inexperi-
enced, too unprepared for such a leap. If I did apply and somehow got
the job, just like the frightened college student years before, I believed
that someone would figure out that I did not belong and send me
packing. In turn, my mentors would tell me that I was ready. "If you
don't yet believe in Richard Carvajal," one of those mentors once told
me, "then believe in me." He added, "I know you can do it."

I did believe in them, and so time and time again, I had trusted my
mentors enough to overcome my fear and put myself out there. I knew
that I had reached the point where my application for a presidency
would even be considered only because all those people had invested
in me, given me opportunities and experiences before logic would say
that I was ready to handle them, and guided and supported me to boost
the chance that I could be successful. Now those same mentors were
saying that it was time for me to pursue a presidency. I was every bit as
afraid of this leap as I had been of any other in my past. In fact, given
the magnitude of the role that I was considering, I would be lying if I
did not admit to, in many ways, being more afraid. That said, I again
conceded that my mentors must know what they were talking about.

Of course, it was a lot to trust. After all, I was that same child who
had cleaned toilets with his dad on school nights. It was I who had

stared at the stars and cried as I wrapped my arms around the reality of homelessness. I, too, had been the young college student who declined the invitation to my college's honors program because I just hoped not to flunk out. Now, having benefited from the transformative power of education and the extraordinary support of those who felt I had much more to offer than I thought could ever be the case, I accepted that it was time to be a president.

Judith Hansen and Jeff Hockaday had convinced me that I should be open to such a role. James Wallace and Bill Christopher had taught me how to lead effectively. Terry Hetrick had showed me that I could do the job well while still being a good husband and father. Gerald Williamson had provided a constant reminder of why I had picked this profession in the first place. Because of their influence, I now accepted that I had the potential to lead, and as one of those mentors had suggested years earlier, that also meant that I now had the responsibility to do so. It was time to take that next big leap.

A DAILY CHANCE TO HELP SOMEONE LIKE ME

So an application was sent off, an interview was granted, and a few months later, there I was, standing behind that podium I described at the beginning of this narrative, having just been invested with the duties and responsibilities of my first presidency. As I said, to understand how I ended up here, it is important to first understand my story—a story that includes poverty, prejudice, the opportunities found in education, and many mentors investing in a kid with potential. Thanks to more good fortune than one person could ever hope to receive, I now have a story that culminates with my finding that "good fit" that the most recent of those great mentors encouraged me to discover, and today I serve as the leader of a wonderful institution devoted to access.

In some states, such institutions are referred to as technical colleges.

Other places call them community colleges. In still other locales, such as the place I now call home, they are known as state colleges. However, what all of these institutions have in common is that their mission is focused on broadening access to higher education, and their low cost and eased admissions standards make fulfilling that mission possible. The faculty and staff who choose to invest their talents at these access institutions often serve students who are ill-prepared and who have numerous personal obstacles to overcome.

I guess I could have chosen to work at a more prestigious institution, and I realize that some who are reading this may even be disappointed to learn that my story does not culminate at such a place. After all, I already mentioned that my first job after earning my master's degree was at the alma mater of a U.S. president. When in graduate school, my classmates and I—just like the scholars in student affairs graduate programs do today—all aspired to work at the *best* institutions we could, so such a landing spot was deemed by many to be a resounding success. In fact, my entire early career was spent at similarly selective private liberal arts colleges.

For me, though, my definition of *best* began to change when my wife got a telephone call one night. She had completed the coursework in her doctoral program and was preparing to write her dissertation. Once finished, her plan was to secure a permanent faculty position at the selective college that employed me. The call, however, was from a dean at a local community college. He had heard about her through a colleague and was calling to encourage her to apply for an open faculty position at his institution.

Cheryl saw the opening as a great opportunity to do what she loved to do: teach. She applied and was hired, and she began coming home with the kinds of stories that are very common at such institutions. One particular story stood out. It was the story of an older man who was too afraid to even get out of his car the first few times he drove to the college. He finally worked up the courage to open the car door, and he was directed to my wife, who became his faculty advisor. The day he walked across the stage to receive his degree was a great one for Cheryl, as she knew she had played at least some role in helping him reach that milestone.

As I heard her tell story after story of folks—like that successful advisee—who overcame much to accomplish their goals, I admittedly became a little jealous. Don't get me wrong: I loved my job, and I loved my students, many of whom I am still in touch with today. That said, working at a place with a $20,000 a year tuition bill meant that I didn't meet many students who reminded me of myself. Our students had gone to good schools, came from middle-class backgrounds or better, and were taught to believe from an early age that they could be whatever they wanted to be. But the students at Cheryl's college were like me: full of potential but also self-doubt. They faced very real obstacles—a lack of quality preparation, poverty, the many lingering effects of Southern racism, learning disabilities, broken homes, a history of substance dependency and/or incarceration, and much more. With these obstacles came the reality that many students would not make it, but when one did, it was life-changing. In fact, often an entire family was changed for the better. As I heard these stories, I remembered why I went into this profession in the first place: I wanted to pay forward the gifts that had been given to me by helping others who needed the same amount of help that I had needed. Why not work at a place, I reasoned, where students most frequently needed such help?

Today, I am doing just that. I—and others who choose to work at access colleges—help the next generation rise above their many challenges and achieve success beyond what they think is possible. These students' stories, like mine, prove why higher education truly is the opportunity business. I often remind my colleagues just how lucky we are to serve where we do. After all, in what other career can one go to work knowing that their mission that day is to change someone's life for the better? To those who are reading this book, I hope that you, too, find tremendous personal fulfillment in the work we do every day. I hope we all continue to recognize how lucky we are to get to do it. Finally, I hope we all continue to invest in those young protégés who similarly have the potential to someday make a difference for other students who long for a better life and a chance to achieve it.

ORO to *Oro*

Gerald Williamson

Oro *is the Spanish word for gold. A thread of this precious element runs through the story of Richard Carvajal. That said,* ORO *could also be an acronym for "Overcoming Rural Oklahoma," which likewise runs through his story.*

IN EACH STUDENT THERE IS GOLD

When matriculating freshmen enroll, they are the ore the institution has to work with for the next few years. Some ores are richer than others. But in each student, there is gold.

W hen the flier for a Washington, D.C., minority internship came in, my office completed an electronic search to identify underclassmen and women who had not only good grades but also—and just as important—campus involvement. East Central

---

After retiring in 2006 from East Central University in Oklahoma, Gerald Williamson has continued to support the university as a leader in institutional advancement. Prior to his retirement, he served as the school's vice president for student services from 1985 through 2006 after an equally distinguished tenure as a business faculty member and basketball coach. In October 2016, Williamson was inducted into the Oklahoma Higher Education Hall of Fame.

University's (ECU's) focus for its students has long been to create the total package: students who excel in and out of the classroom. The returned list was short due to the stringent search parameters I had set, and one name jumped off the page: Richard Carvajal.

During the application process, I realized that Richard and I had strikingly similar backgrounds: small public school education, a less-than-stellar home life, and an older brother—Richard's also attended ECU—who was smarter than a tree full of owls. However, we had our differences. He was brighter and more athletic, had a gift for acting, and was better looking. Someone had given me a chance years before, and I wanted to see if I could pay it forward. This was my chance.

GOLD MINING

The ore had been in the ground long enough; it was time to start mining.

When notification came that Richard had been accepted into the internship program, our preparation began, and two things came into focus. Richard was a fast learner with excellent retention and a truly fierce competitor; he wanted to do well. We set some goals for him to accomplish. Among them was for him to be the best intern—and, unequivocally, the hardest worker—in the group. One advantage of a rural Oklahoma upbringing is that you probably know how to work. Richard did.

The biggest thing we needed to overcome was Richard getting in his own way. He needed to realize the potential that I could already see in him. His growth during this internship was definitely noticeable and incredible. The boy from rural Oklahoma came back from our nation's capital a thirsty-to-learn college student who had proven to be the best in his fellowship program, a program that had included students from Ivy League and other high-profile schools.

Our debriefing on Richard's return to the ECU campus was rewarding for both of us. His exuberance was over the top, and his desire to learn was very evident. He began spending a lot of time hanging around the offices in the student services area. He wanted to see what we did, how we did it, and why we did it. He got his chance.

SHAPING THE GOLD

Pure gold is very malleable; you can do a lot with it.
So are college students who want to learn.

In the early 1990s, NASPA–Student Affairs Administrators in Higher Education identified the need to attract more people of color to careers in student services, so a program was developed—the Minority Undergraduate Fellows Program, today referred to as the NASPA Undergraduate Fellows Program. Because there is not an undergraduate major anywhere in "student affairs," the concept was to provide exposure for students of color to this career possibility, with the goal that such exposure would lead more minority students to consider master's programs in this field. The initial design of the program was for an ethnic minority student to shadow an ethnic minority director or dean two to three hours a week for a semester. This was a great concept—extremely timely for the whetting of Richard's interest—and I was willing to help. Richard did question whether our partnership would be accepted since I was not a minority. I told him with great indignation, "I am left-handed." Then I explained to him that it is always easier to blurt out an apology than to grovel for permission. Actually, I knew we were on solid ground. The designer of the NASPA program and I had attended a summer institute together and enjoyed a wonderful working relationship, and she was willing to let me be one of this pilot program's first mentors.

Truth be told, we didn't follow many parts of the newly conceived script. Richard's internship was for a full year instead of just one semester, he shadowed a vice president instead of a dean or director, we covered a multitude of student services areas where he did real hands-on work instead of just observing others doing work in one functional area, and we put in at least four times the required hours every week.

A trip with a recruiter to a high school was followed up with Richard making recruiting calls. He went on campus tours and scheduled tours for others. Another night—and we did pick a Thursday (ECU students' traditional party night)—Richard completed a ride-along with a university police officer.

Some humorous things happened along the way. For instance, one occurred when Richard organized and ran a 3-point/free-throw shooting contest as part of his time volunteering in intramural sports. There is not a recreation center or YMCA in our small town, and former college students and older high schoolers sometimes attempted to sneak in and play basketball in our recreational gym. It was a problem keeping track of who was enrolled and who was not supposed to be there. That gym served as the location for the event Richard orchestrated. Not surprisingly, it was well run, the participants had a great time, and it was very competitive. Eventually, a champion was crowned. It just wasn't an ECU student. A terrific teaching moment and really "no harm, no foul!"

Throughout the duration of his internship, Richard gained an awareness of what takes place in about a dozen student services areas. He was like a sponge. Each situation became a learning opportunity, and he did not forget what he learned. For example, he would often be in my office when I had a phone call or visitor with a problem or question. He asked me one day how I came to a conclusion and gave a response so quickly. "I cheated," I told him—I had simply faced the same issue before. That said, I encouraged him not to get hung up on problems. "We don't need problems; we need solutions," I told him. He got the point. During his entire career, he has *never* presented a problem to me for which he did not have a well thought-out and precisely articulated solution at hand.

ORO SHINES

We extracted the ore out of the ground and did the smelting; now it was time to get it to the jewelers.

While at ECU, Richard met the woman who would become his wife, and both excelled academically. When it came time for them to select a graduate school, the Carvajals used a Delphi technique. Independent of each other, Richard and Cheryl researched institutions that offered their majors, each creating their own preference list. They compared lists; identified the highest collective five, following a tabulation; and both of them applied to those same five schools. They created a great list, found the school that was best for both of them, and embarked on the next stage of their careers.

Richard demonstrated similar care in making all of his career choices along the way. Each stage of his career and professional maturation has added to his knowledge base, expanded his network of associates, and honed his self-confidence. He has had tremendous mentors along the way. Several of the people who have been instrumental in his rise to success are recognized in his narrative.

However, beyond that, an uncanny occurrence of opportunities has surfaced as he has advanced up the ladder of higher education leadership. At almost every stop along the way, Richard has faced some highly unique challenges. At one institution, in a community where town-and-gown rapport was already dismal at best, rival student bodies met with guns and shots were fired. At another, Richard was designated as the change agent for an institution that had grown since inception to be nationally recognized, but staff from the various departments in the functional unit he oversaw so disliked one another that they had refused to work together—no matter its impact on student success. In yet another, the need to strengthen academic progress standards after uncovering massive abuses in financial aid created significant drops in both enrollment and funding, all while the institution moved from a two-year to a four-year college. In his last position, he was even asked to help consolidate a predominantly White two-year college with a historically Black master's-degree-granting university 4.3 miles away in a city where Martin Luther King Jr.'s first organized attempts to encourage racial integration failed miserably.

Why has Richard Carvajal been the person chosen to navigate these troubled waters time and time again? *Oro* shines! Others could see that he possessed that so often talked about but seldom seen "it factor." He finds solutions to problems instead of a problem for every solution.

Richard is intelligent but has a ton of common sense. He is industrious and goal oriented; he is a tremendous speaker who also possesses the most vital of communication skills—the ability and willingness to listen. He is a problem solver, not a problem seeker. He learns from his experiences and asks questions to further his understanding, not to have decisions made for him. He cares and is most considerate of others—it is never about himself—and he takes care of his people with both praise and support.

In order to be able to make the most of those skills, Richard just needed to know what was out there, to be encouraged, to be shown that he wasn't destined for failure due to what was on his birth certificate, and to not get in his own way. I had the pleasure of finding a young Latino student who had not been raised with a silver spoon in his mouth. He and I took the ore, smelted it, and passed it on to the goldsmiths—his other mentors. They helped to produce a gold star. Simply put, ORO became *oro*.

Paraphrasing the late NFL Coach Bum Phillips's tribute to Hall of

Famer Earl Campbell, "Richard Carvajal may not be in a class of his own, but it damn sure won't take long to call the roll!" That said, the model we used years ago and the additional help Richard received from so many others thereafter, which is detailed in his narrative, can certainly be replicated in the lives of others. Future students and aspiring professionals can become stars of their own with the right help, and their lives, too, can turn into stories that will inspire us all.

Richard Carvajal's narrative, "From Poverty to Purpose," excellently illustrates and confirms what student affairs educators already know about what first-generation students need to encourage their success: motivation, support, and affirmation. Through his descriptions of the role of mentors in his life, Carvajal demonstrates that these same elements of motivation, support, and affirmation are critical for some first-generation college leaders.

Carvajal isolates two characteristics that motivated him to succeed despite poverty and prejudice. First, he saw education as an opportunity to become something more and have a better life. Second, he was competitive and had a need for praise, so he worked hard to excel. He was fortunate to have a friend whose family gave him a home when he was homeless during high school. He also credits his wife for her ongoing support.

Carvajal feels "lucky" to have had valued mentors throughout his career and credits them with seeing his potential and challenging him to take on more responsibility despite his fears—which can be both a hindrance and an incentive. Fear of failing forced him to work hard at everything. He constantly thought someone would find out that he did not belong. Without mentors who saw his potential and cared enough to push him into challenging situations, he may have turned down advancement opportunities later in his career as he had done earlier, when he was offered the opportunity to participate in a college honors program. He feared he did not belong; just staying in college was his only goal.

Mentors encouraged and challenged Carvajal and found opportunities for him, such as the NASPA Undergraduate Fellows Program, where he could learn about the student affairs profession and connect with others from underrepresented groups. Carvajal learned how mentors bring different strengths to the mentor–mentee relationship. His mentors encouraged him to be open to becoming a college president, which was not in his career plan. They taught him how to lead effectively and that he did not have to give up family and personal life as president. Another mentor encouraged him to pursue a presidency as a reminder of why he chose student affairs as a profession.

In addition to confirming what we know about first-generation students, Carvajal's story is a testament to why we need more college leaders who have experiences similar to those of the students whom these access colleges were created to serve.

Gerald Williamson uses the Spanish word for gold, *oro*, as a metaphor to describe the potential in Carvajal and in other students if there is someone willing to work with them to find and "mine" it. Carvajal was fortunate to be mentored by Williamson, who saw his potential and would not allow him to get in the way of his own success. Williamson demonstrates how a mentor has to "extract" the gold by helping students to identify their own potential, to "smelt" the gold by providing the experiences and coaching, and to "get the gold to the jewelers" by pushing students to believe in themselves.

It's heartening to think that with a lifelong mentor such as Williamson, Carvajal will replicate his mentor's work with students of his own.

—Gwendolyn Jordan Dungy

Gwendolyn Jordan Dungy is executive director emeritus of NASPA–Student Affairs Administrators in Higher Education, having served as NASPA executive director from 1995 to 2012. She previously served in senior administrative positions at the Association of American Colleges and Universities, County College of Morris in New Jersey, Montgomery College in Maryland, Catonsville Community College in Maryland, and as faculty at St. Louis Community College in Missouri. She is author of numerous articles and coeditor of several books on higher education. She holds a BS and MS from Eastern Illinois University, an MA from Drew University in New Jersey, and a PhD from Washington University in St. Louis.

Lori S. White

Lori S. White is the vice chancellor for students at Washington University in St. Louis. She previously served as the vice president for student affairs and clinical professor of education at Southern Methodist University; she has also worked at the University of Southern California, Stanford University, Georgetown University, San Diego State University, and the University of California, Irvine. White received her BA from the University of California, Berkeley, and her PhD from Stanford University. She is active nationally in several higher education organizations and served as chair of the NASPA Board of Directors in 2016–2017.

My Soul Looks Back In Wonder, How I Got Over

Lori S. White

I remember the first time I was made to feel different from others. I was 4 years old, and my family had been the first Black family to move into what had been an all-White neighborhood in Long Beach, California. The moving van had barely delivered our boxes when, as a gregarious child, I was outside meeting all of the neighborhood kids. One of the kids asked me, "Are you a Negro?" Not knowing the answer to the question, I responded, "I don't know, let me ask my dad." I don't recall my dad's answer—although whatever he told me did not discourage me from going back outside and meeting the rest of the neighborhood kids. I suppose that interaction with the White kid in my neighborhood was my first *transformational* encounter, as I do remember feeling that the word Negro—whatever its definition—meant I was somehow different from the other kids.

Whenever I am invited to give a talk, I often share that I have a great love for old Negro spirituals. Those old-time, down-home gospel songs not only provide me with uplift and inspiration, they often serve as the theme for the message I hope to deliver in my talk.

As I thought about writing this narrative and took stock of my life and career to this point, the song that came to mind is one titled, "How I Got Over." The lyrics of the song include the phrase, "How I got over. My soul look back and wonder (sic) how I got over."[1] There is another, slightly different, version of the lyrics where the words *in wonder* are used instead of *and wonder*. I have chosen to go with the phrase *in wonder* as I continue to be amazed at all I have been blessed to achieve in my professional career, despite what those, like the kid in my childhood neighborhood, may have thought Negroes were capable of.

FAMILY TIES AND PLANNED HAPPENSTANCE

In my family the PhD is the entry-level degree. My father had a PhD in clinical psychology. In his words, upon receiving his degree, he became the first Black psychologist that he had ever seen. He served as a college professor for many years and, in retirement, was actively engaged mentoring others into the counseling psychology profession and academia. My younger sister earned a PhD in geology and is one of a handful of Black female geologists in the country. She had a long tenure as a college professor and now works for the University of California (UC) Museum of Paleontology overseeing education and outreach programs, and is a role model for young minority scientists.

It was not clear initially that I would follow in the family higher education business. However, my dad expected that, as the oldest of my parents' three daughters, I would. (I have one other sister who is a singer/actress/paralegal/scriptwriter.) My mother, who is a registered

---

[1] The phrase "my soul looks back and wonders" has been used as the lyrics to a song sung by both Mahalia Jackson and Aretha Franklin, among others. The phrase "my soul looks back and wonders" or "my soul looks back in wonder" has been used as part of book titles for a number of different publications on the civil rights movement, African American history, and personal healing.

nurse by training, encouraged her three daughters to pursue our individual passions, whatever those might be.

When I graduated from college (UC Berkeley) with degrees in English and psychology, I really was not sure what I wanted to do career-wise. Truthfully, as an avid sports fan, had there been more opportunities for women in sports when I graduated from college in 1980 and was first charting my career, I would have probably pursued a career as a sports broadcaster.

Career trajectories are often called *planned happenstance*, for while there may be some measure of intentional career planning, much of where we end up in our careers is purely happenstance. Sometimes, career opportunities have little to do with planning—they just happen. My own career in higher education is, in many ways, a prime example of planned happenstance.

Because I did not have any concrete job plans following my college graduation, my dad suggested I get a job working at the college campus where he was a professor. I had not done any of the things I now advise students to do—find a mentor, get involved, access the various campus resources such as the career center. Thus, having no real viable job prospects at the time I graduated, I said yes to the idea of working on the college campus. At the time, I was not quite sure what working at a college campus meant. Those of us who have been to college know, of course, what professors do. I don't think most of us, until we work on a college campus in a nonteaching capacity, realize that there are many people who work on college campuses who are not faculty.

POLITICS

My first position in higher education was working at the information booth at UC Irvine, where my dad was a longtime professor. By way of full transparency, I got the job because the vice chancellor of student affairs owed my dad a *political* favor. That was my introduction to how the real world really works—sometimes political favors are bargained, traded, owed, and paid back in some way, shape, or form. I think we would all like to believe that organizational decisions should be free from any political influence. However, *politics*—which I am defining here as bargaining for some organizational good or need, or arriving at an organizational decision in a way that is not always transparent to all—is a fact of life in most organizations. (Some might argue that politics in churches and schools are some of the most brutal.) Tull and Freeman (2011) wrote a great article on the need for student affairs administrators to develop a stronger political frame.[2] Their research suggests that administrators in student affairs favor the human resources and/or the structural frame, as opposed to the political frame.

THE IMPORTANCE OF HAVING A GOOD NETWORK

The major focus of my first job (a temporary, 12-month appoint-ment) was to provide information to visitors about the campus. To fulfill this responsibility, I discovered the importance of having a good network across the campus on which I could call when I needed a question answered. As part of developing this network, I discovered the group of staff on campus who advised, mentored, and coached students in various capacities. I learned these folks were the student affairs staff on campus—those individuals working in the offices of orientation, residential life, the career center, the counseling center, the cross-cultural center, and so forth. I saw how students blossomed

---

[2] Bolman and Deal (2003) proposed a four-frame model—*political, structural, human resources* and *symbolic*. The *political* frame emphasizes power, competition, and winning scarce resources. The *structural* frame views organizations through the lens of organizational charts and formal rules and responsibilities of individuals within the organization. The *human resources* frame focuses on people and relationships. The *symbolic* frame views organizations through the lens of ritual, tradition, ceremony, and culture.

because of an adult on campus caring about, investing in, and encouraging them. As I observed the work of these professionals, I thought to myself how different my undergraduate experience would have been if someone from student affairs—or really anyone on the large undergraduate campus I attended—had paid attention to me with the same sense of care and support the student affairs staff provided to students at UC Irvine.

For the past 35-plus years, that is what I have been doing—working as a student affairs professional in various capacities. Along the way I went back to school and earned my PhD, and I currently serve as a senior student affairs officer. So, what are some of the challenges and opportunities I have faced along my career journey? Has my identification as an African American woman affected my career trajectory and my leadership?

ENCOUNTERING DIFFERENCE

Growing up in Long Beach and San Francisco, California, I was often the only—or one of only a few—Black children in my classes. I think two things buffered me throughout my childhood from much of the impact of stereotype threat that Claude Steele (1997) described in his research.[3] When my family moved from Long Beach to San Francisco, we moved to a fairly diverse neighborhood with kids from a variety of racial, ethnic, and cultural backgrounds. I was always a very outgoing child and easily forged friendships across racial and cultural lines. Additionally, I was a smart kid and was placed in the highest-track classes, which, unfortunately, included few other Black children. So whatever stereotypes White teachers may have had about the intelligence of Black children were not realized when I was

---

[3] Steele (1997) defined *stereotype threat* as "the threat of being viewed through the lens of a negative stereotype, or the fear of doing something that would inadvertently confirm that stereotype" (para. 10).

a student in their respective classrooms. I am sure it also helped that most teachers became aware at some point that my father had a PhD and that my mother was a registered nurse. I suspect for those teachers who did hold stereotypes about the intelligence of Black children, I may have been the exception to their rule that Black children were not supposed to be smart.

I did have some experiences where I had to confront racism. In high school, my best friend (who was not Black) and I applied at the same time for a summer job. My best friend received an interview and a job. However, despite the fact that each week during the summer I submitted a new application at the same store—an ice cream shop—where my friend was then working, I never even received an interview, let alone a job offer. It did not occur to me until years later it was likely the owner of the ice cream shop did not want to hire a Black girl to wait on her mostly White customers.

In college I went through Panhellenic sorority recruitment (called *rush* back then). After the first round, I did not receive invitations from any of the 13 sororities to continue with the process. In effect, I was dropped from recruitment. While I was personally devastated and suspected the reason I did not receive a bid from any of the sororities was because I was Black, I don't think I was ready to deal with what that might mean to my 1976 viewpoint that the world was a fair place. Growing up in California, the civil rights movement seemed very far away from my reality. As a result, I think I buried that sorority rejection experience and chose to find other ways to become involved in student life on campus.

In thinking back on my life from ages 4 to 22 (elementary school through college), there were other incidents where I was treated differently or unfairly because of my skin color. However, at that point in my life I was probably deep in the racial identity *pre-encounter* stage.[4] Consequently, I either (a) did not have a real conscious awareness of the discriminatory behavior of others directed toward me, (b) did not want to believe that an opportunity denied to me had anything to do with my race, and/or (c) had not had enough of these discriminatory experiences to affect my sense of self.

It was not until I received my first job working at a university, smack dab in the middle of Orange County—one of the least diverse counties in California—that I moved from the *pre-encounter* to the *encounter* stage of racial identity development.

UC Irvine, established in 1965, is one of the 10 branch campuses of the UC system. When I started working at the university in 1980, UC Irvine was still working to establish its presence as a viable choice for prospective college students. The university had to overcome particular challenges to convince Black and Brown students to attend a college in Orange County, which was known for its affluence, conservatism, and lack of diversity.

As a young student affairs professional, I witnessed for the first time the daily struggles African American and Latino college students experienced both on and off campus. Because there were so few of these students on campus, they regularly experienced being the only person that looked like them in their classes and in their residence halls. Each time these students ventured off campus, they had to deal with people who mistook them for anything but a college student. Many of the students were also first-generation college students, living away from home for the first time, and many had not lived in neighborhoods where they were the minority. I saw how these students began to question whether

---

[4]Cross (1971) proposed five stages of racial identity development in his model of psychological Nigrescense: *pre-encounter, encounter, immersion/emersion,* and *internalization, internalization-commitment.* The *pre-encounter* stage is characterized by an unawareness or belief in racial differences. The *encounter* stage is an exploring stage where an individual begins to transition to a pro-Black stance, often because of an experience that makes race more salient to the individual.

they had the skill, talent, and perseverance to make it through the pre-dominantly White university. I realized that, other than the fact that I was a second-generation college student and perhaps had more experience living among White folks, I could have easily been one of those students myself. Just because I was an administrator, I was not immune to what the students were experiencing off campus in terms of hardly ever seeing anyone else who looked like me or trying to figure out where I could get my hair done, go to church, or get some soul food.

To UC Irvine's credit, recognizing the importance of retaining these students of color, it was one of the first colleges in the country to develop a cross-cultural center, establish a counseling center with a clear focus on multicultural counseling, and appoint several administrators of color to prominent positions on campus. That is where I learned the critical importance of targeted support services for underrepresented student populations, faculty, and staff reflective of the diverse student body.

Ironically, my background growing up in a multicultural environment played a significant role in my professional success at UC Irvine. I was able to develop great relationships with the students of color and the White students on campus. Although growing up in a multicultural environment is not a prerequisite to forging positive relationships with diverse students, I think those experiences helped me flow easily among different student groups. The cross-cultural relationships with students proved critical when racial issues that needed to be responded to occurred on campus, as the various groups of students trusted me to be a fair advocate for their viewpoints.

NETWORKING AND MENTORSHIP

After my temporary job working at the UC Irvine information booth ended, I was encouraged by Associate Dean of Student Activities Randy Lewis to apply for the position of director of the cross-cultural center. And I got the job! I had gotten to know Randy and several other key administrators because I had developed an expansive network on campus as a result of my work at the information booth. (Who knew that working at the information booth would end up being such a strategically great first job?) Being tapped by the associate dean to apply for the position of the director of the cross-cultural center was my first awareness of the power of having a network—a collection of people with whom to exchange and share information and who can often also serve as a connection to opportunities. Three UC Irvine administrators (Randy Lewis, Fred Henderson, and Bob Gentry) with whom I had networked in my information booth role became my first mentors (Randy and Bob were White men). Over the years Randy, Fred, and Bob encouraged me to apply and/or tapped me for positions on campus that I would have never considered because I thought I had neither the skill set nor the experience. In the 10 years that I worked at UC Irvine, I had the wonderful fortune to gain a broad and deep set of administrative experiences across several student affairs disciplines—diversity programs, residence life and student housing, student activities, orientation, admissions, Greek life, and others—which provided me with a strong foundation in student affairs leadership.

In the early years of my career (I started working in higher education in 1981), I do not recall hearing the word *network* or *mentor*, although, ironically, networking and mentoring was something I had observed my dad doing throughout all of his years as a faculty member (and something he continues to do even in retirement). My dad told me he learned about the importance of networking and mentoring when he was invited to faculty parties as a new faculty member. According to my dad, he would get gussied up to go to these parties ready to "boogaloo" and "finger pop" (dance). He wondered why, instead of dancing at the parties, the (White) faculty members would be talking in small groups amongst themselves. My dad said he later realized that these small group conversations were where all of the critical departmental information would be exchanged, and where senior faculty would develop connections with the junior faculty and serve as their advocates for research and promotional opportunities. My dad said (his words not mine), "That's when I figured out how the White boys got ahead. While I was finger popping, they were networking and getting mentored." My dad went on to tell me that this was how he finally figured out how the real world really works—that hard work will only get you so far; it is important to also have a strong network and to have folks who are looking out for you.

The challenge for people of color, as my dad discovered, is we may not always realize how the real world works, or we have not been provided or permitted access to the networks and mentors that will get us to the next promotional opportunity. I do not think it is an accident that for so many years most senior student affairs officers were White men. It is not that women and people of color were not smart, talented, or capable—unfortunately, we were not invited into what used to be a student affairs *old boys club*.

I was fortunate in my administrative tenure at UC Irvine to work for an African American vice president for student affairs (VPSA). Horace Mitchell was appointed as the VPSA at UC Irvine in 1984. Although I do not believe having someone who looks like you is a requirement for one to aspire to a particular position, I felt uplifted, encouraged, and proud to work for the first boss who shared my same cultural identity. The seed for thinking I might pursue, and could one day become, a VPSA was planted when Horace became the VPSA at UC Irvine. Until that point, I am not sure I considered a position much beyond the director level, which I had become at such an early point in my career. To be candid, I enjoyed my work and I was still young, single, and engaged in some finger popping of my own. However, working for Horace allowed me to believe that as an African American, I could aspire to become a VPSA.

Horace created a networking circle for us younger professionals on campus. On Fridays, we would gather for happy hour drinking and dancing at a local watering hole. However, unlike my dad's early experience where he was the only one dancing at the faculty meetings, it was made clear to all of us who attended that these Friday night happy hours were very much about networking and mentorship. The older folks in the group all had their doctorates and were at a higher level administratively than my peers and I. In between dances and drinks, these elders impressed upon my peers and me the importance of going on to earn our doctorates. Within the next few years just about all of us in the group who did not yet have our ticket punched (my dad's phrase for getting one's PhD) followed this advice and went on to earn our doctorates. Although I may have eventually decided on my own to pursue my doctorate, being a part of the group Horace put together left me with the expectation that earning my doctorate was something I absolutely needed to do and gave me the confidence to do it.

THE ROAD TO BECOMING A VICE PRESIDENT FOR STUDENT AFFAIRS

I had not been a great student as an undergraduate. I was that student with whom we are all familiar. I assumed everyone was smarter than I, and when I struggled in a course, instead of asking for help, I turned inward and thought I just needed to work harder. Given my less-than-stellar undergraduate academic career, going to graduate school was not something I had ever considered until I became a part of the Friday night happy hour group. Also, finding success in my professional life through on-the-job-training gave me increased intellectual confidence. So I made what I know is one of the best decisions in my life: I quit my full-time job at the age of 33 and became a full-time graduate student.

Planned happenstance kicked in once again in my choice of graduate schools. While I was applying to graduate school, I was doing some consulting work for someone who had earned his doctorate at Stanford University. He suggested I apply to the Stanford program. I was hesitant, as I did not think my transcript and GRE scores made me the candidate Stanford would be seeking. As it turned out, one of my former colleagues at UC Irvine worked in the graduate school at Stanford. During a pre-admission visit to campus, my former colleague introduced me to a faculty member in the Stanford School of Education who later became my advisor. Because I later learned that graduate school admission is dictated by faculty, I am fairly certain that without the introduction facilitated by my former colleague, I would not have been admitted to the program. I never would have thought to apply to Stanford in the first place without the encouragement of the person for whom I had done the consulting work.

Going to Stanford absolutely transformed my life in several ways. While one can certainly be successful regardless of where one goes to college or graduate school (or if one goes to college at all), I did not realize the power of a degree from one of the most prestigious universities in the world. I discovered the Stanford credential almost always ensures I will get an interview for a position for which I apply, even though it certainly does not guarantee I will receive the appointment (as I need to make sure I bring my "A" game to the interview), and a Stanford degree enhances others' perceptions of my intelligence. I continue to find it amazing that our society believes that people who went to Ivy League or Ivy League–type institutions are smarter than people who went to "State U." We all know smart people attend all types of institutions, and that some smart people choose not to go to college or never have the opportunity. However, because at this point we still live in a world where certain perceptions are developed using the proxy of where one went to school, I advise women and people of color to get the most powerful degree they can—a PhD as opposed to an EdD, and one from a highly ranked university. When you are in the minority, it is judicious to use every advantage possible to get the hiring decision makers—who are more often than not folks who do not look like us— to give us an opportunity to compete. The potential impact of what kind of advanced degree I earned, and from which school I earned it, never occurred to me until after I completed my degree at Stanford and I discovered the privileges of the diploma from that school.

Attending Stanford exposed me to a cadre of superstar African American graduate students—Black folks earning PhDs in chemistry, engineering, and computer science, and pursuing PhD or MD degrees, among others. It is a sad commentary on my own educational and professional experience to that point that I had never been around that many smart Black people in one place, or knew Black folks earning doctorates in fields other than education and the social sciences. I was certainly inspired by my fellow Black graduate students to step up my academic game. It turns out I was a much better graduate student than I ever imagined I would be. I was the only one of my School of Education cohort to complete my degree in four years, and my advisor told me my qualifying paper was the best he had ever read. I share this information only to underscore the idea that, at some point, we all have to let go of the imposter syndrome and recognize we are each blessed with incredible gifts and talents.

I developed a mentoring relationship, which has expanded to a sister-friendship, with then-provost at Stanford Condoleezza (Condi) Rice. Condi and I met while I was a graduate student and served as president of the Black Graduate Student Association, and we quickly bonded over our mutual love of sports. Her dad was also a former student affairs professional at the University of Denver, and I think another reason Condi took an interest in me was because I was pursuing the same career as her father.

About a year after I graduated from Stanford, Condi hired me to become director of undergraduate advising at Stanford. I did not have any direct experience in academic advising when she recruited me for the position, but I did have numerous transferable skills directing programs and managing staff, advising and mentoring students in other capacities, and leading critical campuswide initiatives, which Condi thought made me a good fit for the position. As my career has unfolded, there have been many positions to which I have been appointed where on paper it may have looked as if I did not have the job progression or "bullets" of experience a search committee may have been looking for on a résumé. I am grateful to the search committee members who valued my generalist background in higher education and supported the idea that skills and experiences gained in one higher education leadership area could be transferrable to another.

In my opinion student affairs as a profession is becoming much too specialized. People refer to themselves as a residence life professional or an orientation professional, for example, which is contributing to the siloing many of us experience in our divisions of student affairs or on our campuses in general. To serve students most effectively, we have to work in an integrated fashion toward enhancing student learning, development, and success, as opposed to trying to elevate our particular department over the work of another.

Condi gave me mentoring advice that I did not realize I needed. Focus is one of the top five StrengthsQuest[5] strengths. Consequently, once I decided I was all in for a career in student affairs, I started plotting out my life in three- to five-year increments. Condi, someone who started off as a music major and ended up as a university provost and

---

[5] StrengthsQuest is an online assessment that includes 34 different strengths and is focused on one discovering, understanding, and maximizing these strengths.

a U.S. secretary of state, encouraged me to relax a bit on the focused career planning and be open to possibilities that might emerge from directions in which I might not even be looking.

I have chosen to follow Condi's advice, and I now rarely have a concrete plan for a next career move. In the years since earning my doctorate (1995), I have worked at seven different and diverse types of institutions (UC Irvine, Georgetown, Stanford, San Diego State, and Southern Methodist Universities; the University of Southern California; and Washington University in St. Louis). This range of universities includes bigger and smaller institutions, public and private institutions, highly selective and less selective institutions, institutions where resources flowed like a mighty river, and those where I had to figure out how to turn water into wine. I have focused my work, as the phrase says, on "blooming where I am planted." I am committed to making an impact on the institution where I am employed for as long as I feel I can make a significant contribution. When I have left one institution for another, more times than not it has been because an opportunity presented itself when I had not been looking for it— although there have also been times when I have moved on because I knew I was ready for a next step or a new challenge.

MENTORSHIP

Throughout my career I have been fortunate, like so many other authors in this volume, to have many mentors along the way. In addition to those mentors whom I have mentioned previously, other significant mentors include James (Jim) Lyons (dean of students emeritus, Stanford University), Penny Rue (VPSA, Wake Forest University), James (Jim) Kitchen (vice president emeritus, San Diego State University), Michael Jackson (vice president emeritus, University of Southern California [USC]), and R. Gerald Turner (president, Southern Methodist University [SMU]).

Jim Lyons, a true pillar of the student affairs profession, was one of my wise graduate school professors. Penny Rue got me back in the game by giving me my first job out of graduate school after I had been a full-time student for four years. Jim Kitchen gave me my first opportunity to be a senior student affairs professional by hiring me as his associate vice president (AVP) and dean of students, and then graciously let me go when Michael Jackson called Jim to ask if he could pursue me for the AVP position at USC. Later, Michael pushed me out of the nest and told me it was time for me to become a vice president, and Gerald Turner hired me for my first vice president position at SMU.

Collectively from these incredible mentors I learned (a) the importance of understanding institutional culture (Jim Lyons); (b) the value of "management by walking around"—that is, getting out of your office to connect with people (Horace); (c) the art of listening (Penny); (d) that sometimes you have to do battle (Jim Kitchen); (e) the importance of keeping your cool no matter what the circumstances (Michael); and (f) how to balance keeping your eye on the big picture while also not losing track of critically important smaller details, such as learning the names of all of the staff who work in your division and the names and stories of as many students as you can (Gerald). My mentors—women and men, White and Black, gay and cisgender—reinforced the important perspective that mentors do not have to share your same demographic profile.

Along the way to becoming a VPSA, I picked up some important leadership survival skills, such as forging positive relationships with the critical political players on campus (the provost; the vice presidents for administration, business, and finance; the president's chief of staff; the dean of undergraduate studies). Although we may initially be attracted to the work of student affairs because we like to work with people (the human resources frame), when we assume more senior-level administrative positions, we can only thrive and survive in our student affairs role when we understand that sometimes our work is about various kinds of trade-offs among competing priorities (the political frame). My ability to build relationships on campus, outside of student affairs, and discern the political nature of work in higher education organizations has helped me achieve the strategic goals of my student affairs department and/or division.

STAYING THE COURSE

I have had my share of professional challenges and setbacks, made tougher by not ever knowing definitively whether my race or gender had a significant impact. I had a difficult relationship with at least one boss in part because I did not adjust well to his management style and in part because I felt he underestimated my capabilities, perhaps because of my race and gender. There are positions that I applied for and did not receive—one where the person doing the hiring flat out told me that even though I may have been the best qualified for the position of the final pool of candidates, he could not hire me because his bosses preferred another candidate (ironically, in this particular search I was the only woman and the only person of color in the final pool). As a fairly new vice president, after making the tough decision to suspend a fraternity, I was "loud talked" in front of students by the fraternity advisor who was angry with my decision. I wondered whether my predecessor, who was a White fraternity man, would have been treated similarly. And there is the constant question of "Which number is your son on the team?" each time I attend a football or basketball game at the institution where I am working, instead of the person who is asking the question first assuming I may be attending the game because I am an alumni or employee of the institution (as I am 5 feet tall, it is unlikely any son of mine would be playing on a college football or basketball team). As a VPSA I, like many of my VPSA colleagues of color, have experienced being the first and/or only person of color appointment on a president's or chancellor's cabinet, and have recognized the challenges and opportunities that come with this appointment.

While I fully acknowledge that racism and sexism exist in the organizations in which we work, what continues to keep me together psychologically is that I am determined to move forward, despite knowing that I may experience racist behavior or suspecting that others may behave differently toward me because of racial or gender stereotypes. I have seen other colleagues who have allowed racism and/or sexism to debilitate them; I am determined not to allow that to be the case for me, particularly when I know we have important work toward making higher education more inclusive, not just for ourselves, but also for our students and colleagues. Yes, there are times when I feel "I have been in the storm so long."[6] However, "I keep on keepin' on" because I believe deeply that I have a responsibility to do what I can to help make the road a little smoother for the next person who follows me in this work.

MY SOUL LOOKS BACK IN WONDER

I have come far from my first job working at the information booth at UC Irvine. Since that time, I have been a director of several student affairs departments, have served as an assistant vice provost for undergraduate education in academic affairs and as an AVP for student affairs at two different institutions, and am now on my second appointment as a senior student affairs officer.

My respective supervisors have told me that I have been an impact player at the various universities where I have worked. More important, I have forged wonderful relationships with countless numbers of students, as my holiday card list continues to grow each year.

In 2016, I was elected chair of the board of directors for

---

[6] From the Negro spiritual "I've Been in De Storm So Long."

NASPA–Student Affairs Administrators in Higher Education. As I accepted the gavel I looked into the audience and saw in the faces of the young professionals gathered in the room, myself 30 years ago when I, too, was a young professional. I never in my wildest dreams would have imagined I would have been able to have a career so personally and professionally fulfilling, and my soul indeed looks back in wonder, how I got over.

References

Bolman, L., & Deal, T. (2003). *Reframing organizations: Artistry, choice, and leadership* (3rd ed.). San Francisco, CA: Jossey-Bass.

Cross, W. E. (1971). The Negro to black conversion experience: Towards a psychology of black liberation. *Black World, 20*(9), 13–27.

Steele, C. M. (1997). A threat in the air: How stereotypes shape intellectual identity and performance. *American Psychologist, 52*(6), 613–629.

Tull, A., & Freeman, J. P. (2011). Reframing student affairs leadership: An analysis of organizational frames of reference and locus of control. *Research in the Schools, 18*(1), 33–43.

The Transforming Power of Higher Education

Condoleezza Rice

My grandfather was a sharecroppers' son in Eutaw, Alabama. For some reason, he decided that he wanted to go to college—and get book learning. He researched where a colored man could go to college. He learned about Stillman College in Tuscaloosa—about 30 miles from where he lived. He made his way there and—after making a little bargain to become a Presbyterian minister in exchange for a scholarship—successfully completed his degree. He somehow understood the transforming power of education.

Granddaddy Rice knew that a higher education would never be taken from him, that his future success depended on having knowledge and skills, and that he would pass on the benefits of that education to his children and grandchildren. My father would become a senior administrator at the University of Denver. My Aunt Theresa would

Condoleezza Rice is currently the Denning Professor in Global Business and the Economy at the Stanford Graduate School of Business; the Thomas and Barbara Stephenson Fellow on Public Policy at the Hoover Institution; and a professor of political science at Stanford University. She is a former Stanford provost, and from 2005–2009 she served as the 66th U.S. Secretary of State.

earn a PhD in English literature at the University of Wisconsin. And I, too, am a part of his legacy. The value of a higher education cannot be overstated. It is, very simply, the gift of limitless horizons for a lifetime.

Because education is so powerful, we must make certain that colleges and universities are places of opportunity and equality for those who attend. A student's ethnicity, race, sexual identification, or religious background should not matter as they learn, study, and create. Students come from varying socioeconomic backgrounds just looking for a chance to make their own name, provide for their families, or change the world for the better.

We need to think of our work as university administrators as a trust—a responsibility to give every student an opportunity to succeed. As provost of Stanford University, I saw firsthand the efforts of our faculty and others in the administration to support our young people— and to remove barriers to their ability to accomplish their dreams.

No one was more central to that effort than Lori White. I first met Lori when she was a graduate student in the School of Education at Stanford University and I was provost. I remember our first encounter. She asked me a very tough question—a skeptical one about inclusion and diversity and what I was doing *personally* to deliver. I loved it.

I thought to myself, "I have got to have Lori as a part of my team." Lori would become the director of undergraduate advising at Stanford and, of course, move on to ever more responsible positions in higher education.

I would learn that we shared a passion for education and a similar background. Her father, too, was a university professor and her mother valued education for her girls. My parents had always said that I had to be twice as good to succeed. It was a statement about prejudice that I didn't question or debate. I took it on board and tried to live up to that expectation. Lori has the same ethic. No one works harder. She knows the power of her own education. More important, she wants others to have that gift. Everyone should work twice as hard, not because of prejudice but because it is a key to success.

Lori's career has been one of breaking down barriers and shattering glass ceilings. The wonderful thing, though, is that she has not done so out of ambition, but out of a deep desire to help others. Lori has told me on many occasions that she thinks of me as a mentor. I am grateful for that and honored. But this has been a two-way street. I have learned a lot from this passionate, intelligent, and determined woman. Gerald Turner, the president of Southern Methodist University, for whom Lori worked, once told me that he, too, had learned a lot from Lori and been inspired by her commitment. I know how he feels.

Lori White is a determined advocate for inclusion and diversity. She mentors her staff, peers, and students—showing them that color or gender need not stand in the way of success. She shows universities that diverse communities are better communities where learning and growth flourish.

University leaders are charged to make the transforming power of higher education a reality for students. We are to make sure that nothing gets in the way of the limitless horizons that it creates and the great futures that it makes possible. We must demand excellence of our students and tell them that, no matter their color, gender, or sexual identity, there is nothing wrong with trying to be "twice as good." We can then step back and watch them flourish, knowing that we are doing our work well. That is the attitude and commitment that Lori brings every day to this important work. She is a leader in our field because she takes her responsibilities in the right spirit—it is a trust. I am immensely proud of Lori White, and honored to call her my friend.

When I read the title of Lori White's narrative, I caught my breath because I have been working on a memoir with a similar title stimulated by the song, "My Soul Looks Back and Wonders How I Got Over." In my variation on the title of the old Negro spiritual, I, too, changed the words "and wonders" to "in wonder." As I read the chapter, I continued to catch my breath as I read about the experiences that have been transformational in White's life and career. Although she shares lessons for new as well as experienced professionals across all demographics, she pays particular attention to the unique challenges that people of color, especially African Americans, and women may face. As she so generously shares her experiences as a student and as a new professional, readers learn that regardless of how privileged a student may appear, Black and Brown students in particular, who inevitably face challenges on and off campus, benefit from mentors or others who care and who are willing to provide support.

White shares how particular habits have been critical in her career success, and I think following her lead has the potential to transform the trajectory of one's career. For example, she discovered early in her career that politics in organizations is a fact of life, and understanding and using it need not be negative. She shows how important it is to understand the politics of one's organization, not only for personal advancement, but to be able to assist students as well. Networking also sometimes has negative connotations. However, White gives examples of how networking is not only something to be embraced, but essential if one expects to be successful as a resource for students.

Another important piece of advice about networking illustrated by her dad is that "hard work will only get you so far." How often have we heard colleagues or have we said ourselves that we didn't understand why we were not selected for some opportunity because we know we worked harder than the person selected? The brutal truth might be that the person selected had someone looking out for them.

White and other authors in this book attest to the fact that effective mentors need not be of the same cultural background. However, more often than not, mentors and role models who are of the same cultural identity as those they are mentoring have a powerful impact. Sometimes the impact is realized when mentees, for the first time, see someone similar to themselves to emulate. Sometimes the impact is realized when the mentor is proof that someone similar to the mentee can succeed in a particular role that, at first, appeared out of reach.

Lori White has had some incredible mentors and opportunities, and she graciously shares the lessons she learned from each of them. Perhaps most poignant for women and people of color is that she, too, shares the burden of not knowing whether her race or gender had an impact on what she calls professional challenges and setbacks. We can all be encouraged as she declares, and has demonstrated, that she has allowed neither racism nor sexism to keep her from moving forward.

—Gwendolyn Jordan Dungy

Michael L. Jackson

Michael L. Jackson is president and CEO of the Boys & Girls Clubs of Monterey County, California. He previously served as vice president for student affairs and professor of higher education at the University of Southern California for 18 years and as dean of students at Stanford University. Jackson is a past president of NASPA–Student Affairs Administrators in Higher Education and served as a commissioner of the Western Association of Schools and Colleges Senior College and University Commission. He received his bachelor's degree in anthropology from Stanford University and his master's and doctoral degrees in educational administration from the University of Massachusetts Amherst.

Guideposts for Life and Career

Home, Love, Friends, Work, Openness to New Possibilities, and Peace of Mind

Michael L. Jackson

During my career as a student affairs professional, professor, and leader who is African American, several guideposts provided structure, balance, and a sense of security. These guideposts served me well, and I have tried to pass them on to my staff, colleagues, students, alumni, parents, and others with whom I have worked. As my career developed, it became very clear over some years that the most important aspects of my life were family, home, love, faith, friends, work, and peace of mind. Whenever I made big decisions, I reflected

This chapter is adapted from "Reflections on a Life and Career in Student Affairs: Guideposts and Structure," by M. L. Jackson, 2016, *Journal of College and Character, 17*(2), pp. 75–81. Copyright © 2016 by the National Association of Student Personnel Administrators, Inc. Adapted with permission.

on how these decisions might affect these guideposts because they are expressions of my values and character.

THE FOUNDATION

Over the years, I continually asked myself a series of questions: How do I want to live my life? With whom do I want to spend my work time and personal time? Is the work I am doing important? If so, why? If not, why not? Are my decisions in the service of a higher good beyond my own personal needs and desires? Can I remain calm and focused when confronted with highly charged and emotional situations? When I am alone with my thoughts do I feel at peace, or am I anxious because I am not following my internal compass?

If persons slight me, how should I react? Do I take their jabs personally or try to understand why they may have acted in a certain way? (As we say in the office, "Do you think they woke up that morning and decided to mess with you on purpose?" Probably not.) How do I ensure that I am guided by low ego and high results? Have I helped my staff and colleagues be as successful as they can be in their careers and lives?

These guideposts and questions provided a template that allowed me to quickly determine where I was emotionally when confronted with new and daunting problems, and how to deal with them without fear or worry for my personal safety or what would happen with my career. I was lucky to have been raised in a family that stressed being prepared, not being afraid to discuss uncomfortable topics and issues, keeping one's ego in check, and knowing that my talents and gifts were to be used in the service of others.

I certainly never imagined the kinds of situations I would have to confront in my career. I never imagined that there would be so many exhilarating moments, such as watching students graduate who came from circumstances that made getting to that ceremony seem harder than going to the moon; celebrating the worthy contributions of

Nobel prize winners with faculty friends; celebrating the Chinese New Year in Hong Kong while watching fireworks at The Peak, the highest point on the island, with dozens of University of Southern California (USC) alumni, parents, and students; securing a $10 million gift to establish a center for learning and creativity for students with dyslexia, ADHD (attention deficit hyperactivity disorder), and other learning differences; and being elected president of NASPA–Student Affairs Administrators in Higher Education, which allowed me to contribute to the broader field of student affairs. I also never imagined I would experience dark, almost paralyzing tragedies including dozens of student deaths resulting from car crashes, suicides, accidents, and murders, and brutal sexual assaults on women.

If it were not for the guideposts, I am not sure I could have thrived in my role as a dean and vice president for so many years. It was my responsibility to take the initiative in each of the examples cited above. I could not be a bystander who waited for others to take on the tough challenges or complex projects. My guideposts provided the grounding I needed to feel confident and act without lots of second-guessing and self-doubt.

For example, when I was dean of students at Stanford University, a group of students held a sit-in to protest the university's lack of diversity in the faculty and curriculum. It took place in the main quadrangle where the president's office, the School of Humanities and Social Sciences, and Memorial Church are located. When I approached the students to learn what their protest was about, some said they would talk only with the president; others ridiculed me, called me names, and said I was just a "lackey for the man." I calmly told them that they could call me any names they wanted, but if they wanted to talk with the president, they needed to work with me in my role as the dean of students. I asked them to tell me their grievances so I could facilitate a respectful dialogue despite the tensions and high emotions, and make sure their concerns were honestly represented so that we could negotiate a solution together that would allow all parties to "save face" and feel reasonably good when the sit-in was over.

Despite many long hours of shuttle diplomacy by me and members of my senior management team, the sit-in lasted four days. When it was over, one of the key university vice presidents, for whom we all had great respect and admiration, said to me, "You are one of the bravest persons I know. I can't believe how you were able to help bring the sit-in to a conclusion, given how rudely students treated you." I was surprised to hear his comments, because it never occurred to me to be afraid. I did what any good dean should have done. And I knew that it was my responsibility to help get the community and students back to their normal activities while making sure that student concerns and grievances were taken seriously and handled with respect.

As I look back on it now, it is clear that the guideposts and values that provided structure for my life and work were in place, and that they helped me do my job without worry. I had neither fear nor concern about personal safety, because I was focused on keeping the students safe and helping them accomplish much of what they wanted. I also wanted to help them learn how to channel activists' concerns into positive outcomes that can make life better for other students and the institution. I believed that once we ended the protest, the good work would speak for itself.

FIGURING OUT THAT ONE HAS TALENT: EARLY SIGNS

It is one thing for your mom and dad to tell you that you are wonderful. It is another thing when a teacher or someone outside your family recognizes your potential and tells you so. I can remember that as early as fifth grade, when I was appointed a student crossing guard monitor at a busy intersection near my elementary school, teachers were taking stock of students beyond what was represented by their grades. They were deciding based on our academic achievement and social behavior which students should be given leadership responsibilities and which ones would be asked to take on tasks beyond the classroom. I hoped that one day I could become a crossing guard monitor, but it was not clear how. When teachers explained why other students and I were chosen for such a responsibility, I realized that my life could be affected by the evaluation and judgment of adults and peers. It was a revelation that I still carry with me to this day.

I also remember two eighth-grade physical education teachers/coaches pulling me aside and telling me they were disappointed because I did not want to play baseball and run track in the same season. Their teams were short-handed, and they needed help. Although it was tough to hear their criticisms at the time, I never forgot our interaction and what they were trying to convey. They wanted me to realize that I had talents and should not be selfish. They wanted me to think about others and what they needed from me as a teammate with skills that could help their teams be more successful.

ANOTHER SIGN: REMAINING OPEN TO THE POSSIBILITIES

During my senior year at Stanford, a professor for whom I worked as a work-study student in the School of Education said that I should pursue a doctorate in educational administration at the University of Massachusetts (UMass) Amherst, where he had been recently appointed dean of the School of Education. He told me that he thought I was smart, he liked how I worked, and he believed that I would be good as an education administrator, while developing a rewarding career for myself. He talked about the positive impact I could have on others and society. I thought I was headed to law school like most of my friends, so this conversation was like a thunderbolt that changed the course of my life, gave direction for my talents and interests, and opened up a world of possibilities.

When I started graduate school, I received an assistantship at UMass Amherst to work in the Clinic for University Teaching, a Kellogg Foundation–funded program to develop and promote faculty development programs at the university and at other land grant institutions in New England. I also volunteered to become the graduate student representative on the board of directors of the Center for the Collegiate Education of Black Students (CCEBS) at the university. This federally and university-funded program provided support services (academic, personal, career counseling, advocacy for students with other offices, crisis support, and summer work-study programs) for students of color—primarily African American, Hispanic, and Asian American— and some low-income Caucasian students.

I had served on the board for two years when the executive director resigned to take another position. The board, which consisted of 10 tenured professors of color and me, were wondering who within the group could lead the program until a new director was hired. None of the professors thought they could devote the time necessary to lead the program, so they asked me if I would consider taking on the role.

I had never led a program or supervised a staff. But I decided, after thinking about it and consulting with my dissertation committee chair and a couple of other close friends, that I would do it. I also remember thinking, "Why not me? I can do this." It was a life-changing decision that helped me learn about leadership, managing complex budgets, decision making, supervising professional and graduate student staff, university politics, racial identity politics, how to set standards, and how to make presentations that could persuade others to act.

I had to completely revamp the staff and improve the standing of the program in the eyes of faculty and administrators who believed the program had poor standards that enabled and advocated for students who performed poorly in the classroom. For example, when I reviewed the records of the 600 students in the program, I found a number of students had failed all their classes for more than one semester, yet they were allowed to remain in school because of advocacy by the CCEBS director. I stopped that practice, which made some of the African American students very angry as they felt I was betraying them and our race. One guy even tried to attack me in my office because he was severed from the university.

At the same time, some African American faculty and students said, "It's about time someone had the guts to clean the place up and set higher standards for the staff and students." I also benefited from the advice of Chancellor Randolph Bromery, who had a PhD in geophysics and constantly advocated that all students, particularly students of color, strive for excellence and not settle for mediocrity and "getting over." After three years we turned the graduation rate from 35% to 65%. It was a remarkable achievement that we all relished.

After completing my doctorate and taking about six months off, I returned to California and was hired at Stanford University, where I held five different jobs in 15 years: assistant director of The Row (a collection 34 of student houses that included fraternities, co-ops, and academic themed residences), assistant director of overseas studies, assistant to the provost, associate dean of students, and dean of students.

The key to my time and professional progress at Stanford was being open to White administrators and faculty who saw potential in me as a talented person who also demonstrated that a person of color could be a successful leader in a prestigious, predominantly White institution. Three pivotal conversations during my time at the university exemplify this point.

The first was with James (Jim) Lyons, who was dean of student affairs when I arrived in 1980. He told me to make sure I got experience working with non-minority-focused programs to demonstrate that I could work with all kinds of students. He said that you have to be prepared for the day when you will have responsibility for programs that serve all students of all races and backgrounds. Jim is an incredibly sincere person, and he really made me think in a more strategic sense about developing my career.

The second conversation was with Stanford President Donald (Don) Kennedy. At the time, I was serving as assistant to the provost, and my office was between his and the provost's office. I worked regularly with Don, his senior team, and other university deans and faculty leaders. After being at the university for about 10 years, Jim asked me to take on the associate dean of students job. I questioned whether it would be a good career move and consulted Don, who gave very direct advice: "You have proven that you can be a great assistant and you are welcome to stay in the president/provost office. But if you want to build you career, you need to go 'wrangle a line.' You now need to demonstrate that you can lead other staff, programs, and budgets at a higher and more complex level."

The third conversation was with Condoleezza (Condi) Rice when I was dean of students and she was provost. After 14 years at Stanford, I began to explore leaving the university. During my job search I was offered a vice presidency at a small public liberal arts university in the Pacific Northwest. When I talked with Condi about the job offer, she congratulated me and then said, "I think you should pass on this job and find an institution that is more well-resourced, highly ranked, and considered a player as a major research university."

Condi reminded me that I had worked hard to get to this point in my career, that major research universities provide more professional opportunities, and that I had been a finalist for vice presidencies at two other major research institutions. She was prescient, as the USC offer to become vice president for student affairs came a few months later and led to an amazing 18-year run. As a result, I have had an incredible career, traveled to many parts of the world working on educational projects, and met many wonderful people who are leaders in our society.

EXPECTATIONS FROM PEOPLE OF COLOR

In my work, I dealt with complex personnel issues involving African American, Asian American, Native American, Hispanic, and Caucasian staff. The issues in each case involved whether they were competent administrators, strengthened our team, and were viewed by students, faculty, and staff as helpful and productive.

Given our organizational ambitions to provide the best student affairs programs possible, a key question was, can we rely on this person to provide great support and service to students, faculty, parents, alumni, and their colleagues? In most cases, institutional leaders dodged dealing with these staff issues, particularly those involving staff of color, because they did not want to be accused of racism.

Not handling these personnel issues forthrightly was insidious. The result was that staff, who happened to be minorities and others, remained in their positions, which deprived students of better educational and developmental outcomes. These staff members did not improve despite training and other developmental opportunities to do so. Their poor performance and lack of credibility reflected badly on the organization and other staff.

I did not shrink from these challenges, even though they were tough and politically sensitive personnel situations. I reminded all involved that our goal was to strive for excellence as educators, meet high institutional standards, and not allow colleagues to remain in key program positions if they could not perform at a very high level.

I had to be truthful with myself about the work and what it required, and proceed accordingly. Otherwise, I would have violated the trust the institution bestowed on me as an institutional leader.

When you are in these roles you cannot keep passing the buck, especially if you are an administrator of color. Your colleagues, your bosses, and the students are watching. And if you are mentoring younger staff, they are paying close attention to how they see you handle such sensitive matters.

You can get through these situations by making effective use of human resource advisors, legal staff, and public relations staff, and by keeping your president and provost informed about how you are proceeding. You would be surprised at how much support is there for you when tackling such personnel matters.

WE ARE CALLED!

Careers as student affairs leaders in higher education are not for everyone. My belief is that most of us are called to this work because we want to help individuals and create thoughtful, caring communities of purpose that are focused on the betterment of humankind. We want to promote peace in the world one person at a time. We believe there should be few limitations when it comes to helping students of all backgrounds feel cherished and figure out who they are, what they want to do with their lives, and why they want to do it.

There is no "end" when it comes to helping students who are struggling with a personal crisis or self-doubt. Sometimes, that help means allowing a student to take some time away from campus to sort out problems, but the goal is to help them evolve and live a life of usefulness, purpose, and prosperity, in community with others in mutually supportive environments. There is great meaning in serving others and knowing that if you approach all persons with an open heart and mind about making a real human connection, no matter how fleeting, they and you will thrive.

WE ARE AMBITIOUS. THAT'S A GOOD THING!

Wanting the best for others and ourselves is very motivating. We student affairs professionals are ambitious, and that is a good thing!

There is nothing selfish about wanting to be successful while working on behalf of others. It stimulates us, makes us take action, and creates energy that can sustain us and attract others to our side.

To be an effective student affairs leader, you have to be honest with yourself about your ambition. What motivates you and why? How do you feel about money? Do you seek a particular job because it pays more, has a larger staff, has a fancier title, or is located in a more prestigious office on campus or at a higher-ranked school? Do you want to make a difference in the lives of others and strengthen educational communities? Are you, as they say, "all in?" Are you inspired by a school's mission and believe you can help achieve it? Are you motivated because of the inspiring vision of a leader for whom you want to work? Do you believe that you are the one person who can turn a struggling organization into a thriving one that is admired on campus for its accomplishments and contributions to the institution's overall goals? These are a few reasons that might motivate you to take on more responsibilities and make the sacrifices necessary to prepare yourself for them. My sense is that the vast majority of us who work in student affairs do so because we feel a sense of purpose and satisfaction when we help turn a student's life around or help resuscitate a struggling student organization or staff group that needed inspiration, direction, support, and the knowledge that someone in authority cared enough to help them.

As I have said to many staff and student groups, we do not pursue careers in student affairs because we seek accolades and awards. We go into the work because we are ambitious about making a difference in the lives of others. We do not do it for recognition. That is not to say that we do not like being singled out for good work, but public recognition is fleeting. And in our line of work, the next issue or crisis is just around the corner. If at some point others recognize our dedication and work, it is appreciated. But the real satisfaction comes from knowing that you gave heart and soul to the task of supporting others and helping them get or stay on the right track.

NURTURING THE NURTURERS

Student affairs work can be intense and, at times, feel all-consuming. Therefore, it is crucial that we support our colleagues in their professional work and personal development. I have helped dozens of staff members get promoted, complete master's and doctoral degrees, earn special professional development certifications, and serve on university, regional, and national committees to broaden their institutional learning and networks. This contribution has made my journey even more rewarding and fulfilling. For example, I had an associate dean who asked to reduce her time to 50% so she could spend more quality time with her young boys. She passed up being considered to become my associate vice president twice. She was a superb professional and, a decade later, she became vice president for student services at a leading liberal arts university. In addition, four of my former associate vice presidents became vice presidents for student affairs at top-tier private and public research universities.

Mentoring and supporting those who have worked with and for me has been one of the most important and enjoyable parts of my career. None of us who reached senior levels in student affairs, myself included, did so without having excellent mentors! I have always felt that I should help and mentor others throughout my career. I started way before I became a dean. This is what helps our profession grow and stay vibrant.

DEALING WITH STUDENT DEATH OVER THE YEARS

I have dealt with more than 120 student deaths in my career. As many senior student affairs officers can attest, dealing with student deaths is among the most difficult issues to handle; the loss of a young life is a great tragedy, and there is much to mourn. There is nothing worse than calling parents and telling them that their child is dead. You never really get over hearing them respond with tears and anguish, "No, there must be some mistake," and then asking, "Why, why, why?"

However, because the death of a student is an extremely sensitive issue for families, police, university administrators, friends of the deceased, and the broader university and local community, depending on where the death occurred there is little public discussion about this topic. During these times we do some of our most important work as we handle gut-wrenching circumstances, communicate personal and institutional values, and visibly express how much we care for members of our educational communities.

The death of a student is a test of emotions and stamina for you and your staff and the student's family and friends. The loss calls upon the institution to be concerned about the personal hardships of those who are suffering, not just its own well-being. Student deaths are an emotional drain because you must help families, friends, and others grieve and find solace in the wake of loss and misery. You are called upon to employ pastoral skills that help guide the family and the community through the process of shock, grief, acceptance, and moving on without the loved one or friend.

The most important thing to do is to always tell the truth about a student's death, no matter how horrific the circumstances. And, if you do not have an answer for the family about something related to the student's life on campus or the circumstances that led to his or her death, get the answer and provide it as quickly as possible.

You must make every effort to comfort the family and visibly demonstrate how you and the institution care for the student. For example, I have accompanied the body of an East Indian freshman to his home country, attended out-of-state memorial services, sent a senior staff member to Bulgaria with the body of a graduate student who had committed suicide, and traveled to Mexico to meet the family of a student who had died in an accident on spring break. I have had a father tell me that he never wanted to hear my voice again as long as he lived. Another dad of an international student who died told me he wanted to get a graduate degree from the university to complete the journey his son was unable to finish because he saw the terrific support his son was provided when he was alive.

The guideposts that undergird my professional and personal life helped me to maintain balance and equilibrium in dire circumstances and to work cooperatively with my colleagues on such cases. And, once the crises ended, we hoped we had performed to the best of our abilities and gave the family and others affected by the tragedy as much support as they needed to be able to cope as best they could with such loss.

BALANCE DOES NOT COME EASY

One day during a class of master's students in higher education management a student asked, "Dr. Jackson, how did you find balance in your career?" It was a great question, but I was taken aback by it at first because I had not given it a lot of thought. I then said, "Each of us must figure that out for ourselves." I told them that I found my work as a new professional totally consuming and fun. I was single, living on my own, and had great friends and an extended family I could visit. Early in my career, balance came from doing what I loved and believing I was making a difference, or so I thought. I lived on two residential campuses—UMass Amherst and Stanford—where there always seemed to be something I could do for and with students and to support other colleagues in their efforts. My supervisors were encouraging, and I figured that since I wanted to become a dean of students someday, I had to get that kind of experience and mentoring.

But it wasn't until I fell in love with my wife, got married, and started a family that I realized that I might have been in balance as a single person, but not as a husband who wanted to deepen his relationship with his spouse. So, over time, I recalibrated how I worked. I became more efficient, focused, and effective, got involved in non-university activities, and took real vacations. I also now had a partner with whom I could share my life and all the highs, lows, and random occurrences that impacted each of us.

To me, finding balance is something you must constantly work on. You must be deliberate and invest in it just like your retirement funds. The more money you invest, the more your portfolio grows through compounding. The more you devote to finding balance in your personal and professional life, the more you will find peace of mind and the resilience needed to deal with the myriad issues and challenges you will encounter.

BE TRUE TO YOURSELF: YOU MAY NOT GET ALL YOU WANT, BUT YOU WILL SLEEP BETTER

A colleague and I were talking many years ago about another person with whom we worked. We had a professional, but not friendly, relationship with him and did not trust him. I told my colleague about some advice I gave our coworker to improve his chances of gaining a promotion to a higher-level position he was seeking. My colleague was surprised. He said, "I can't believe you did that given how difficult a person he is and the fact that you know he has worked against you." I said, "That's me. I help people and always try to find the best in them and encourage them to find the best in themselves." Our coworker had asked for advice and I couldn't have lived with myself if I did not give it. I gave him the best advice I could, and he got the job.

In many ways, this vignette sums up how I approach working with people and why the guideposts like the kind discussed earlier are so important for each of us to incorporate into our lives, no matter where we are in our personal and professional journey.

A LIFE OF FIRSTS AND CONTINUAL REFLECTION IS IMPORTANT

I have had a life of firsts like many other African Americans in my generation: the first African American to integrate an elite all-White male prep school, the first of 36 first cousins on my dad's side of the family to attend college and earn a terminal degree, and the first African American to hold certain positions at Stanford and USC.

I would not have had any of these firsts if others had not seen potential in me as a person who could contribute to the advancement of a program or organization. They would not have occurred had I not worked hard to prepare myself for opportunities and encouraged mentors and others to talk bluntly to me and not sugarcoat the truth about what skills I needed to learn and improve. I hope these musings and stories stimulate reflection on your personal and professional life.

If you are a seasoned professional, I hope my words make you think about your guideposts. Remember, regardless of whether you have consciously developed a system or structure to help guide you, your actions and decisions convey your values, what matters to you, and why it matters.

If you are a mid-level student affairs professional, I hope I have given you a glimpse of how much thought and focus it takes to progress in your career and to assume increasing levels of responsibility.

I hope new professionals will be inspired and understand that to have a fulfilling career in student affairs, you must thoughtfully and deliberately think about what you are doing and why you are doing it. You cannot approach your work in a haphazard fashion and hope that everything will work out fine. You must act within a philosophical and ethical structure that helps you deal with the inevitable chaos and confusion that result from working in organizations that focus on educating young people.

In the spirit of speaking bluntly and succinctly, never let race become a crutch to fall back on and prevent you from tackling difficult issues. Our line of work and careers require us to act or step aside. If we do not handle matters deliberately and constructively, we are not living up to our roles as student affairs administrators and educators. And we are not being true to ourselves as leaders who want to bring out the best in others and the organizations we lead.

A Teacher At Heart

James Lyons

Michael Jackson is a teacher. That's the pinnacle of praise. Why, then, the label *student personnel administrator*? The full meaning is rooted in history and was trumpeted by Kate Mueller, one of the earliest thinkers of our profession. She titled her landmark book *Student Personnel Work as Deeper Teaching*. The message: administration is a means and not an end. Fulfilling an institution's academic and social missions is the end. Michael learned that early in his career. His was a calling and not a job. The calling was grounded with intellectual and philosophical passion. The zest to teach shaped what he did.

Along the way Michael had opportunities for posts with impressive titles and good compensation, but narrow scope. He turned them down in favor of building experience and more learning. These decisions paid off. He moved to posts with significant challenges and opportunities.

What are some distinctive qualities that served him and his institutions well? Near the top is the surging appetite to learn that marks

---

James Lyons was a senior student affairs officer for 28 years: 10 at Haverford College and 18 at Stanford University. He also taught in and directed a master's program at the Graduate School of Education at Stanford for an overlapping 13 years. In 1988, he was the recipient of NASPA's Scott Goodnight Award for Outstanding Service as a Dean.

all good teachers. He recognized that all members of a collegiate community are immigrants; everyone came from somewhere else. Hence, campus cultures change constantly as members immigrate and emigrate. History, geography, traditions, rites, rituals, heroes, and heroines constantly evolve. So do the norms of academic and social behaviors. Michael knew that he was in an institutional perch that allowed him to see and make sense of the whole. Few others on a campus have such a catholic view of the cultural landscape and the whole of the student experience. Michael was a valued resource for his faculty and administrative colleagues. He was able to permeate and transcend the corporate-like silos that so often harden institutional arteries. He emerged as a central figure because he saw and made sense of the whole.

The unending pressures of our work lure many to mistake activity for accomplishment. Nowhere is it more obvious than the overuse of electronics to interact with others. The quickness is alluring but phony. It negates the all-important human touch that is the core of what deans should be modeling: speaking face-to-face, listening attentively, and using all of our senses to understand. Michael takes time to be human. He didn't send an e-mail to a grieving family; he visited them. He recognized the importance of giving one's all to every human encounter. Now, he reaps the reward that so many of us experience when we hear of a long-forgotten encounter that had a significant impact on the recipient.

Another key attribute of Michael is his skill as a team player. What does this mean? He does not fear asking for advice, sharing center stage, exposing his reasoning, admitting fallibility, involving colleagues, and practicing transparency. The mark of such leadership is when the team says, "*We* did this ourselves."

Our profession is better because of Michael Jackson's service. He made a difference. He taught us all.

Michael Jackson values family, home, work, and friends. His faith and love for people have brought him peace of mind as he has executed various roles as a leader in student affairs. In his essay, he refers to home, work, friends, faith, love, and peace of mind as "guideposts." These elements form his foundation and provide him with wisdom and equanimity in times of challenging decisions and tragic circumstances. His "guideposts," "internal compass," and "template" have been the baseline and standard by which he always measures important personal and career decisions.

Particularly relevant today is the example of how his guideposts sustained him during student protests early in his career as dean of students at Stanford University. His guideposts helped him focus on goals that would have positive outcomes for both students and the institution. Because of his desire to find positive outcomes for all parties, he had the courage to confront students when others were reluctant. More important, he understood his role as an educator and recognized this event as a teachable moment for students.

Jackson's guideposts did not suddenly materialize. He was able to see beyond his day-to-day experiences at an early age. He had the ability to synthesize his experiences in a manner that made them more than events in his life; they became lessons learned. He has been fortunate that people who could mentor and advise him have singled him out as a result of his intelligence and dedication to excellence in his tasks. He demonstrates that you never know who will say just the right thing to put you on a path to your destination career. Paying attention to a professor's suggestion and following through on advice led him to his first advanced degree, the institution from which he would receive the degree, and the area of study that would lead to—in his reflection—an "incredible career." He summarizes this good fortune as the ability to "remain open to the possibilities."

For newer professionals in student affairs who are weighing their decision about whether to stay in the field, Jackson lists a set of questions that could reveal important answers about the decision. He gives a holistic view of the profession, shares the joy and rewards of nurturing promising students who struggle to graduate, and describes the most difficult and heart-wrenching part of the work of student affairs— being responsive to constituents following the death of a student. Being available to families, friends, and the entire academic community during these times was critical, and Jackson relied on his guideposts to sustain and direct him to do what was best for both the family and the institution.

Michael Jackson generously shares his career ladder and the keys to his progress in professional positions. As an African American in the rarified atmosphere of being "the first" in numerous all-White opportunities, he has a special message in his narrative for professionals of color. He also shares how one's relationship to work can change as one defines other priorities such as family. Being a student affairs professional is an ever-evolving process. What remains constant are one's values and character. Jackson kept these front and center as his guideposts throughout his successful career.

—Gwendolyn Jordan Dungy

Robert D. Kelly

Robert D. Kelly serves his alma mater, Loyola University Maryland, as the university's vice president and special assistant to the president. Kelly previously held executive leadership roles at Union College in Schenectady, New York, as the president's chief of staff; Loyola University Chicago as the vice president for student affairs; and Seattle University as the vice president for student development. In addition to his bachelor's degree in political science, Kelly received his master's degree from The University of Vemont and his PhD from the University of Maryland. He has enjoyed leadership roles in numerous higher education organizations, including serving on Loyola's Board of Trustees as well as on the NASPA–Student Affairs Administrators in Higher Education Board of Directors.

Living and Leading from Within

Robert D. Kelly

I have a strong interest in the study of leadership. I read leadership books and have taught leadership courses at both the undergraduate and graduate levels. I have both sought out and been thrust into opportunities to serve. While I enjoy leading groups and organizations, I also have a desire to understand the context in which my leadership is most effective. I am cognizant that not all ways of leading are conducive to the uplifting of people or systemic institutional success. I want to not only be an effective leader by leaving the group or organization better than I found it, but I also want to lead with integrity and vitality. I need to enjoy the act of leading. To lead in this manner, I find I need to be reflective about myself and the context in which I lead.

I have been fortunate to learn from others who have led with a sense of joy, humility, and deep introspection. Through the act of leadership, others have shared wisdom about a variety of topics including vision, strategic planning, relationships, and ethics, not to mention race, gender, ethnicity, and ability in the context of leading others. These mentors showed through their own struggles that finding congruence in the public and personal spheres of life in higher education is not easy. It is especially uneasy when you need to look within yourself.

It is not uncommon for each of us to be our own worst critic. As a proud product of a Jesuit education, I wholeheartedly believe in the notion of reflection in every facet of my life. St. Ignatius of Loyola encouraged deep introspection in what he named the Daily Examen. Each day, I was encouraged to find time to be "with myself" and reflect on what I had to do, interactions I might encounter, and hopes for myself and others, as well as think deeply about the next day. All of this reflection was done in relation to God's hopes, expectations, and dreams for me. Of course, in that process of deep reflection, we often remember or place too much importance on the negative things. Personally, I tend to look at those negative things as items to consider, but I do not allow them to define me. I was not always in this space, but I have come to it—over time. The important step is to contextualize self-criticism, self-doubt, and the negative audiotapes we play over and over in our mind. Our mentors are guides on the journey and, at each stage of our journey, they can help us reflect and make sense of the world. In this essay, I analyze the notion of authenticity and the importance of mentors, self-reflection, and comfort with ambiguity as one thrives at the intersections of the personal and the professional, happenstance and expectations. I also discuss a drive to do more and be greater, while at the same time trying to understand the cultural and practical implications of change.

AUTHENTICITY AND INTERSECTIONS OF CLASS AND RACE

I remember sitting in my office at a small private highly selective liberal arts campus wondering, "Did they hire the right person?" While I felt confident in my educational and experiential training, I had a sense of not being prepared for my first professional role. I had grown up in a middle-class home as the youngest child, with nurturing and supportive parents and a protective older brother, and I had made all the "right" choices about where to go to be educated. As I reflect on the environments in which I have settled, I believe I made wise choices about my mentors and role models. Still, at that time I had this feeling that I was an imposter, or at least that the human resources office had made a mistake. I shared these thoughts with a mentor, and she said, "Believe in yourself. The institution will be stronger with your contributions, no matter what they are." I would hear these words again later in my career.

Fast forward a number of years to a different institution where I served in a leadership role for the division of student affairs. As I sat in my office, my supervisor said, "We need to engage our staff in a conversation, a dialogue of sorts, which advances the issue of diversity among the staff." For months, the leadership team in the division read, analyzed, researched, discussed, planned, and rehearsed an approach to explore the issue of diversity from both an affective and a cerebral perspective. We wanted not only to challenge conventional thought about diversity, but also to touch the hearts of the staff members, ideally in a way that might move them toward action. This action would manifest in structural and psychological changes in how we addressed and understood diversity. Additionally, it was believed that a real discussion on race, if effectively delivered, would enhance the experience of all staff, regardless of their racial or ethnic backgrounds. From the leadership team's perspective, the diversity dialogues were effective. From the perspectives of the staff members with whom we spoke, the diversity monologues were a paradigm shift and less supportive. We had spent a great deal of time thinking about what we wanted to tell the staff and what they needed to learn and understand, but we saved no time for an actual conversation. Although well intentioned, our diversity dialogues were one-sided and lacked the interchange between differing points of view. As a result of what were perceived as monologues on racial diversity, some staff members were asking themselves, "Is this the right institution for me?" But from where did this line of thinking come? I asked my supervisor about this, and he said, "Disrupting what others think about their place in the world is hard. It is even more challenging when the disruption is due to the construct of race. He went on to offer that as a person of color, I would carry an additional weight as I assumed leadership roles because of the personal and professional work on race that others were not offered or did not take on. I learned to not allow the additional weight to bring me down or stop me, but instead considered it an opportunity to strengthen myself. I learned early that some struggles can make us stronger, more agile, more thoughtful, and more aspirational. My supervisor offered, "The institution will be stronger for contributions you make."

FINDING MY AUTHENTIC SELF

I have come to believe that, overall, institutions and the leaders who are privileged to guide them want all searches and hires to be successful. Most supervisors want their employees, faculty, and staff to thrive because it makes the institution stronger. The same hopes and dreams we have for success and development in our students, we also have for our educators. That said, not all environments are ready, at any given moment in time, to be challenged, pushed, advanced, or engaged. This is where I have found I need a healthy balance of sage advice from mentors and the input of my inner self. I believe we, as educators, need to take responsibility for our own journeys and ask ourselves: Who will be our guides? From whom will we get perspective on various opportunities, challenges, and encounters? What is the right environment for us at this point in our lives? And, based on what we want to share and learn, where can we be most effective? The same supportive parents, protective siblings, and partners who believe in us and colleagues who enrich us can answer many of these questions when we are open and receptive to the feedback. I found one of these individuals when I began college.

The people we encounter on our distinct paths can encourage or discourage the time spent on reflection. I firmly believe that I am here in my current position because people believed in me. These people took the time to get to know me, not just superficially but at my core, they saw something—my authentic self. Susan is one such person. Susan was the quintessential dean of students and, at the same time, so much more, taking a broad view of the institution and its well-being. She oversaw everything from how the students lived in the residence halls to their personal problems, behavior, leadership, activities, recreation, and athletics. She was kind, generous, and interested in things like inclusion, diversity, high expectations, and positive student behavior. She had a love for her work in higher education. As an undergraduate student leader, I took an immediate liking to her and one day she invited me to lunch. I remember being really excited about this lunch with the dean whom I had met on more than one occasion. I RSVP'd that I could attend the lunch and then learned that it was not a private lunch but a monthly gathering she held with many students. Although disappointed that it was not a one-on-one lunch, I was intrigued.

One day after class, I decided to stop by Susan's office. She had mentioned in larger speeches that students should stop in any time, and I decided there was no time like the present to take her up on her offer. I wanted to learn more about the monthly lunches and what might be in store for me. I stopped in and Susan's door was closed. Her assistant, Peg, invited me to sit down and talk. This surprised me, and I was impressed with the care Peg took to get to know me. A one-day pop-in turned into a daily check-in. At one such meeting, Susan's door was open, and she warmly greeted me into her space. I became enamored that her job was to be with students. On her wall hung a number of interesting items—photos of student celebrations, various scenes highlighting the beauty of the campus, sporting events, and her academic degrees. The collection illustrated her interest in the campus and her appreciation for students' lives.

One item on the wall was a black-and-white photograph of people acting out a scene from *The Wizard of Oz*. I asked her why she put that particular scene of Dorothy, the Scarecrow, the Tin Man, and the Lion on her wall, and she explained that the photo, taken years earlier, was actually of staff members who were performing a skit for the parent summer orientation program. I was still confused until she clarified by sharing that the skit was based on a section of her dissertation. Dorothy, like many students on campus, had the ability and strength within her to accomplish her goal. But Dorothy did not realize it, or the environment was not such that she was able to recognize her own strengths. Students, at times because of the choices they make, are not always in the right situations to access or utilize their strengths. Susan explained that the environment and changes to it can unlock significant potential in students. She shared that at the end of each lunch she hosts for students, she gives them a keychain, and on this keychain they will place the "keys" to unlock their own potential, to change their own circumstances—the keys for Dorothy to get home, for the Scarecrow to think, for the Tin Man to feel, and for the Lion to be brave. It was the "a-ha" moment for me and one that influenced how I began to think about my own life and work. Environment matters, and we as leaders in higher education have within us the ability to shape it. Faculty champions, staff mentors, and everyone on campus play a role in the development of the student. I became a fixture in the dean's office, helping out in whatever way I could or sharing my own leadership stories from student government. Supported by Susan, early on I formed a conceptual framework for understanding leadership and service.

Quinton is another person who assisted me in finding my authentic self. Quinton and the entire leadership team had been discussing for some time the lack of structural diversity in the staff within the division. I remember thinking to myself that this was a significant issue given all of the research we know about diverse working environments. And, as for learning environments, diversity is key. But watching Quinton at a meeting, I was struck to see a White man speak with passion about the value of diversity. Obviously, this was something that had not just affected his mind; it also touched his heart. Quinton led a series of conversations about diversity with the leadership teams on campus. He offered that ending discrimination needed to be a personal responsibility that he and others needed to own.

Like Susan, Quinton was also in touch with who he was at his core. He had a great sense of self that added credibility to his leadership style. Having a conceptual framework of issues about justice and fairness is one thing, but to share openly about where and how you learned these concepts is deeper and more complex, and contributes not only to changing minds but to changing hearts and actions as well. As I worked with Quinton, he showed me that diversity is more than a category or group; it is the collection of stories that each person holds, the experiences that shape their lives, and the expressions of similarity and difference that serve as a foundation for mutual understanding.

DIVERSITY AS TEACHER

I have come to believe that diversity speaks to the deepest, most human part of the other person and ourselves. It gives me the opportunity to listen and understand how the other person experiences the world, makes meaning, finds fulfillment, deals with tragedy, and hopes for the future. Knowing how someone defines diversity or how the person identifies along various aspects of diversity (e.g., race, ethnicity, age, gender, sexual orientation) provides perspective and context. A true desire to understand the place of the other allows me the opportunity to explain who I am, where I came from, how I think about the world, what is important to me, what frustrates me, and what love, hate, and compassion each look like to me. Diversity allows me to think about my daily routines and to attend to the details of my life and to make adjustments based on what I am learning. Diversity has become the way I connect to people and reach deeper understandings of the human experience. Diversity allows me to soar with my greatest hopes for my children and my partner.

In fact, I believe some of my best work occurs when I address diversity and inclusion. I think how we address diversity and inclusion successfully is one of the biggest questions facing the human race the world over. The big societal institutions of government, religion, business, family, and medicine, among others, are not going to solve the issue, although each could contribute significantly to making our world equitable, just, and inclusive.

FROM AWARENESS TO ACTION

As leaders on college and university campuses, we hold positions of power. Understanding issues of equity, privilege, oppression, and social justice is critical as we continually shape and refine campuses for student success, faculty enrichment, and institutional success. I can recall being in meetings where faculty and staff discussed issues of power and how, knowingly or unconsciously, leaders can shape the experiences of others.

I believe understanding the various components of our own identity is important to changing the status quo. In any given situation, I try to ask myself, "Am I seeing and hearing the hopes and aspirations of other people, or am I focused on my wants and desires?" Understanding my own motivation from where I sit has been an important lesson in leadership because of the importance I place on fairness and justice.

I recall from childhood asking one of my first mentors, my brother, to play a game with me. If he said he would play the game, I could count on it happening no matter what. But once, I recall him not playing, after he said he could. I reminded him that he made a promise. He told me it was the best way for him to teach me that sometimes people place little importance on words and that I needed to look at actions. For me, a person's word was everything and, while I still find myself focused on what people say, I realize that actions are also important. Placing too much emphasis on language has created its share of challenges. I tend to believe others until I am given reason not to—so liars, cheaters, and other unscrupulous folks might get ahead at first, but then I wise up. Fool me once, shame on you . . . you know how it goes.

That said, I continue to think about diversity and leadership through a lens of fairness and justice. I recognize my roots of fairness and justice come from my immediate family and were informed by my early life experiences with family, church, schools, friends in the neighborhood, and episodes of *The Brady Bunch, The Cosby Show, Family Ties,* and even *Happy Days.* Real-life experiences, of course, continually offer more tangible expressions of values of love, honesty, loyalty, faith, and the worth of every human life. In different phases of my life I grappled with different experiences and ways of thinking about and acting on those values. I love differently now than I did when I was younger. I share who I am with certain people. I am loyal and true to a fault with some, and I value the lives of others more than I ever have. At the same time, I make decisions quickly, I can close myself off to a person when I become disappointed or when I perceive someone to be an obstruction- ist or closed off to another way of thinking—yes, I am in touch with my humanity and realize my shortcoming of not giving second chances.

I make mistakes in both my professional and personal lives. George Bernard Shaw said, "A life spent making mistakes is not only more honorable, but more useful than a life spent doing nothing" ("George Bernard Shaw quotes," n.d.). More applicable to a search for authentic- ity is Shaw's quote, "Success does not consist in never making mistakes but in never making the same one a second time" ("George Bernard Shaw quotes," n.d.). Looking back, I can see times when I shared too much, did not share enough, made rash decisions about another, did not make any decision, or did not attribute the best motive to another. And, mind you, these are all things that I tell students and colleagues not to do. Still, I am a firm believer in the potential to always do more, to always be better. The shortfall in that line of thinking is that my notion of *more* or my notion of *better* is limiting—it's about me and not you, and not you and I together. I have grown comfortable with my limitations, but it took time. I am often willing to offer grace to others who make mistakes but struggle with providing that same grace for myself and embracing my authentic self.

LESSONS ARE EVERYWHERE, JUST LOOK

Dealing with your own humanity, the negative audiotapes, and self-doubt is never easy. Fortunately, I have worked with a supervisor who was a mean-spirited, narcissistic bully. I recall him once saying to me, "I don't pay you to disagree with me." In a moment of not thinking before I spoke, I responded, "You don't pay me enough not to disagree." Even in the moment, I realized I was wrong to reply in such a way. It was not who I aspire to be, and there are numerous ways I could have responded in a more professional, helpful, graceful, and generous way. The same supervisor once told me that I was "too honest." A colleague said that I cared "far too much." And someone I supervised asked me if I could just "give it a rest about collaboration." Each of these encounters hurt, but in each situation I came to the notion that I needed to keep moving forward. I needed to be myself even if who I am is not appreciated in the moment. I needed to be me because it would feel awkward to do otherwise. I needed to be my authentic self because, as mentors and supervisors earlier told me, "The institution will be stronger for the contributions you make."

After reflecting on the context of the situation in which these comments were made, I came to learn that sometimes the supervisor was not the malicious, dishonest, uncaring person I initially made him out to be. Sometimes supervisors and leaders have a particular way and in a particular time frame they need things to be done, and these same people sometimes struggle with communication. It's grace that I want to be afforded, and affording it to others is an important step in the leadership journey. I came to recognize the ability to afford grace to others through work on campus climate. Community and campus climate are issues that shape our lives and hold great meaning for me.

One such story that now plays a critical role in my life happened years ago. With friends in my car, I drove my vehicle into a parking lot. Failing to negotiate access to the parking gate box, I handed the card key to a friend in the back seat who inserted the card, which raised the gate so that we could proceed. Almost immediately I was stopped by a White male campus security officer who began to interrogate me about my presence on campus, the origin of the card key, and other questions that I found unnecessary and demeaning. Certainly, the officer was doing his job, but as I look back, the manner in which he approached me and the accusatory tone in his voice made me feel different and unwanted. In short, he violated the sense of community I had always felt as a student.

In any community where there can be inclusion and exclusion, we need to constantly examine the messages we overtly and covertly send about racial diversity. Community in all of its forms is an essential part of college life, often making the difference between success and failure. For students who arrive on campus without clear direction or form, a community is a foundation to which they can return as they explore the world around them and attempt to come to terms with their place in it. In every area of life in general, the presence of community and the feeling of inclusion it offers is important, and that is especially true in higher education. The university is a place of many communities—spiritual, academic, and social, to name a few—and that is its great strength.

Although I managed to adjust easily to life in higher education and became a part of the larger communities, the developmental issues faced by others were different for me. There were times when I felt "I'm not like them" or "there's no one else here like me." Everyone at one time or another feels that way, but as an African American the feelings were magnified tenfold, especially when it became evident that the larger community did not always welcome those who were racially different.

With regard to diversity issues, the larger community falls into four distinct groups: those who understand the benefits and actively work to promote diversity, those who may not identify the benefits but work actively because it will better the institution, those who agree with the goal but disagree with the methods for reaching it, and those who disagree and offer resistance at every opportunity. When groups oppose the goal, they send the message that because you are different, you are not welcome. And that those who are different have nothing to contribute, and so their exclusion or mistreatment is justified. I believe that because of the diversity of my experience and my being, I have meaningful contributions to make.

AUTHENTIC LEADERSHIP

One person in particular, Steve, recognized an important contribution I could make. Steve gave me the proverbial seat at the table: my first vice presidency and my first opportunity to sit on the executive cabinet of an institution. I appreciated the lessons from Steve years ago and do so even more now. Steve was excited to be president of the institution and his joy was infectious. Steve's authenticity emanated from his willingness to animate the atmosphere or the spirit around him. Steve had certainly held numerous leadership positions and he reveled in inflection points, times that transformed his life. Steve told stories about these moments in his life that he thought might provide meaning or fulfillment for others. He was always instructive and always pastoral in his approach. He was comfortable in his own skin, confident in what he knew but assured that he did not know everything.

I remember a situation where the executive leaders of the institution were discussing strategic priorities. The team was trying to determine if items such as diversity and technology were foundational or differentiators in our strategic planning. After an hour of arguing numerous sides of the issue, Steve said, "We need to make this decision based on our principles and not react to what others will say. We never need to act from a place of fear." That moment crystalized for me how Steve looks at the world. He is joyful because of his faith and he is confident in his principles. I saw him as centered. His ability to lead from his center inspired me then and continues now as he grapples with such issues as how to differentiate his institution and foster a leadership in others that endures. I have a certain kinship with Steve's leadership because it is life giving. It's the kind of active and engaged leadership I aspire to incorporate in myself.

COMMUNICATION IS KEY

Equally powerful but very different is the leadership that emerges from studying people and their customs, beliefs, mores, and work. This is the kind of leadership and authenticity that flows from Charles. After working with Charles, I realized that he possessed an ability to communicate about the institution in an infectious manner. He was excited and confident in its direction and momentum. But unlike Steve, Charles did not emphasize the inflection points in his life; instead, he reflected on his life as a whole as a lesson. I remember him once saying to me, "The challenge for you is to both 'hit the ground running' and 'be the anthropologist' before rushing to make changes."

Charles wanted me to be good at both making change and also observing and allowing for change to happen in the right time. Through reflecting on my conversations with Charles, I was able to incorporate his feedback into my own thoughts about what I could do better for the organization. Charles's thoughtful guidance and laser-sharp focus on outcomes spoke to me. As I reflected on my ability to hear the feedback, it brought me to the issue of context.

Charles knows my background, and I know his. Charles can make sense of the current place and time, the short-term future, but he also has the power to dream. His ability to put words to a dream animates his leadership and allows others to follow.

WORK IN PROGRESS

Every day I feel I am getting closer to my authentic self, but I am still searching. I have been given a great gift in life, which is to love people who return that love—a partner, two wonderful children, my parents, brother, extended family, friends, colleagues, strangers, even occasionally students. I recall after a student's failed attempt to change a policy she said to me, "You've made a difference to me. I would have given up, but your care for me as a person showed me that I needed to at least try and let the chips fall where they may. Thanks for caring, being human, and being honest with me." I struggled to accept that compliment because I could not remember being honest with her. But I did remember feeling rushed, and I remembered being abrupt, direct, and eagerly wanting to move on to the next terribly important thing on my list that day. I remembered thinking that this student was taking a great deal of my time, and that her visits were taking me off task.

This student's compliment reminded me why I love what I do: I have the privilege of shaping environments that work for students, faculty, and staff, whether it's teaching a course, raising money for a scholarship or a building, working with colleagues on complex issues to enhance university life, or grappling with tough budgetary issues and prioritizing strategic initiatives. Students are the campus's reason for being, and taking some time to pause and reflect is important. Moments to pause are sometimes self-imposed, and other times they land on me like a ton of bricks.

In this situation, this student provided me a very valuable lesson. She saw my actions as helpful and caring, but more so, she provided me with more grace than I had given myself. Sometimes, as college and university leaders, we don't see and hear our authentic selves, and it is important that we recognize when others do. Mentors, guides, and others do that for me day in and day out. They hold up mirrors for me and allow me to keep trying, striving to do more, improving, succeeding, and even stumbling from time to time. And this was a lesson about being a work in progress. It's not easy but success comes to those who are all-in in the continual journey to find their authentic selves.

In reflecting on my career thus far, I am continually integrating what it means to live and lead from within the context of higher education. As a leader I need to be allowed to experiment. I need to be able to laugh even in the midst of deep, unsettling pain. I need space where I can be open and exposed, where judgment is suspended for a time. Like others, I have come to know we all need to be celebrated, cherished, and honored. We all need to be embraced. Ultimately, we need to be accountable. So hold me accountable, but *hold me*. I will do the same for you.

Reference

George Bernard Shaw quotes. (n.d.). Retrieved from https://www.brainyquote.com/authors/
george_bernard_shaw

The "I" and the "It" of University Leadership

Stephen V. Sundborg

think one of the first things Rob Kelly would say about me is that I don't read leadership books. I have the world's best unread collection of them, because people give me one about every week. I don't know if they do that because they think I am a leader or because they think I need help to become one. After 19 years as a university president, I have my own understanding of what is the core of leadership, especially university leadership. It explains both why I don't read leadership books and why I invited Rob to the table of the cabinet of Seattle University as our vice president for student development many years ago.

I hold that leadership is not a set of skills or practices, not even a number of habits—although these are important and helpful if they have a core or a center to adhere to and to branch out from. I believe that leadership is one of the most personal of realities that tests and shapes us, makes us vulnerable and self-possessed, puts us in hundreds of enriching and challenging relationships, and deepens our humanity.

Stephen V. Sundborg, SJ, a Jesuit and theologian, became president of Seattle University in July 1997. He leads a comprehensive, independent university of more than 7,500 undergraduate and graduate students and 1,000 faculty and staff members.

It is not easy to write about leadership because it is so personal and particular to the individual person.

The core of leadership is the integration in an individual of what I call the "I" and the "it." The "it" is the set of expectations and parameters, roles and relationships, and responsibilities and opportunities of a leadership position. They are endless and they come from others, especially from all of the constituents to whom a university leader must attend. If you seek primarily to satisfy the "it" of a position, you are necessarily living in a secondhand way, because you are, in effect, living and seeking to fulfill the expectations of others. You are living their wants rather than your own. That is deadening, killing. I should know, because I fully served the "it" of my presidency in my first year and had a heart attack at the end of it!

On the other hand, the "I" of a person in a leadership position is who a person is—how he feels, imagines, thinks, loves, relates, is present to himself, ponders and prays, relaxes, suffers, and enjoys. The "I" is how a person is linked to her past and her family, remembers, treasures, holds, values, aspires, dreams, and dares. You can't responsibly carry out a leadership position simply by being the "I," being who you are, and doing what you feel or want. That works for about a day. There are boundaries and requirements to leadership.

The sole, critical core around which leadership must manifest itself is the integration of the "I" and the "it," each of them informing the other, not flip-flopping from one to the other as an unpredictable leader, but forming a whole, a unity, a reliable single center. From that integrated center a leader acts with consistency, with personal energy, with persuasive power because the person draws from her deepest self and fills the position of responsibility with herself, with her life. In my experience, especially as a long-serving president of a university, this is the sole indispensable reality of vital leadership. Without the integrated "I" and "it," there is nothing to which all of the needed skills and practices of leadership can attach themselves. If a leader has this core, I am convinced from experience that others will rally around him, enjoy working with him, because by magnetism and dynamism there will be a shared power for a common purpose. It's this core that is crucial. Another way of saying this is leading from this integrated core is leading from one's spirituality. It means being plugged into one's deepest source of power in living up to the demands and opportunities of leadership.

This is precisely what I saw in Rob Kelly and why I invited him to be vice president for student development at Seattle University and to take a seat at the table of our cabinet. Rob had been with us only for half a year, but I spotted in him what I had learned university leadership requires, and so I tapped him. In the very difficult and often misunderstood and underestimated aspect of university leadership in student life, Rob was Rob; Rob was alive; people loved working with him; they had energy because of him; he filled out his position of responsibility with his person. And what a person that was: relaxed, outgoing, fun-loving, gregarious, optimistic, engaging, committed, and talented! He was comfortable in who he was, in his body, as a man of color, in his culture, among students, and with colleagues who worked with him. We all agreed that no one could recruit others to work for them as well as Rob could. People want to work with a leader who is a person, who gives them agency, who allows them to be who they are in the leadership position they have. That's Rob. I turned the tables on the master recruiter and recruited him to join our table of central university leadership.

Rob brought to the table of our cabinet that same integrated, alive leader. He could be uncertain at first, but he got the hang of it. I remember him leaning over to me as I sat next to him at the table after two days of bloody budget deliberations to whisper, "Did I just get everything I was asking for?" I whispered back, "Yes, but this is the last time!" Rob was good, that good, and we were good to him that first year! The university leader who acts out of an integrated "I" and "it" makes it look easy, natural, and unburdened because he is not carrying the weight of the responsibilities (the "it") on his back. Instead, he has metabolized them so they are part of who he is. Rob is very natural; he makes it look easy. So do I, though it took me at least five years to do this, to live my own leadership rather than to serve others' expectations. Rob was quicker because of how alive he was in himself.

My one caution for the reader—and perhaps for Rob, too—is that this personalized way of leadership can be too personal, too idiosyncratic, and may not attend enough to structures, systems, policies, practices, and processes. My own experience is that the integrated "I"-and-"it" leader needs to surround himself or herself with people who are especially attentive to—and good at—the latter. When Rob left us to go to Loyola University Chicago, I knew it was the right move because there he could take on greater responsibilities, work with bigger and more complex systems, and seek to integrate greater demands. The "I" and the "it" would require a more difficult integration and further growth as a university leader.

I also wonder after 19 years what such a personalized way of leadership requires in regard to succession planning and in the abilities of the next leader. A university, for its health, requires both very personal leadership and strong, clear systems. I sometimes wonder whether my way of university leadership is too personalistic and not systemic enough.

My successor will know. Maybe Rob Kelly is that successor as president of Seattle University. Then it might not be the last time, Rob, of getting everything you ask for in budget deliberations! But, then, it still might be, because presidents, too, don't get all they want.

Rob Kelly is a deeply spiritual person who refuses to be hindered by the negatives in life. Like other successful professionals, his ability to rise above and go beyond barriers has come with time and experience. Self-reflection and the influence of mentors have been critical in his gaining the confidence to look past the negatives in his life—when shadows of self-doubt emerged, and when his institutions were not ready for change, especially regarding diversity. Because of his personal encounters with racism as an African American man, Kelly prioritizes the need for all within the academic community to focus on inclusion and to be diligent about examining "the messages we overtly and covertly send about racial diversity." His conception of diversity is the lens through which he "connect[s] to people and reach[es] deeper understandings of the human experience," which is also the principle on which his leadership rests.

One can admire Kelly's humility in admitting his own faults as he learns to work with a supervisor who was a "mean-spirited, narcissistic bully." Through it all, he continues to use advice from his mentors as his mantra: "The institution will be stronger for the contributions you make." One of his mentors exhibits the characteristics he aspires to incorporate into his own style of leading. He sees this leader as centered, joyful because of his faith, and confident in his principles. As Kelly works toward these aspirations he continues to submit to self-examination, all the while holding himself to a higher standard than what he expects of others. It is clear to me that Kelly will continue to strive as he climbs to greater heights in the profession.

Stephen Sundborg, in explaining why he hired Kelly to be vice president for student development and included him in the president's cabinet, shares a succinct and cogent description of how he views leadership. He admits that he does not read books on leadership because he has his own understanding of *core leadership*. Readers might hope that he will write a leadership book with his ideas in the future. To Sundborg, leadership is particular to the person and the context, and no formula or set of rules can apply to all. What he saw in Kelly was an integrated person who was "comfortable in who he was, in his body, as a man of color, in his culture, among students, and with colleagues who worked with him." Kelly's ability to integrate who he was with the expectations and other requirements of his position convinced Sundborg that he possessed that integration of the "I" and the "it."

Sundborg believes that if one possesses this core leadership, others will be drawn to the person and be willing to work toward common purposes. He recognized that Kelly had this kind of impact on others. Sundborg could see similarities between his own core leadership characteristics and those that Kelly possessed. He could see the upside and he could also see that caution might be necessary because such a personalized approach to leadership could have the downside of not attending as much to structures and systems. In his final comments giving a nod to the fact that Kelly is presidential material, he suggests that Kelly will know how to balance the "I" and the "it" or ensure that there are others around him who can assure that there is attention to all parts of Sundborg's concept of core leadership.

—Gwendolyn Jordan Dungy

Mamta M. Accapadi

Mamta M. Accapadi currently serves as the vice president for student affairs at Rollins College. She has served as dean of student life at Oregon State University and worked in multicultural affairs at The University of Texas at Austin. An active member of NASPA–Student Affairs Administrators in Higher Education, she has served as chair of the NASPA Undergraduate Fellows Program Board and on the faculties of the NASPA Institute for New Vice Presidents for Student Affairs, the NASPA Alice Manicur Symposium, and the Dungy Leadership Institute. She has held academic appointments in ethnic/Asian American studies, women's studies, and educational psychology. She received her BA, MEd, and PhD from The University of Texas at Austin.

A Journey of Reconciliation and Healing

Mamta M. Accapadi

Everyone has a story. Our stories are glorious tales of reconciliation of others' expectations of us, our own internalized perceptions of ourselves, and our aspirations of who we want to become. When I was invited to contribute to this book, I found myself in a collision of these tales. Surely, the invitation came by mistake. Even if it was not by mistake, the invitation must have come because other colleagues were not able to participate. A major theme in my life story has been not being the "first choice," but rather the "promising alternate who surprised people." So, it took a few days to fully process that the invitation to participate in this project was real; it then took more time to figure out how I could show up wholly and authentically and in a way that would honor the hopes of the mentors and colleagues who extended the invitation. I continue to be shocked and humbled that, even decades later, I am still in dialogue with the young timid woman who lives in my heart, trying to figure out what others see—things that I either take for granted or don't recognize in myself at all.

I went to college to fulfill my immigrant parents' hopes and dreams of becoming a medical doctor. When I was leaving for college, my mother said to me, "I can now die in peace. My daughter is going to become a doctor." Although we did not have much in terms of financial resources, my parents invested everything they had in me. Tears still come to my eyes when I think about their countless sacrifices. I wish I could have been resilient enough, brave enough, smart enough, but during my college years, I experienced multiple breakdowns that I would now identify as depression and anxiety, triggered by my struggle to navigate an environment that was so deeply foreign to me while carrying the pressure to honor my parents' wishes. Despite having grown up on a college campus where my father served in an administrative support role, I had no idea how to navigate my undergraduate journey. I am grateful for the compassionate educators who supported and mentored me along the way, particularly women of color and specifically Black women. Although we educators who work with underrepresented groups often hear a version of my story, what was missing throughout my specific journey were people skilled enough to understand my perspective from my particular identity frame.

And this is why I chose this profession.

In the following pages, I will share vignettes from different stages of my life and career that have shaped my trajectory and transformation as an educator.

IN MY SHOES

Like many of us, I stumbled upon the field of student affairs. My first job, as an orientation advisor, introduced me to the wondrous world of the dean of students' office. I was at the brink of self-harm after such a difficult first year in college, so finding this home full of mentors and student affairs educators was the saving grace for me. I was enamored by "Jane," one of the senior administrators in student affairs. She was passionate about students. Jane had funny stories. She lit up a room with her vivacity and spirit. Jane was a staunch supporter of women. She embodied strength and commanded respect. Upon meeting Jane, I knew I wanted to *be* Jane.

"You can tell which of our students are leaders by their shoes; their choice of shoes can tell you how they make decisions."

Those may not have been her exact words, but I remember this moment as if it were yesterday. Jane—mentor of my dreams, in a conversation about leadership—made a statement about how she was able to discern student leaders based on their shoes. I was heartbroken. I remember looking at my worn-out sneakers that I wore everywhere, trying to reconcile that I would never be considered leadership material because my shoes told a story that did not align with Jane's standard of leadership. My "shero," the person I aspired to be, probably without ever realizing it, was implying that I was not a leader. I accepted the heartbreak, and because I was determined to impress her, I saved money from my paychecks to buy shoes worthy of her praise.

Over the next few years, my career advanced. I graduated and, while continuing my studies, became the university ombudsman for student–university matters. By this time, I was earning a meager annual salary in this role, but not only did I have name-brand shoes, I had also figured out a way to buy nice clothes—though often not in my size, and on clearance, so I had to hem and tuck as needed to adjust the fit.

In my ombudsman role, I often served as a mediator between parties in conflict. There was an instance in which Jane, another student affairs administrator, and I served as an arbitration body to resolve an issue between a student and a campus department. Initially, because the department had not technically violated any policy, the team was leaning toward upholding the department's decision. I was afraid to speak up, particularly in disagreement with my mentor, but I managed to share a different opinion, asking our team to consider the spirit of the policy and what it implied, not just what it technically said. This comment led to more lengthy discussion and a final determination in favor of the student. At the end of that meeting, Jane pulled me aside and said, "Nice job, Mamta. I really appreciated your thinking and approach to fairness. And by the way, nice shoes!" And she smiled.

Even today, when I think back on those early years in my career, I still feel a longing for validation from Jane. I have so much gratitude for what she taught me, but I know now that Jane was not my mentor. Her mentees were women like her. Jane hired her mentees as student workers. Jane had meals with her mentees. She met and knew her mentees' families. As much as I loved her and wanted her to love me, Jane was never my mentor and I was never her mentee.

At the time, I lacked the critical lens necessary to critique Jane's narrow assessment of leadership. I also failed to see who held what roles in the office, particularly who was holding me—and others like me—up behind the scenes without the pomp and circumstance and show-womanship. It was only later that I began to notice the patterns. Why did only White women from historically White sororities have access to leaders like Jane? Why did I not notice how much support, challenging work, and opportunity I was actually getting from my mentors, both of whom were Black women? Why was I so ashamed of who I was? Why was it that the only thing that I could imagine as leadership was erasing my story and forcing myself into metaphorical shoes that never honored my journey?

PERPETUATING STATUS QUO VERSUS DISRUPTING STATUS QUO

As I look back on my early experiences, I have both compassion and criticism toward Jane. I cannot imagine what her journey must have been for her to reach her position. Jane's sacrifices certainly paved the way for women like me. I have compassion for her story even though

I do not know it. I have some criticism because I can now clearly see that although she appeared as a confident leader, her leadership style was informed from a place of pain. She may not have presented herself as angry or in pain, but her actions reveal a clear commitment to making sure that others like her would not experience the same pain and/or lack of access that she likely experienced as a woman in our male-dominated field.

When we experience pain from oppression, there are two dominant paths we take to navigate and reconcile that pain. One path is replicating the oppressor. In its mildest form, this can look like a practice that legal scholar Kenji Yoshino refers to as *covering*, where we downplay characteristics or behaviors attributed to stereotypes of our minoritized identities (Yoshino, 2007). This may look like women "not showing emotion" or people of color changing their "ethnic-sounding names." It may look like physically and behaviorally conforming to a gender binary. In Jane's case, she encouraged a certain tone of voice for women, and she valued a certain professional appearance informed by corporate norms that generally appeared to be defined by men.

In a more harmful path, the replication of oppression takes the form of internalized oppression and horizontal aggression. Along this path, individuals who have internalized their oppression use dominant group behaviors—ostensibly to transcend their oppression—and may engage in horizontal aggression to enforce the dominant group. In Jane's case, while she was a staunch advocate for women, her advocacy required that women lead like men in cute shoes or that legitimate student leaders come from certain parts of the university student population—specifically, upper middle-class White women in sororities.

In both paths, although Jane may have challenged sexism at the individual level by supporting specific women, she actually amplified sexism systemically by making decisions that maintained behaviors of the status quo—decisions informed by sexism, classism, racism, cisnormativity, and so forth—allowing only groups with certain backgrounds access to leadership and other opportunities. As educators, we have a duty to disrupt the status quo and dismantle those very systems and norms that have perpetuated lack of access for minoritized communities.

In student affairs, we rely on theories to understand how we might best support students at our institutions. We have theories of leadership, identity development, moral development, and other topics. While theories are not perfect, they give us pathways of inquiry and insight. In *Teaching to Transgress*, bell hooks shared how she came to engage theory as a liberating tool. She wrote:

> I came to theory because I was hurting—the pain within me was so intense that I could not go on living. I came to theory desperate, wanting to comprehend—to grasp what was happening around and within me. Most importantly, I wanted to make the hurt go away. I saw in theory, then, a location for healing. (hooks, 1994, p. 59)

So, how can we leverage theory as a tool of liberation? I draw guidance from Sufi wisdom to inform my practice. Rumi suggested that "the wound is where the Light enters you" ("Rumi quotes," n.d.). Although he invoked the divine in his poetry, I find his invocation relevant as we think about how our identities inform our leadership practices. If we are to disrupt the status quo, we must recognize that the status quo has been a source of harm and that we, through our privileged identities, are the conduit of that harm. Then we must also commit to reconciling how oppression has affected us. Put differently, an advocate of the status quo might lead from the mindset "I did it, so you can do it, too," whereas the disruptor of the status quo might lead from the mindset "I need to name my pain, do my own healing, and I will support your journey to do the same." hooks (1994) reminds us that, indeed, "it is not easy to name our pain, to theorize from that location" (p. 74).

SELF-WORK MATTERS

What I have learned, reflecting on Jane's experiences with me and on my own experiences as an educator, is that we need to do our self-work in order to lead fully and authentically on our campuses and in our communities.

By the time I began working in multicultural affairs, I had become the "angry woman of color." That anger was triggered by pain when I realized that I was never someone Jane considered to be a future leader in our field. It came from the pain of realizing that as a mild-mannered and safe student of color of Asian descent, I had a different kind of access than that of my Black and Latinx/a/o peers, who were advocating for racial justice, and the stereotypes of our identities were being juxtaposed against one another in a way that positioned my Black peers, in particular, to seem uncooperative or angry. It came from the pain of not being seen as a legitimate person of color on a campus stuck in a Black–Latinx/a/o–White paradigm. The pain and the anger were legitimate; however, as legitimate as that pain may have been, it kept me from leading at my institution. I imposed my pain on the stories of those students with whom I worked. This imposition was not only unfair, it was inappropriate because I allowed my pain to eclipse their lived realities, and I also used my position of power as a staff member to do so. As I think back on that time, I wish I would have created space to honor my own pain and healing so that I could have better served students of color on their own terms, in their own truths.

I recall another moment, when the dean of students, Teresa Graham Brett—a woman whom I initially critiqued but whom I am now able to honor with great admiration—was facilitating a training session on privilege and diverse populations. It was the first time I was introduced to these concepts, and she had us engage in an exercise to reflect on our comfort levels in working with specific identity-based populations. We were discussing lesbian, gay, bisexual, and transgender students, and I confidently proclaimed that I had no discomfort in supporting these particular groups of students because since I was a person of color, and since I had worked with gay and lesbian students before, I *completely* understood what they were going through. A few days later, Brett stopped me and asked me to think about my comment. She challenged me to consider my reaction if a White colleague would have claimed to understand students of color because he or she had another subordinated identity, or because he or she had a relationship with a handful of students of color. And I know what my reaction would have been: it would have been one of judgment and anger. I share this narrative to point out that I was so consumed by my own pain as a person of color, I was not able to recognize when I showed up in my dominant identity—in this case, my heteronormative and cisnormative identities. Brett had a profound impact on my career even though I never appreciated her style of leadership when I worked with her. I was tethered to my pain in a way that was keeping me from being an agent of liberation. Similarly, Jane had not done the self-work on her identity as a woman or as a White person, so she could not recognize when she was engaging in oppressive practice, advocacy, or allyship; she was only able to lead from a space of unexamined and unreconciled pain.

I think doing this kind of self-work is not only the most difficult part of being a leader but also the most rewarding and most liberating part. And we cannot do this kind of work alone. We need coaches and counselors to help us along the way. My mentor and former supervisor, Larry Roper, continually reminds me that I cannot lead from the place of pain and that I always have the ability to lead from a space of joy, no matter what circumstance I may be in. Doing the self-work to follow this advice has required me to do some of the most difficult self-examination I have ever done in my life—and to be honest about where I still have to heal and grow.

A CALL FOR INTERSECTIONAL REFLEXIVITY

I recall a tough conversation I had with a White woman colleague who came from a low-income/working-poor background. At her institution, almost all of the people of color on her team had expressed frustration in working with her, particularly feeling minimized around coded racialized and classist behavior. At the same time, she often remarked on what it was like to navigate the "good old boys," referencing her male-dominated work environment. When I challenged her to think about whether she was able to take in feedback about the impact her Whiteness was having on her colleagues, she was resistant to hearing it. When I asked her if she had shared feedback about the good old boys environment to her male colleagues, she said that it was difficult to do so because of the gender power difference. I asked her why she could see the difficulty from a gender power difference and not draw that same parallel in what her staff of color were not able to share with her. She resisted further, noting that she had friends of color and that nobody had ever shared this feedback with her before.

As higher education leaders, educators, activists, and scholars, we cannot separate our identities—and perceptions of our identities—from our leadership practice. My colleague, very quick to name classism and sexism, chose neither to name nor own her cisnormativity, Whiteness, and internalized classism. Consequently, because she chose to not name her dominant identities, she could not fully embrace how the intersections of her identities impacted others' perceptions and actual experiences with her. Her naming of sexism but lack of reconciliation of its profound impact on her identity resulted in the performance of patriarchy in a form more harmful than a man's performance of patriarchy. Additionally, she was not able to recognize how her unexamined performance of Whiteness and her assertion of upper-middle-class norms further contributed to her colleagues' experience of her as deeply oppressive. While she had an opportunity to pause and understand these dynamics, she chose to affirm her right to lead in this way "because men do it all the time."

Self-work requires intersectional reflexivity. This means that our greatest self-work requires us to honor our identities (the ones that are salient to us and the ones that may not be salient) and come to understand how we have experienced those identities, how those experiences have shaped how we engage with others, and how we show up in the world. It also means that we have to look at how the intersections of our identities further situate how we are perceived. As an Asian American woman vice president of Indian descent, I am initially perceived by people to be submissive, meek, and conflict avoidant. When I am treated this way, I experience deep trigger, and I have to manage my anger because I have dealt with this stereotype my whole life. It also means that just as I honor those intersections, I must purposefully recognize how my upper middle-class, heteronormative, U.S. citizenship status gives me amplified access to opportunities and norms that I take for granted.

Now more than ever, students from a broader range of backgrounds and identities are going to college. Whether or not we share commonalities in the stories or identities of our students, we as leaders must recognize the complexities of our identities. As I offered earlier, while I experienced racism as a person of color, I also really needed to understand how I participated as an oppressor of lesbian, gay, bisexual, and transgender people. I needed to understand how my identities take up space for me, for my colleagues, and for the students I serve—and how I might leverage my leadership to create equitable space for my colleagues and students to thrive.

OUR LEADERSHIP IMPERATIVE AS TRANSFORMATIVE EDUCATORS

I often share with graduate students and new professionals that we as educators do the greatest harm from our unexamined, dominant places even if we have good intentions. This harm occurs precisely because we are not able to challenge what we are afraid to name, and we choose not to name what we are not able or willing to own. At a previous institution, I received many complaints about a faculty member who referred to his Black male students by names of Black celebrities. Students complained that they felt dehumanized, and when I discussed the matter with him, he shared his history of being involved in the Civil Rights Movement during his early career; he felt that the students were being too sensitive. In college, when I was in the middle of the many breakdowns I experienced from the pressure of trying to fulfill my parents' dream of me becoming a doctor, I reached out to my academic advisor, who told me that "[my] people do just fine." She further affirmed that I was "an adult, and in America, where we can make our own decisions." In both of these scenarios, the professor and my advisor came from a caring place with good intention—even though many of us may not see it that way. What they did not do was come from an intersectional place or from a place where they examined their own identities. When we lead in this way, the only outcome is detriment toward the very students or colleagues we are trying to support or mentor. Our leadership imperative as senior educators requires us to lead from a space of cultural humility and to champion mutual liberation.

CULTURAL HUMILITY

Because of my background in multicultural affairs and social justice education, I have been profoundly influenced by the field of social work. As I continued to seek resources to develop curriculum around dismantling privilege in student affairs, I initially encountered the concept of cultural humility through social work, which was first introduced in the field of multicultural education for medical practitioners. Tervalon and Murray-García (1998) proposed that care providers need to move beyond cultural competence and toward cultural humility for a 21st-century approach to medical care. The three major pillars of cultural humility include a lifelong commitment to self-reflection and self-critique, acknowledgment of power imbalances within the care provider–client relationship, and development of mutually respectful and dynamic partnerships on behalf of clients and communities.

For me, *self-reflection and self-critique* means that I commit to being a lifelong learner. This means that my learning is not only academic but also personal—and that it comes from every dimension of my life. This process also means that I must really examine the roots that shape my values, which, in turn, inform my opinions and actions, and it means that I must be humble enough to recognize where I may have gaps of self-awareness. When I have experienced challenges in all of my past positions in student affairs, I can trace back the roots of those challenges to not being in a space of self-reflection and critique.

When I think about how I *acknowledge power imbalances*, it means recognizing that everyone brings wisdom to the table. This also means that I always need to be in check of the power that is ascribed to me in my positional leadership identity as well as in the one that I assert. I used to struggle with this concept because I never wanted to acknowledge I had power, or I tried to operate in a space without power. Because my salient professional identity is that of a social justice educator, I have generally internalized a negative connotation of the term *power*. While I am still on my own journey with how I engage that term, I have come to reconcile that my role is to leverage power by redistributing it, diffusing it, naming and critiquing it, and/or asserting it appropriately, depending on the circumstance.

Finally, *developing mutually respectful and dynamic partnerships* means that I must take all of these concepts and be in relationship with my colleagues, students, fellow educators, and beyond to facilitate systemic change. Our opinions and values are only as effective as the impact we make for the greater good of our communities while in an authentic relationship with those communities. Student affairs is not a profession that was ever intended to maintain a status quo. Every dimension of our field, every functional area commits to the development of the students we are privileged to serve. Development, by definition, implies a shift or change of perspective, awareness, or consciousness.

CHAMPION MUTUAL LIBERATION

Higher education institutions occupy a place of tension: They are mission-driven entities committed to the success of their students, but they attempt to fulfill this mission with countless policies, procedures, and bureaucratic practices. In student affairs, we create, hold, and implement our institutions' fair share of those practices. My very first professional job in the field, as university ombudsman, taught me to consider a different approach to our work. After hearing many appeals of grades from students whose professors may not have developed clear grading expectations in their syllabi and policy disputes because a student submitted a form too late or to the wrong office, I realize that our work is about transcending the policy enforcement dialogue and advancing the mutual liberation dialogue.

I want to be clear that I am not advocating that we throw all infrastructure to the wind; rather, I am suggesting that we elevate the spirit of our work. This is the artistic practice of our work. For example, when I have worked with international students who are involved in student conduct matters, I think very critically about what it means to uphold my institution's community standards, while also considering the disproportional impact on that student—particularly as it relates to sanctions of suspension or expulsion. It is our job to sit in the tension of our values and our infrastructure while honoring and adjusting both of them.

I have developed a commitment to being a detached educator working toward a practice that may someday lead to mutual liberation of myself, my colleagues, my students, and beyond. This perspective comes from my Hindu upbringing, specifically a text widely used to guide one's spiritual and physical commitment to living a purposeful life, the yoga sutras by Patanjali. This text is a compilation of 196 sutras, or sayings, across four chapters that prepare one for spiritual liberation. Because I see our work as grounded in mutual liberation, this text has had a profound impact in shaping my approach as an educator. The second chapter offers the eightfold path of yogic practices that "yoke" us on our path. To apply these eight limbs as a template for practice in our field, consider the following:

1. *Yamas*: These are ethical guiding principles. What principles guide your practice as an educator (e.g., "Do no harm")?
2. *Niyamas*: These are virtuous habits. Which habits shape your practice as an educator (e.g., transparency, social justice praxis–informed leadership)?
3. *Asana*: In yoga, the asana is the pose or position one is in. More broadly, how are we situated to lead with steadiness, ease, and joy from our own positions?
4. *Pranayama*: This is the regulation of one's breath and breathing. In our own work, how do we engage in the regulation of our own breath—meaning, when do we create space to inhale and exhale, to notice what is happening around us?
5. *Pratyahara*: This is the practice of withdrawing from the external senses. Sometimes we can be distracted by the many demands on our time. When do we create space for contemplation away from external distraction?
6. *Dharana*: This is being in a state of mind of unwavering focus. How can we align our goals to be in unwavering focus of

advancing the mission of our institutions and the success of our students?

7. *Dhyana*: Closely linked with *dharana*, this is the process of mind that sustains one's unwavering focus. How do we commit our actions to the goals on which we have chosen to focus?

8. *Samadhi*: In meditation practice, this is a harmonious union between the person engaging in meditation, the practice of meditation, and the subject of meditation. In our field, what would it mean if we could cultivate an ethos on our campus communities that is so aligned that one could not distinguish among our leadership as vice presidents, our work as organizations, and the student experience? That all of this would be, or could be, one seamless series of energetic moments? (Yoga Sutras, 2:29–3:3)

WE ARE THE CONSCIENCE OF THE INSTITUTION

When I worked as dean of student life at Oregon State University, I remember a faculty member, Lani Roberts, sharing with me that my then supervisor, Larry Roper, was the conscience of the university. I remember thinking to myself, "What a profound compliment, and what a great responsibility—to be the conscience of the institution!"

When I transitioned into my vice presidency at Rollins College a few years later, I found myself on a campus that was in deep need of hope and restorative energy. As a new vice president, I found myself intimidated by a small number of critical faculty, and I unfairly overlaid judgment on the entire faculty. I quickly internalized a fear-based narrative and felt that I had to lead from a place of asserting power. Initially, I felt that I had to just "sound more scholarly" or push back more confidently, or find evidence of how I was their equal as an educator. When I was beginning to cede my sense of hope, I ended up having lunch with two women faculty members who essentially said to me, "Stop trying to be a vice president, and be you." A day later, one of my own trusted colleagues in student affairs also said, "Don't show the faculty what we do in student affairs; show how we are all in partnership together, and *be* what we do in student affairs." A long-time member of the president's cabinet and one of my most treasured mentors, Lorrie Kyle, said to me, "You are the conscience of the college; you have to stay above it all." To be the conscience of the college—this is our work. It is our calling. And we are only as clear as our self-work allows us to be. We can only lead as far as our own personal growth will take us. Our mutual liberation as individuals and the health of our communities depend on it. This is the path to *samadhi*.

As an educator, I always think back on that day I went off to college, carrying the hopes and dreams of my family with me. Back then, they felt like a burden that I did not feel equipped to bear. Today, I realize that it was actually those hopes and dreams that were carrying me all along—as the foundation of my wholeness and humanity. When I learned to be in reconciliation of all of my stories, I was able to commit to a path of authentic leadership in my own wholeness and be a champion of that journey for all the students we are lucky to serve—no matter what shoes they come with.

References

hooks, b. (1994). *Teaching to transgress: Education as the practice of freedom*. New York, NY: Routledge.

Rumi quotes. (n.d.). Retrieved from https://www.goodreads.com/quotes/103315-the-wound-is-the-place-where-the-light-enters-you

Tervalon, M., & Murray-García, J. (1998). Cultural humility versus cultural competence: A critical distinction in defining physician training outcomes in multicultural education. *Journal of Health Care for the Poor and Underserved, 9*(2), 117–125.

Yoshino, K. (2007). *Covering: The hidden assault on our civil rights*. New York, NY: Random House.

Reflections

Welcoming Mamta Accapadi

Larry D. Roper

D uring my more than 40 years in higher education, I have had the fortune and misfortune of a front-row seat to the evolution of conversations around diversity. When I began my professional journey in the mid-1970s, I had no awareness of specific conversations about diversity as a broad construct; the diversity-related conversations to which I was privy focused mainly on how to increase the number of Black students on predominantly White campuses. Much like the prevailing social/institutional conversations at the time, diversity was constructed to be a Black–White dichotomy. Obviously, our conception of diversity has evolved significantly since that time; now, we not only see diversity as a complex, multidimensional entity but we also attach social justice as a related component.

Diversity has always been important to me personally and professionally, though I must confess that I have needed to invest significant effort into expanding my personal conception of diversity from the narrow view with which I was socialized. Like that of most other student affairs professionals, my commitment was deepened and enriched by the experiences I've had with students. As a residence hall professional in the early part of my career, I had the opportunity to live in high-density settings with students, observe their struggles to live in community with each other, and directly respond to the unique cultural needs they presented. I was tasked to make sense of and honor life situations and cultural backgrounds with which I had little or no history. I was challenged to learn from, grow with, and support those whom I supervised in responding to the diverse needs presented by students. My early experience with diverse residence hall communities showed me that it is imperative to hire staff members who reflect and respond to the diverse students who attend our colleges and universities.

My consciousness of the need to hire diverse staff grew stronger as I moved through various professional roles and was probably most heightened during my time as a coordinator of multicultural affairs. In that role, I became aware of the significance of having other colleagues who understand the importance of diversity, who are committed to diversity, and who can work competently and sensitively with students from diverse backgrounds. However, while the aforementioned issues provided valuable insights, the most significant takeaway related to my observations about how those who serve in diversity-specific roles are regarded—and the implications such regard has for the long-term career prospects of those in multicultural affairs–type positions. As coordinator of multicultural affairs, I became highly sensitive to the perception that my job involved serving only a particular segment of the student population and that my knowledge was largely restricted to those who were defined as *diverse* students. I found this attitude to be restricting, dismissive of my knowledge and commitments as a student affairs professional, and a disservice to our institution because it diminished my potential contributions to student success on our campus. This coordinator experience and the observations I gleaned while serving in this role informed my perspective on hiring and staff selection.

It was not long after meeting Mamta Accapadi, when she came to Oregon State University to interview for the dean of student life position, that I had an intense gut instinct that she was the leader we needed in that role. Before meeting her, I was intrigued by the rich mix of professional and academic experiences she possessed. Her academic credentials and the level of responsibility her previous positions required in terms of deep engagement with issues that can enhance or divide campus communities struck me as being vital to success in the dean of student life role. However, I was relying on the interview to validate whether what appeared on paper as potential was reflected in interpersonal interaction as reality.

During the interview we asked each of the finalists to participate in a student affairs leadership team meeting so that they could get a sense of the leadership culture they would potentially be entering and so that their potential colleagues could get a sense of the candidates' perspectives. Additionally, I had dedicated one-on-one time with Mamta during the process. In simple terms, Mamta exhibited the three qualities I consider essential in hiring a new employee: she revealed herself to be smart, demonstrated a sound work ethic, and exhibited the ability to treat others with care, respect, and thoughtfulness. Even more powerfully, Mamta revealed that she understood what it meant to work on behalf of students.

Because of Mamta's background in multicultural affairs, I made a particular effort to be sensitive to how that experience might shape the range of institutional issues to which she might have been exposed. Clearly, there were candidates in our pool who had what may have been perceived as more experience with dean-like roles and responsibilities. However, the candidates' most recent experiences had less relevance for me than did the depth of thought that the successful candidate would bring to the position, his or her passion to learn and grow, and the qualities of leadership that a successful candidate would embody. Mamta's career revealed powerfully that she is committed to service to—and the success of—students of color. Her responses to issues during the interview process showed that her knowledge and potential for professional impact went far beyond the multicultural domain.

Our goal in hiring a dean of student life was to identify a person who was committed to the art of "deaning," which to me means someone who is willing and able to move in and out of various student and collegial communities and to build connections among those groups. We were seeking an individual who could listen acutely to the voices of the many constituents and discern the important issues being communicated. These basic needs and expectations for the position suggested that the successful candidate must bring with him or her a commitment to the entire student body, that he or she must possess a spirit of service and an ethic of deep care for the well-being of the individual and the community.

During our interview process we asked candidates to do a public presentation and to participate in public forums so that various stakeholder groups could have the opportunity to interact with them and so that the candidates could get exposure to the community's top-of-mind issues of concern. These events were very important for letting our community see the quality of individuals whom we were considering for the role. The public interactions also allowed our community members to see the diversity within our pool and to hear the diverse perspectives of the candidates. It has been important to me since the first opportunity I had to be involved in hiring that I use my role to enhance the diversity of the campus. At the same time, my greatest responsibility is to equip our staff with the highest-level competence we can attract in order to shape and advance our mission commitments.

As a leader, I can think of few more gratifying experiences than the opportunity to offer a position to a highly qualified person who enhances the diversity of an organization. Such was the case with hiring Mamta. I would be less than honest if I did not affirm that her diversity was important in her hiring, but I can also say that without her knowledge, skills, and demonstrated commitment, her diversity would not have mattered. Mamta was hired for her brilliance and for the demonstrated leadership that she has exhibited in the past and that was on display during her interview process. The fact that she would bring diversity along with those other personal and professional attributes was merely a bonus. For me, the bottom line was that our campus and the student affairs organization needed the attributes that Mamta possessed.

For me, the commitment to diversity is not about hiring individuals with an identifiable set of personal attributes; it is about hiring a unique mix of knowledge, skills, commitments, values, and behaviors/ways of being that are presented in ways that may not be detected by viewing individuals through traditional frames. A commitment to diversity means looking more closely for evidence of competence and potential, listening more deeply for knowledge and commitment, and reflecting more thoughtfully in considering the potential value that individuals might bring to the student affairs organization. Hiring for diversity must be more than hiring individuals to be representatives of a particular identity group. Commitment to diversity means hiring in a way that creates an organizational culture where the work will be informed by a broad range of perspectives, represented by a rich array of human histories, informed by knowledge from a breadth of areas, and committed to practice that reflects the cultural richness of those who participate in the life of our campus.

When we welcomed Mamta Accapadi to join the student affairs community at Oregon State University, I had no doubt that we were getting a colleague whose expertise would instantly make us a smarter organization, whose presence would make us a more caring organization, and whose work ethic would make us a more diligent organization. Now, in hindsight, I can affirm that even my most optimistic hopes were exceeded. Our organization did indeed get a tremendous dean of student life, but what I didn't anticipate is that I would gain a wise counselor, a valued colleague, and a dear friend whom I will cherish for the rest of my life. Oregon State University and I are forever changed because Mamta chose to join our organization.

In her narrative, Mamta Accapadi encourages the personal and professional soul searching that can lead to a commitment to tackle the complexities of our identities and how they influence our service and leadership practices. Major themes in her narrative are the duty of student affairs professionals to disrupt the status quo and to commit to doing self-work for inward clarity. Accapadi asserts that we cannot separate our identities and the perceptions of our identities from our practice.

Accapadi's description of her compassion and criticism of an admired mentor is an excellent example of how good people with good intentions can unwittingly hurt and exclude others from opportunities when they do not recognize their own prejudices—prejudices that stem from personal, often unacknowledged, experiences. If Accapadi's mentor had done the self-work to be the kind of leader who could leverage her position to change systems of exclusion, then she would have realized that she was not opening her perceptions to see strengths in women who were not like her. The beauty of this example is how Accapadi's perceptual frame shifts from wanting to be like the mentor to being able to critique the mentor while retaining compassion for her. Accapadi demonstrates the complexities involved in recognizing and owning one's own pain and healing while accepting others who bring with them different truths.

Accapadi introduces *cultural humility*, a particularly useful concept from the fields of social work and multicultural education for medical practitioners. While Accapadi describes the pillars of this idea, for me, the essence of the concept can be understood in her statement, "I must be humble enough to recognize where I may have gaps of self-awareness." Her essay emphasizes the act of deliberately connecting all the parts of one's life in order to be fully available to serve students—even if it means disrupting the status quo.

Having known both Larry Roper and Mamta Accapadi, as I read Roper's piece I thought about how lucky Oregon State University was to have both leaders at the same time. Roper relates that the goal was to hire a person committed to the art of "deaning." I pulled *Leadership Is an Art* by Max DePree from my shelf and thumbed through the book to find a statement that would define both Roper and Accapadi as exceptional leaders: "Leadership is much more an art, a belief, a condition of the heart, than a set of things to do" (DePree, 1989, p. 148).

During the process of selecting the dean of student life, Roper was looking beyond the candidate's most recent work experience; he was looking for that belief and condition of the heart that Accapadi brought, in part, as a result of her background in multicultural affairs. Using his own experiences as a professional in multicultural affairs, he looked for her spirit of service and her "deep ethic of care for the well-being of the individual and the community." These attributes go beyond the operational aspects of the dean's position. What he found during the interviews with her was that condition of the heart that assured him that she would indeed be committed to the art of deaning.

Roper's statement regarding the deliberative processes involved in hiring Accapadi clearly articulates what a commitment to diversity hiring means. He explains how it is much more than hiring representatives of particular identity groups. Roper's concluding comment about Accapadi is a strong testament to her professional skills and to her as a leader and a cherished friend.

—Gwendolyn Jordan Dungy

Reference

DePree, M. (1989). *Leadership is an art*. New York, NY: Dell Publishing.

Larry D. Roper

Larry Roper is a professor in the School of Language, Culture, and Society at Oregon State University, where he serves as coordinator of the undergraduate social justice minor and coordinator of the college student services administration graduate program. Previously, he served as vice provost for student affairs at Oregon State University from 1995 to 2014. He received his BA from Heidelberg College in Tiffin, Ohio; his MA from Bowling Green State University in Bowling Green, Ohio; and his PhD from the University of Maryland. Roper currently serves as a commissioner with the State of Oregon's Higher Education Coordinating Commission and on the Heidelberg University Board of Trustees.

Navigating Identity and Leadership

Larry D. Roper

When I was a child, my family and I spent a number of years living in the home of my grandmother. The house had two bedrooms, a small attached room that had to be entered from the back porch, and a full basement. During our stay, as many as 15 people were living together in that cramped home at any given time. The key architect of that living environment was my grandmother, Luberta Ellis, affectionately known in my family and in our neighborhood as "Ma Bert." She lovingly welcomed not only my family into her home but also cousins who had tragically lost their parents, aunts and uncles without means to provide for themselves, and other family members who would have been homeless otherwise. In addition to the extended family residing in the home, there was also a boarder living in the room just off the back porch and a single mother and her three children living in the basement.

The experience of living for several years in the densely packed space that was 311 Dean Street in Akron, Ohio, profoundly shaped my values, behaviors, and attitudes. As I have navigated through life, I can identify specific aspects of my worldview and leadership behaviors that directly result from my early life experiences, particularly the influence of my grandmother. Because my early life experiences were powerful and formative, I feel it is essential for me to acknowledge them, as I believe aspects of my personal story show up with me when I come to an organization, institution, group, or personal relationship.

A FOUNDATION FOR LEADERSHIP

My early childhood and family life offered some fundamental and foundational messages that have become recurring themes in my career as a student affairs professional, among them: bringing order to situations that have the potential to be chaotic; facilitating the development of loving, respectful relationships among a diverse group of people; navigating difficult personal and financial times, while still staying rooted in hope; being aware of the power of community and the shared strength that grows out of a group of people who are committed to one another; understanding the importance of hard work and the responsibility of each person to contribute whatever they are capable of to the group; needing to think beyond oneself and to give time and attention to the needs of others; and being resilient, which includes holding oneself and others together during challenging times.

Throughout my education and my career, I have had remarkable experiences with highly educated and accomplished individuals. But it is imperative that I acknowledge that the foundation of my leadership perspective is most deeply influenced by my grandmother, who never went beyond third grade but who possessed wisdom about the world—a true gift for bringing and holding groups of people together—and demonstrated a remarkable ability to breathe life into the dreams of others, no matter how difficult the circumstances.

Although I did not have the personal insights to fully understand all of the realities of my life in my early years—including the depth of poverty in which my family was embedded—I was able to recognize that I was blessed to have as the major influence in my life a woman who had deep love and commitment for her family, a home life that was rooted in love and respect among an indescribable mix of personalities and dispositions, and guidance from adults who modeled the importance of hard work. I must also note that while religion was an important facet of my early life, the more significant and overriding message with which I was instilled related to the importance of faith: that my life should be guided by deep belief and that my values should be influenced by an ethic of love and forgiveness.

During the first 18 years of my life in Akron, I had to work consistently to reconcile the powerful positive messages received from my family, the intense poverty of the various neighborhoods in which I lived, and the rhetoric of the American Dream and the Great Society that I heard both in school and in the political discourse of the time. As much as I wanted to believe all that might have been possible for me and those like me, I was surrounded daily by overwhelming evidence that the communities in which I lived were the object of isolation, neglect, and negativity.

I can recall watching with interest as a child as the president of the United States described some of the core elements of the Great Society—among them, a War on Poverty (later to be followed by a War on Drugs and a War on Crime). I personalized those messages to mean that the president had declared war on my neighborhood. My naïve mind could not distill positive intent from what President Johnson was promoting as hopeful aspirations for our nation. The subsequent civil unrest that affected my city and other metropolitan areas (referred to in the media as "race riots") only further reinforced my feeling that war had been waged on my inner-city community.

The family and neighborhood circumstances under which I grew up, the conditions of the schools I attended, and the social and political climate of the time all greatly influenced me. I left high school confused yet aspirant. I was hopeful that college would empower me to change the world; I believed that I would pursue a career that would allow me to right the wrongs I saw in the world.

HIGHER EDUCATION AND IDENTITY FORMATION

When I entered Heidelberg College as a freshman, I was fully focused on the goal of studying history and returning to my hometown to be a high school history teacher and football coach. I wanted to have the same positive influence on young people that my coaches and a handful of teachers had had on me. However, like many people who turn to the student affairs profession, I had some significant interactions with student affairs professionals early in my college career that inspired me to consider other paths. My undergraduate experience included being a resident assistant, a student athlete, and a student leader, thus giving me access to mentoring, encouragement, and support to pursue a master's degree in student affairs.

Even more, my college experience provided me with a role model for the type of student affairs professional I wanted to be, and it offered me insight into the powerful and transformative role that education can have when it is facilitated by caring, thoughtful, student-focused individuals. My undergraduate dean of students was and continues to be the most influential person in my professional career. While I have had the opportunity to work for and with some truly remarkable supervisors, I modeled the template of myself as a professional on the dean of students, as he performed his role with such mastery.

My undergraduate institution was a predominantly White college that enrolled approximately 1,100 students; among them were nearly 70 African American students and hardly any other visible racial diversity. Because of the era during which I attended college, no one acknowledged the possibility that there were gay or lesbian students on campus, so the possibility of having transgender students was not even considered. Thus, my intellectual formation and initial professional identity formation took place in an environment that was literally and figuratively a Black-and-White world.

Although I grew up in an overwhelmingly Black neighborhood and attended overwhelmingly Black schools, the coaches and teachers who guided me to pursue college were all White. So, the idea of forming a close relationship with my dean of students, a White man, felt quite natural to me. When I met Robert Oleson—or "Dean O" as he is fondly called—I was struck by his humble and soft-spoken nature. He possessed a natural gift of inviting others into relationship with him by demonstrating deep listening and true openness to hearing their stories. I struggled mightily to adjust to the college culture, so it was incredibly comforting to have Dean O reach out to me and provide me with thoughtful counsel and support. I was even more comforted when he introduced the issue of my Blackness into the conversation and challenged me to think about the role race might be playing in my adjustment challenges and to consider, too, the ways that my background might serve me well in finding success in college. Although I did not recognize it at the time, in 1971, Dean O led me to assume a strengths-based approach for looking at my education and how I looked at the world. In various ways throughout my career, I have tried to frame my leadership and the questions I pose in that same appreciative, strengths-based way.

The fact that Dean O showed the willingness to raise the issue of race (diversity) helped me to understand that leadership requires relationship courage. He raised the issue in a way that allowed me the option to explore whether race was a factor, encouraging me to take ownership over what I believed to be true about my life and social circumstances. It was truly empowering to be exposed to a person who gave me the stimulus and space to interrogate my experience. Dean O was my first mentor, and he has been my consistent mentor throughout my career.

I left college with the idea that my ultimate professional goal was to be a dean of students.

After completing my master's program, I still focused on the same professional destination even though I was aware of the professional possibilities beyond the dean of students role. I assumed my first full-time position at the same institution where I had held a graduate assistantship, and that job launched me on my journey.

JOURNEY TO LEADERSHIP

My career has been characterized by movement among a wide range of institution types, including small, private, denominational, land-grant, selective, financially fragile, and regional, among others. My choices to accept positions have been a combination of well-advised and uninformed decisions, and my length of stay at an institution has ranged from one year to more than 20 years. The common elements and consistent themes in my decisions to join, leave, or stay at an institution typically came down to the degree to which I felt the position would support movement toward my personal vision, whether I felt my growth was being promoted, whether I felt congruence between my values and the institution's mission, whether I had collaborative and supportive colleagues, and the degree to which I was afforded leadership autonomy.

As I navigated my career, I relied heavily on self-mentoring. Again, while I had some wonderful supervisors, I have never had a Black supervisor or a person of color serve in that role for me. My self-mentoring arose from the intense mix of issues with which I wrestled throughout my career and my doubts that anyone could truly understand them at the level I was feeling them. Although today I am certain that was not the case, at the time I was incapable of believing otherwise. Certainly, there have been pivotal people in my life who have imparted wisdom and guidance along the way, but—in the classical sense—I have traversed my career largely without a mentor.

My own maturity and growth, the people with whom I have been fortunate to work, my professional networks, and myriad unexpected and unanticipated circumstances that worked in my favor have influenced the trajectory of my career. While my career path has not been linear, there has been a thematic consistency in my professional journey, with common issues arising repeatedly. I never consciously developed a career map for reaching my goals, but I did have a sense of the type of experiences I needed and wanted to seek out. The themes in my career provide me with the best frame through which to describe and make sense of my journey.

PERSONAL VISION

While I began my career with a fairly fixed view of where I wanted to end up, I eventually found that I needed to make room to allow my personal vision to be influenced by what I learned along the way and the insights that others provided. Frankly, my goal of being a dean of students was based on the isolated world of my undergraduate experience. As I gained greater exposure to higher education and the wide diversity of institutions, I began to alter my view of the career possibilities that might be available to me. At the same time, as a first-generation college attendee and graduate, attaining a master's degree far exceeded my expectation of the level of education I would achieve. Thus, when it was suggested that I consider doing doctoral work, I had to reconsider my view of what the future might hold. Ultimately, I recast my vision to include a doctorate and the aspiration to become a vice president of student affairs. However, within that revised vision, I held fast to the idea that I could perform the vice president role while modeling the same leadership ethic that I experienced with my undergraduate dean of students.

As I ventured through my career it became clear to me that I would need to be flexible in terms of my goals. Although each of my positions, starting with residence hall director, provided distinct opportunities, none was a direct path to becoming a dean of students. So, I created a mindset that challenged me to develop the kind of generalist profile that I believed was necessary to become a dean. This thought process spurred me to move from Ohio to California, to Maryland, to Delaware, to Pennsylvania (all in less than 10 years' time) and, ultimately, to pursue a doctorate as a full-time student. This series of moves allowed me to experience diverse institutions while assuming a variety of roles that helped me gain valuable experience in many aspects of student affairs.

After completing my doctorate, I was offered my first dean of students position, though it was only a one-year interim role. Fortunately, near the conclusion of my term, I was offered a position as vice president for student affairs/dean of students. The design of that position and the way the president communicated the expectations for the role were extremely critical for me, because in my mind I had drawn a stark distinction between the responsibilities of a vice president and those of a dean of students. When I inquired about the rationale for the combined job title, the president stated simply, "Our college needs someone to lead as a vice president, and our students need someone to serve as a dean." That explanation and the conversation that ensued on the drive back to the airport after my interview not only breathed life into my personal vision but also enriched my view of the ways in which my leadership might be expected to influence that institution and any ones at which I might someday be employed. That question of how I am leading my institution and how I am serving the students who attend it may never have been part of my evolving leadership vision had I not, without foresight, asked what I thought was a simple clarifying question about the rationale for a position title.

This episode is one of many that I could offer to illustrate the importance of allowing your vision for your role, responsibilities, and career possibilities to be influenced by the wisdom and insights of others. I believe that as one's vision evolves, so too does the sophistication of one's leadership and the possibilities for the relationships that might develop.

MISSION AND VALUES CONGRUENCE

I have had truly wonderful opportunities to work at many different types of institutions. My first job was at a Midwest college affiliated with the Brethren Church; it also had a seminary. My next position was at a West Coast public university whose curriculum had a significant focus on the agricultural sciences. Then I went on to a small public liberal arts college in the Mid-Atlantic region. I subsequently had positions at two different Catholic colleges in the East and Northeast. As a result of these moves, I had occasions to be both thoroughly disappointed by my perception of mission commitment and deeply moved by the intensity with which mission can be pursued. My relationship with and understanding of institutional missions grew as my own awareness of the complexity of institutions evolved. Early in my career, I interpreted mission statements as statements of reality that described the campus environment and its current state. This outlook proved to be a source of disappointment for me. I found myself being frustrated that the institution described in the catalog seemed to be at odds with the actual institution at which I found myself working. However, as I grew to understand mission statements as assertions of aspirations—the institution's proclamation of a commitment to what it would like to be—I found myself in a position of having a different relationship with the institution.

In my two significant senior leadership roles, one at a public university and the other at a Catholic college, the congruence between my personal values and the espoused commitment of the institution proved to be pivotal. However, I found that I was most challenged in the context of Catholic higher education, as Catholicism did not represent my own personal faith, and some of the specific institutional policies that flow out of that religion required me to support institutional values with which I did not always personally align. Yet, it was in this context—where I felt dynamic tension between my own personal values and the mission commitments of my college—that I had my most profound growth.

During my experience at this Catholic college, where I came to realize that institutions did not hire me to lead in the direction of my personal values, I became a better professional. It was significant for my leadership and professional identity development once I recognized that I was not hired to lead based on my personal opinion. My maturation as a leader and professional colleague was greatly enhanced once I embraced that my major responsibility was to lead in the direction of greater mission fulfillment and apply the institution's core values. However, it is important for me to acknowledge that one of the most significant struggles of my career has been wrestling with the tension between what I stand for and what I believe the institution stands for. The most disheartening of times in my professional life have been those occasions when I have taken on as my personal charge to change what I think should be the commitments of an institution—essentially, when I have attempted to create a new mission for the college or university.

As leaders, we all have personal views of the type of world in which we want to live and the values we would like to see demonstrated by our institutions. Yet, I believe it is very important to view institutional performance and our institutional leadership in the context of the institution's mission. First and foremost, we must ask: How do I help my college/university be what it says it wants to be? This has been especially helpful when I have had to address issues about which I feel strongly.

For example, when contentious racial incidents have occurred, I have found myself experiencing intense personal feelings. In those moments I know that if my response is based on personal values and feelings, it may not be as thoughtful as it should—or would—be in a situation that does not provoke the same intense feelings. When confronted with such situations, the question I ask is: How do we resolve/address this issue in a way that allows us to demonstrate our commitment to be who we say we want to be (or to affirm that we are who we say we are)?

For me, mission and values congruence is a matter of finding a way, with integrity, to advance the commitments of my institution—even when its values appear to differ from my own. I believe this is most easily accomplished when one's personal values closely parallel those of the institution; however, not all actions on the part of the leader, who must act on behalf of the mission, will match up perfectly. In the end, I discovered that the gap was not as wide as I had thought and that the possibilities for congruence were much more accessible than I had anticipated.

Early in my career I was a self-described "sucker for mission statements," which meant that I read those declarations as statements of fact. This naiveté meant that I would quickly become disillusioned by institutional actions that did not make sense to me. Once I developed a better understanding of the power of missions and their aspirational nature, I was better able to have grace for the flaws of my institutions and to implicate myself as having responsibility for the pursuit of institutional success.

PERSONAL GROWTH AND TRANSFORMATIVE EXPERIENCES

Clearly, the most consistent theme in my personal journey has been growth. How I think about student affairs as a profession and my relationship with my institution, how I approach my various roles, how I engage in relationships, and the knowledge I now possess are all dramatically different than they were more than 40 years ago, when I started in student affairs. As I described earlier, when I entered the student affairs possession, I entered a Black-and-White world that largely lacked any acknowledgment of the diversity that existed in society or on campus. The policies that we administered allowed for heavy-handed behavior and still had remnants of in loco parentis. During the course of my career, I have seen dramatic shifts in who attends college, the expectations and requirements for serving students, public policy, how policies influence our operations, the complexity of student expectations, the breadth and depth of knowledge about students, and how to effectively educate students, among innumerable other changes. My point is, the world in which I find myself leading today significantly differs from the one in which I entered the student affairs profession. If we don't grow, we will find ourselves becoming obsolete, functioning in ways that are uninformed by contemporary knowledge and acting in ways that do not reflect the realities of the current situation.

An indispensable contributor to my professional growth has been my involvement with professional associations, particularly NASPA–Student Affairs Administrators in Higher Education. Such involvements have provided me with opportunities to learn from other practitioners, engage with faculty and scholars, assume leadership roles that allowed for skill enhancement, be involved in group writing and other collaborations, and have international experiences that broadened and enriched my perspective. The value of involvement with professional associations cannot be overstated. When used in the right way, the resources and opportunities afforded by these associations can significantly enhance one's growth and stimulate one's potential for professional advancement. At the same time, I have observed some student affairs professionals who have become over-involved in associations—in ways that have been detrimental to their campus performance. I strongly contend that our best work should always be done on the campus. Service to our profession is crucial, but our highest priority must always be fulfillment of our campus responsibilities.

The direction and focus of our efforts to grow should be in the direction of our aspirations. In my case, I started my career with the goal of being a generalist, but as I progressed in my journey I began to envision myself as a vice president as well as a scholar–practitioner. As my personal vision expanded so did the range of possibilities from which I could draw professional growth opportunities.

Some of the most transformative experiences in my career took place when I was fortunate enough to work on behalf of our profession—when I had to consider pivotal questions or confront difficult issues. Specifically, chairing the 2012 NASPA Annual Conference after the controversial decision to have the conference remain in Arizona, in the aftermath of anti-immigrant legislation, was a very positive and transformative experience for me. The conference planning team and the subsequent theme "Ignite Leadership Influence Change" provided me with a reframing of leadership at a time when I was seeking deeper inspiration. That theme (with the intentional absence of commas) was intended to reflect core obligations in a fractured world—to be a catalyst (ignite), to lead responsibly (leadership), to use our voices (influence), and to make the world different in positive ways (change). The challenge of working with others to reconcile support for my professional association, while demonstrating awareness of the deep hurt and fear that many of my professional colleagues were feeling, spurred my own personal growth. It is difficult to quantify the transformation that comes from deeply engaging with others to preserve and enhance community in the midst of circumstances that threaten to severely fracture relationships.

Another NASPA experience that has been a powerful source of transformation is my near 30-year involvement with what has evolved into an annual summit for African American men. This effort began as a conference program session aimed at sharing information about the challenges to and strategies for success of African American males in student affairs. Eventually, this program evolved to a daylong pre-conference summit. The sense of brotherhood with members of the summit leadership team has been an incredible source of motivation and support. There is a lack of Black male colleagues on my campus, so having a dependable reference group with whom I can think about the unique aspects of my identity and my career has been truly profound.

Because I worked extremely hard to attend to my professional development and to develop a profile as a scholar–practitioner, I earned the rank of full professor at my university. In an unexpected event, the provost offered me the opportunity to serve as interim dean of the College of Liberal Arts at my institution. Though I had strong doubts about my fitness for the role, I ultimately accepted it. The 18 months I spent in the position were truly transformative—not only did I develop a more sincere appreciation for academic colleagues and the unique challenges they face, but also my appreciation and affection for student affairs work and for my student affairs colleagues was deeply enhanced. The dean role validated my belief that student affairs leaders can be effective in roles across the university and that effective leadership is based on understanding the needs of the organization, forging effective relationships, and demonstrating care for those things that the organization holds most sacred.

Although my focus on growth was largely driven by my desire to stay relevant and to put myself in a position to pursue my professional vision, I was not tuned in to the reality that those around me were also operating with a vision of what they believed might be possible for me. Subsequent conversations with my provost revealed that, as my supervisor, he had a goal of supporting me to move toward senior academic leadership or a presidency—though, for me, neither of those roles is attractive. Nevertheless, it is important for leaders to realize that opportunities for transformation may arise most unexpectedly and require us to venture into arenas beyond those with which we are most familiar. In my case, unfamiliarity bred transformation.

COLLEAGUES AND COLLABORATION

I have been at my current institution for more than 20 years. A question I often get from job candidates who visit our campus is, "What attracted you to Oregon State University?" I used to rattle off the list of reasons that spurred me to accept the job offer and move to Oregon, but some years ago I decided to respond differently. Now my reply is, "Since I have been here as long as I have, the better question might be, Why have I stayed at the university?" I then explain that the reason I stay is because of the colleagues. There have been struggles at every position I have held and at every institution with which I have been associated; what has made the difference is the character of the colleagues with whom I have shared these challenges.

During the constant assault of budget cuts that my institution has endured over the years, I was required to work with colleagues at all levels of my university to determine priorities, identify approaches to implementing reductions, and, in some cases, rethink organizational structure. During such situations, it becomes fairly obvious who is being collaborative or self-serving. At the same time, in those organizations where members declare a desire to be collaborative, challenging times reveal the degree to which those same members are willing to hold to those values even when conditions would dictate that they might more easily retreat to the safety of self-preservation.

As a leader, I have found that collaborative environments allow me to feel more liberated than those situations where I might wield power independently. In collaborative situations, the senior student affairs officer is able to participate in the life of the organization and be more engaged with the creativity and innovation that ensues. But collaborative environments do not just occur—they must be nurtured into being, and they must be honored and cared for if they are to endure. As a leader, I have found that there is a natural suspicion of leaders. This suspicion arises from the incongruence between the rhetoric of leadership and the reality of how individuals actually lead—particularly because most interview processes put candidates in the position of endorsing collaboration as a leadership philosophy (by including it as one of the important selection criteria). Prospective leaders will declare themselves to be collaborative on their way into the organization, but once in their roles they resort to their socialized ways of leading. The natural instinct that I have observed among many leaders is to collaborate on the low-stakes issues and to hoard decision-making authority on high-stakes matters.

Truly collaborative leaders must be committed to sharing power and honoring the collective wisdom of the organization, even when that wisdom is different from what that leader might decide individually. In this case, collaboration is more than just sharing power; true collaboration involves giving up power, which is a frightening proposition for many leaders. However, if colleagues observe a true, consistent commitment to collaborative leadership during the best and worst of times, then trust in the leader and organization will grow—and so will commitment to the success of the organization. Collaboration allows members to be better colleagues to each other, but it also enables organizations to function at a higher level than they would if members are isolated and fragmented in their efforts.

I stayed at my institution because of the collaborative nature of the institution and the deep commitment to collaboration among my colleagues in student affairs. Also, I have had the opportunity to engage with truly generous and caring colleagues who have allowed me to work side-by-side with them to do the important work of the university.

This experience let me avoid the kind of isolation that can sometimes characterize a senior leadership role.

AUTONOMY AND VOICE

While collaboration is a key factor in creating successful organizations, so is autonomy. Individual leaders need the ability to cultivate their unique voice and approach to leadership. In my role as a vice provost, it was very important to me that I could lead the student affairs organization in a manner that I could sustain over the long haul. At the same time, I felt it was my responsibility to put those whom I supervised in the position to construct their own unique leadership styles. One might think that such an approach to supervision would be welcomed, but in many cases I found that it created anxiety.

While many leaders may state a desire for autonomy, some will find that being given autonomy requires a level of confidence that they have not achieved. When presented with the opportunity to make autonomous decisions, some leaders would press me to tell them what decision I would make. Further discussion would reveal concern about the consequences associated with making a decision that did not align with the decision I would make. Leadership autonomy should be a gift that is given to a leader and not a potential hammer to be used by supervisors to punish those whose decisions do not mirror their own.

I have cherished the autonomy I was granted to work with my colleagues in student affairs to construct a culture for our organization that allowed us to build the relationships, programs, and services to advance our shared values and commitments. With that autonomy, we were able to cultivate our unique voice and respond to issues in ways that matched our unique outlook. At the same time, I was fortunate to work within an environment that was not punitive, and it was incumbent on me to grant my supervisees the same grace afforded to me. As a leader, when I decide not to give my perspective on a supervisee's decision, I also give up my right to second-guess it and any impulse I might have to negatively judge the outcomes of the decision later; that is how both autonomy and voice are validated. Having autonomy and voice within my institution was a true gift that allowed me to grow and refine my identity as a leader.

STRUGGLES AND SUCCESSES

Throughout my life and career my leadership experiences have been characterized by a mix of struggles and successes, with struggle being the more consistent of the two. In my view, struggle is a fundamental aspect of life—but struggle is not to be confused with drudgery. To me, struggle is that attribute that calls us to stay on course with our values, desired destination, commitments, and hopes in spite of the prevailing circumstances. Struggle is also that synergistic quality that is revealed when a group of colleagues engage the dynamic tensions in their divergent perspectives on an issue with the goal of uncovering the best possible decision for their organization. Struggle is the source of innovation, the stimulus for community, and the impetus for organizational success. In my leadership, I have tried to stimulate exploration of big questions, challenge my colleagues to achieve deep engagement with one another, and share ownership for the matters that sustain our organization. Each of those challenges represented unique struggles that revealed individual and organizational strengths. While individual episodes in the life of our organization represented particular struggles, the most persistent one I encountered as a leader was associated with working with my student affairs colleagues to hold our organization together amid the ups and downs of our institution. The economic turbulence to which we were consistently exposed constantly pulled at the fabric of our organization, as members of our division regularly feared for their livelihood and the fate of our organization.

I have always found it difficult to describe my professional successes. My view of organizations requires that if, in fact, they are collaborative, then the successes of the student affairs division where I have served as vice president should be presented as those of the organization, with me as just one of several contributors. The successes that I can most confidently claim are those associated with the personal journey I have traveled and the success I have had in navigating social and institutional dynamics. I have pride in my success in winning the struggle to hold on to the core values that were instilled in me as a child in the face of forces that pushed me to do otherwise. I am proud that I was able to construct a leadership approach that honored the legacy of my grandmother and that I believe allowed the wisdom of colleagues—no matter their background or educational level—to influence our organization's thinking and performance.

Included in my successes was my ability to stand up to the challenges that I encountered as an African American. There have been many instances in my career when I was the only African American administrator or faculty member on my campus. During the entire 19 years of my role as vice provost, I was the only Black or U.S.-born person of color serving as a senior administrator at my institution. Too often, this distinguishing factor put me in the role of institutional leader on all matters of race. I had to consistently make clear the conditions of my presence, which included the fact that my presence would not be used to take my institution off the hook for equipping other leaders to develop skills to lead in the area of diversity. I had to work to not be a token—to be seen as a leader in areas beyond diversity—and to not be invisible and voiceless. At the same time, I had to lead with the recognition that as the sole person of color in senior leadership, members of my campus community would view my behavior and leadership differently from that of my colleagues. Because of my race, people of color on campus, particularly, had high expectations of how I used the perceived power of my role.

SUSTAINED BY CORE VALUES

My identity as a leader is strongly influenced by the values and lessons I learned from my family. That background in poverty challenges me to be aware of and responsive to inequities, isolation, invisibility, and inaudibility within organizations. My leadership has been built on a commitment to creating space for those who might otherwise be marginalized and giving access to community to those who might be abandoned—values I acquired from my family as I observed my grandmother create a sense of home. The unique family circumstances under which I was raised provided me with an atypical perspective on and approach to leadership. The power of those childhood experiences continues to resonate for me.

I have been blessed to have a marvelous career as a student affairs professional—a career marked by struggle and success, learning and growth, transition and transformation. My career was characterized by magical encounters with amazing colleagues. Those encounters have shaped me and stimulated my continued evolution. I have also been sustained by a set of core leadership values that were nurtured within me during my childhood—leadership values rooted in hope, faith, and community, much as my home life as a child was. At the conclusion of my journey as a senior student affairs leader, I was able to achieve a profound appreciation for the significant ways that within poverty richness can be found. I can say without a doubt that any strength I brought to my organization came from the strengths of my family and the lessons of my upbringing.

Diversifying a College in Transition

William L. Pickett

I hired Larry Roper as vice president for student affairs and dean of students at St. John Fisher College in Rochester, New York, at the end of the 1986–1987 academic year. I was completing my first year at Fisher and my first year as a college president. I was the fourth president of the college and the first one who was not a member of the Congregation of St. Basil, the Roman Catholic men's religious order that had founded Fisher in 1951 as a Catholic college for men. It became coeducational in 1971.

I came to Fisher from the University of San Diego, where I served as vice president for university relations. My previous 20 years of higher education administrative experience were in development and advancement in four Catholic college and universities in Kansas City, Denver, Detroit, and San Diego. My experience at the University of San Diego was especially important for my thinking about institutional leadership and culture. Central to that thinking was a focus on institutional values and their expression in a mission statement. Similar

William L. Pickett served in Catholic higher education for 30 years, including 10 years (1986–1996) as president of St. John Fisher College in Rochester, New York. He was one of the leaders in adapting Total Quality Management to higher education. In 2006, he retired from the Roman Catholic Diocese of Rochester, where he served as director of pastoral planning.

to the experience Larry describes in his own understanding of a mission statement, I came to see it not just as a statement of aspirations but as a statement of the standards to which the community, especially those in formal leadership positions, would hold themselves accountable. Those values were the standards by which we could critique ourselves and our decisions.

I had lived and worked in a variety of urban settings. Because my work on behalf of my institutions brought me into direct contact with the world outside the university, I had developed some notions about the role of higher education within the larger cultural and economic context. I had seen the future, especially in Southern California, and that future was much more diverse in every way than the Rochester community and the college community could possibly imagine. In many respects, Rochester had been insulated from some of the social forces—such as a high unemployment and crumbling urban infrastructure—at work in America because of the dominance of Kodak and Xerox which, at the time, controlled their markets. Of course, that reality was already changing even if it was not yet apparent to most people.

The culture of the college reflected its recent past of male and clerical leadership. The all-male past was intensified by transformation to a coeducational campus begun barely 15 years earlier. Although the gender makeup of the student body was roughly balanced, the faculty and staff were still overwhelmingly male. The female faculty tended to be younger and not yet tenured, and many felt intimidated by their senior male colleagues. The student body was racially homogenous, with less than 8% students of color in a metropolitan area with more than 15% people of color. The authoritarian and paternalistic leadership style of previous presidents had resulted in an administrative staff and style that had not yet become professionalized, which had already happened in many other Catholic colleges and universities, including the ones where I had served.

In the midst of the many other priorities and demands on my time and attention, I identified two major priorities that could have lasting impact on the college. First, the developmental culture at the college was not preparing students for the world in which they would live out their personal and professional lives. The lack of racial diversity at the campus hindered the development and learning of all students, both majority and minority. During my first year, I asked a group of alumni of color to meet with me to talk about their experiences at the college. I met with a group of six or seven and listened to their stories, which were both good and bad. What I remember most, however, was an alumnus telling me that he had a good experience at Fisher, had both White and Black friends, and looked back fondly on those years. But then he said, "But Dr. Pickett, when I walk past those same guys on a street downtown, they pay me no attention. It is as if I didn't exist." He said this with a profound sense of sadness and hurt. Clearly, however well things went on campus, majority students were not dealing with the realities of racial diversity, and they were certainly not being educated for leadership in the community—no matter what the brochures said.

Second, the administration of the college needed to be professionalized and strengthened to match the academic quality of the faculty. Very few administrators were members of national professional organizations, and almost none attended professional development conferences and seminars. In fact, senior administrators found such professional development activities to be an unnecessary waste of resources. Management systems were underdeveloped, and lines of communication were obscure and confusing. When I interviewed, I found both an academic dean and a dean of the faculty. When I asked a group of department chairs to identify which one was the chief academic officer, they admitted that they weren't sure. The college needed a strong and professional group of vice presidents who, along with the president, could work collegially to strengthen the administrative and management infrastructure.

For a variety of reasons, different in each case, I named new vice presidents in finance, academic affairs, development, and student affairs. There had not previously been a vice president for student affairs. The dean of students had reported to a vice president for student services along with admissions, financial aid, student academic services, and registrar. While the other functions remained in a separate reporting line, I created a vice president/dean of students with reporting lines from residence life, athletics, and activities. Although I do not remember that conversation with Larry on the way to the airport, his recounting of my response accurately reflected my thinking about this position: We needed someone who would serve students and be able to operate comfortably at an institutional level.

In fact, I had similar expectations for each vice president. He or she would function as an advocate for his or her constituency or area of concern as well as think and plan at an organizational level. Admittedly, this is often difficult and complex, but that was exactly what I meant by professionalizing the administrative leadership. In addition, each vice president would be able and willing to educate the other members of the senior staff about his or her constituency or area of concern so that, together, we would develop a rich and complex perspective on the entire college and its role in the community. In my 10 years, we had a remarkable set of people in these senior roles. Each of them had or developed the insights and skills to serve as chief executive officers, and five of them subsequently went on to such roles. I was one of those who saw that clear potential in Larry but fully respected his assessment of his own desires and inclinations.

The search for these positions employed campus search committees under a set of ground rules. I told the search committee that I would not go outside the process to appoint someone who had not been recommended by the committee. By the same token, I would not necessarily appoint any of those recommended. We might have to go through the process again, but I would respect the process and the committee's role in it.

In the search for the vice president/dean of students, however, I added an additional caveat: I would not consider any final set of candidates that did not include a person of color. From my own contacts in higher education, I knew there were candidates of color who met the educational and experience requirements of the position. I also knew simply pledging nondiscrimination would not be enough to attract such candidates—a proactive approach was required. While there were some who objected, the committee listened to my rationale and accepted this challenge. The result was not one but two highly qualified candidates of color in the three recommended by the committee. One of them was Larry. He was offered the position and accepted.

Larry exceeded expectations. He was a strong and articulate advocate for students and the ways institutional policies affected them. He used his intelligence and background to function at the institutional policy level. His discussion of his understanding of a mission statement and how he could relate to it as a college officer reflected that growing understanding. He taught me and his colleagues about student issues in ways that I had never experienced. Because of Larry, we became involved with William E. Sedlacek and his research at the University of Maryland on the importance of noncognitive variables in the success of nontraditional students in higher education. Although we initially focused on students of color, this research and our interaction with Larry and William helped us understand the term *nontraditional* as describing a student for whom the organizational culture was not designed and about whom stereotypes would develop. Further, we began to appreciate that this dynamic would be largely unnoticed by those for whom the culture was organized—in other words, White men. Much of the later success of the college can be attributed to the seeds planted by our engagement with this research.

I realized when Larry was hired that he would not be at Fisher for the long term. His abilities and skills clearly qualified him for service at more senior levels at larger institutions. His effective service at Fisher was based on his own undergraduate experience at a liberal arts college, but he was drawn to the complexities and challenges of larger universities—and rightly so. His colleagues, among whom I count myself, speak of him fondly to this day and count ourselves blessed to have served with him.

William Pickett's reflection about Larry Roper as vice president for student affairs/dean of students provides additional context about the environment in which Roper wrestled with his understanding of mission statements and what purpose they served. As president, Pickett interpreted the mission statement as a statement of aspirations and a "statement of the standards to which the community, especially those in formal leadership positions, would hold themselves accountable."

Roper became part of a college that was largely White, led by a president who would use the values in the mission statement as standards for critique and decision making, and it was a college in need of professionalizing the administration. This was a great time for a new administrator—as Roper was back then—to see how leadership could evolve at an institution.

Pickett also saw that although student affairs might have been providing services for students, it lacked sufficient emphasis on the developmental needs of students. Roper was the perfect administrator to work with student affairs to create an orientation toward the "whole student" concept.

Pickett not only saw Roper as someone who could reorient the work of student affairs, but as someone who could be an institutional leader and fulfill Pickett's vision of a professional group of vice presidents who could collaborate and build a strong management team. Having selected Roper for the position, Pickett writes that Roper exceeded expectations in the position, both in being an "articulate advocate for students" and in "function[ing] at the institutional policy level."

167

Obviously, Roper was a good fit in his leadership role at St. John Fisher College in Rochester, New York.

—**Gwendolyn Jordan Dungy**

Anna K. Gonzalez

Anna K. Gonzalez is the dean of students at Lewis & Clark College in Portland, Oregon, where she also serves as a founding faculty member and program director of the master's program in student affairs administration. Her previous positions include associate vice chancellor for student affairs at the University of Illinois at Urbana–Champaign, associate dean of students at the University of California, Irvine, and dean of students for three Semester at Sea voyages. She received her BA from Loyola Marymount University in Los Angeles, California, and her PhD from Claremont Graduate University in Claremont, California. She has served on national boards for organizations including the Association for Asian American Studies and NASPA–Student Affairs Administrators in Higher Education.

Strategic Leadership

Purpose, Values, and Community Engagement

Anna K. Gonzalez

O n April 29, 1992, a jury acquitted four Los Angeles police officers of assault despite video evidence showing them physically
assaulting Rodney King. Soon afterward, riots broke out in
communities all over the United States. Students at colleges and universities joined in community marches or held protests on their campuses.
I still recall the shock I felt at the failed justice system; I wanted to do
something, and all I could think of was to protest, to shut the system
down. Despite pleas from family members to stay in my apartment and
caution from friends and advisors to consider the risk to my student
leadership role on campus if I engaged in this activity, I helped lead the
demand that the university acknowledge racial injustice. I joined the
hundreds of students who together laid down our bodies in front of the
main gate so that no one could leave or enter the campus.

Days after the protests ended and the fires were extinguished in the
burning cities, we met with members of the administration. We weren't

sure what our punishment would be, but we prepared ourselves for the worst, acknowledging early on that shutting down the campus could result in disciplinary sanctions. The meetings we had with members of the administration—particularly with my mentor and then dean of students, Barbara Avery—proved to be the transformational encounter that affirmed my decision to pursue a career in student affairs. Through those meetings, I learned how to listen, to voice my passion with reason, to be accountable, to stand by my values and beliefs, and to understand power relations that are embedded within the culture of an institution. More important, I saw the significance of an administrator who taught us both understanding of and accountability to members of our community. Over time, I have come to appreciate colleges and universities as places where individuals are allowed the grace, space, and time to engage critically on important topics as part of the charge to transform society for the better.

More than 20 years have passed since the Rodney King verdicts and the L.A. riots. I am now the dean of students and senior student affairs officer at a selective four-year liberal arts college. Reframing my role from one of an activist who protested against the institution to that of a change agent whose job is to highlight student voices and experiences as part of the university was a difficult and sometimes painful journey.

My narrative is about the leadership values that inspired me to become a values-based senior student affairs officer. Reflecting back on my career, I realize how important it was for me to choose carefully where I would work within the institution. Although I was offered three different positions, I chose first to work in a multicultural center because I had a vision that such a place should move from the margins to the center of the university. I believed then that I had the energy, creativity, and a little bravery to help make that happen. Little did I know how much I would be transformed by what I learned at the center itself and how my own understanding of race and power structures would evolve over time.

LEADERSHIP MATTERS: HOW AND WHY

My first full-time job, as the program coordinator at the University of California (UC), Irvine Cross-Cultural Center (CCC), quickly taught me that I was no longer a student. In fact, as my own mentors would remind me, I had a responsibility to be an advocate for the students without taking away their educational opportunity to engage the world with agency and accountability. bell hooks (2003) wrote,

> My hope emerges from those places of struggle where I witness individuals positively transforming their lives and the world around them. Educating is always a vocation rooted in hopefulness. As teachers we believe that learning is possible, that nothing can keep an open mind from seeking after knowledge and finding a way to know. (p. xiv)

It was at UC Irvine that I first valued having an awareness of my leadership style. During a time when policies and practices related to race were being challenged in higher education and when affirmative action was voted down by the citizens of California through a referendum, it was even more important to have leaders who could be both effective and inspiring. Many students, staff, faculty, and alumni were fearful and angry that the growing tide against race-based policies and practices would result in the demise of programs and services such as ethnic studies, educational opportunities programs, and the CCC.

Students and other stakeholders thus engaged in protests that demanded an expansion of services aimed at the recruitment and retention of students of color, the growth of ethnic studies, and the support of cultural centers. While a part of me admired their commitment for social change and the level of activism at which they were engaged, I also needed to lead in a way that framed their work and their educational experience within an ethos of hopefulness. I wondered how I could connect the students' activism and my own commitment and responsibility to be an educator. Even more important, I needed to take the lead in explaining the role of multicultural centers in higher education. As the first multicultural center of its kind in the UC system, the CCC faced high stakes not only to continue to exist but also to move from the margins to the center of the sociopolitical life of the university. I will now offer a narrative that speaks to the process of how I lead and to its relationship to the purpose of a cultural center in the lives of students and the communities from which they come.

Since I started my first full-time position more than 20 years ago, I have come to appreciate having a leadership paradigm that combines both *transformational*, or visionary, and *transactional*, or performance-based, leadership. This hybrid style enabled me to build motivated and values-centered teams that understand that student affairs work is about the educational welfare of students—both those who are currently enrolled and those who have not yet been admitted. More important, having this hybrid style allows me to better prepare students for a complex world with multiple components, challenges, and opportunities.

In order to see how the two leadership approaches can coexist and be complementary, it is important to understand the core of each one. A key outcome of transactional leadership is expectations and rewards. The relationship between the leader and follower is material and contractual. Simply put, rewards are given to those who perform well in their positions or tasks (Bass, 1985). The transformational leadership style is markedly different. It relies on the leader having a high level of charisma and an ability to inspire others. According to Burns (1978), transformational leadership includes a clear sense of purpose, is values driven and visionary, and is able to deal with complexity, uncertainty, and change.

These differences have led some to argue that transformational and transactional leadership really do not belong in one continuum. They exist as polar opposites; as such, it would not be possible for a leader to utilize both theories in managing one team. However, others suggest that while the two approaches *seem* to be at odds, transformational and transactional ways of leading can actually be complementary (Lowe, Kroeck, & Sivasubramaniam, 1996). Bernard M. Bass (1999), one of the experts of transformational leadership theory, which builds on Burns's work, argued that these are actually two separate but inter-related concepts. As two separate leadership styles, transactional and transformational leadership can, in fact, coexist within one leader. Furthermore, Bass (1999) posited that the best leaders actually manifest a combination of these two leadership styles.

During one of the most critical times in the history of the university, I needed to develop a plan that would result in having the campus community understand and support the role of the CCC in the educational development of students. By utilizing the combination of transactional and transformational leadership styles, I initiated a plan that resulted in the expansion of the physical structure and programmatic offerings of the CCC. How did this happen? Using the concept of transactional leadership, I reminded members of the institution of the key benefits and rewards of having a center whose mission is to foster a diverse and inclusive university. Furthermore, we were able to offer data that showed that the center provides important educational opportunities for *all* students—particularly those in leadership positions. These programs included cultural competency training and intergroup dialogue. Even more important, these educational encounters happened within a space that encouraged debate and civility. By highlighting what the CCC actually did through quantitative and qualitative data, I was able to show the benefits the institution actually received from its existence and would gain from its expansion. In thinking through the action and

reward component of the transactional leadership paradigm, I successfully argued that the center should be recognized and rewarded for its
positive contribution to the fulfillment of the university's mission.

My use of transactional leadership in this case took on an added twist
by infusing a version of Rousseau's (1762/1974) concept of the social
contract, which directs a set of agreed-upon principles of the common
good to uphold a democratic society. The social contract between the
university and its own students was established in the mission of the
institution as the state's premier educational institution and in subsequent documents such as its diversity statement, which was adopted
in 2006 by the academic senate and president. The statement declares,

> Diversity should also be integral to the University's achievement
> of excellence. Diversity can enhance the ability of the University
> to accomplish its academic mission. . . . Educational excellence
> that truly incorporates diversity thus can promote mutual respect
> and make possible the full, effective use of the talents and abili-
> ties of all to foster innovation and train future leadership. (UC,
> 2006, para. 3)

During this time, it served me well to note that the performance
and reward component in transactional leadership was embedded in
hierarchical structures. By being informed by data and incorporating it
into an argument for the centrality, not the marginality, of diversity, my
team and I were able to communicate to the community and members
of the administration the CCC's myriad contributions to the mission
of the institution. Furthermore, through the work we were accomplishing at the center, I successfully ensured that the institution met
the social contract it had in relation to its shared value of diversity and
the citizens of the state. The data that my team and I gathered proved
that the CCC was a high-performing unit that added to the institution
and its mission. As such, the center was rewarded: It was supported in
its efforts to expand its physical structure and programmatic offerings.

My leadership process took into account the performance-based component of the transactional leadership style as well as the reminder of the social contract that existed between the institution and its citizenry.

At the same time that I was using transactional leadership to explain the CCC's role and importance, I also needed to be a leader who upheld the principles and components of transformational leadership. In working with and engaging others who questioned the purpose and role of the CCC, I needed to be inspirational, motivational, and authentic in my leadership strategy, so I relied on my own belief in the CCC and its role in transforming the lives of students and the institution itself.

In our daily work with students, we student affairs professionals are often guided by the transformational power of education. As an immigrant, it was ingrained in me at a young age that education was the key component in transforming the lives of my family with particular emphasis at that time on social mobility. Through my activism and the examples set by my advisors and mentors in student affairs during my college years, I learned that the transformative power and transformational promise of higher education can literally change the world for the better. And, in that process, transformational leadership is not just about the charisma and style of the leader but also—and equally important—about the process and manner by which one leads with vision and authentic commitment to the mission of the institution.

My work at the CCC, particularly during a critical time when policies were being implemented that questioned the center's very existence, allowed me to examine what multicultural centers could contribute to transforming the experience of students and to transforming my own leadership. Cultural centers have often been characterized as spaces created to segregate minority groups from the White majority. Indeed, these centers were created to provide supportive spaces for students of color in order to boost their retention and graduation rates.

Many students of color experienced stereotypical threats and racial microaggressions, which impressed upon them the message that they did not belong in the community or the institution. The creation of cultural centers was therefore necessary to realize the promise of an equitable educational experience for these students, particularly those matriculating in historically and/or predominantly White institutions (Patton, 2010).

As centers evolved over time, many expanded their missions and work to explicitly include the development of programs that sought to provide educational programs for the entire campus community. The reason why this element was added to the CCC's mission was critical to ensure its relevance and success for the 21st century university. We felt that building a more culturally competent student body and having campus conversations on issues of race and equity need not be limited to inside the walls of cultural centers; the engagement of all members of the community in these issues was—and is—important. While respecting and keeping to the original mission of cultural centers to serve students of color, we also felt that these spaces should not be the only places where conversations on diversity and inclusivity were being critically examined. We felt that students of color should feel equally safe at other parts of the campus beyond the cultural centers. Transforming colleges and universities by centering the critical issues of power and privilege *throughout* the cultural and programmatic framework of the entire institution is one of the most important yet least recognized roles of cultural centers.

Throughout my time working for centers such as the CCC, I made sure that those programs that were initially focused on student retention and leadership development expanded their connections with the research- and community-minded mission of the institution itself. In the practice of transformative leadership, I invested deeply in the bifocal mission of the center and sought to inspire others to embrace how the life of an individual and the entire institution could be changed for the better. Infusing my own narrative as an immigrant, a person of color, and an activist into my role as an administrator was both necessary and challenging. I had to be vigilant about maintaining a level of professionalism and making sure that I treated all individuals, groups, and situations in a fair and consistent manner.

I must confess also that the experience of working at the CCC, particularly during the time when its existence was being questioned, was perhaps the turning point, the transformative point, in my career. I had to look at the big picture of the purpose—not only of cultural centers but of all other initiatives in higher education that dealt with issues of access and inclusion. I could no longer rely on responding to these attacks merely by providing an answer that was filled with anecdotes, passion, and moral justification; rather, I had to learn how to connect the purpose and history of all programs related to access and inclusion with the mission of higher education, learning outcomes, the American promise of fairness and opportunity, and the future strength of this nation. In leading others to understand the transformative power of cultural centers, my own understanding of the purpose of colleges and universities was redefined and has since served as my own motivation for my work.

HIGHER EDUCATION TRANSFORMING COMMUNITIES

My mother used to ask me if my work resulted in having other mothers lose their children the way she lost her own daughter. In many ways, the daughter who left home at 18 to go to a university didn't fully come back to her family. As a first-generation college student, I saw going to college as leaving behind my entire family and, in many ways, never really going back. Even when I physically came back home during the summer, my life had changed and my interests had become inextricably connected to what was going on at the university. I felt a part of my family, yet apart from my family. I couldn't help thinking that they could not possibly understand what I was going through and what I was learning at the university because none of them had attended college in the United States.

Students and their families typically view going to school as a life-changing experience. First-generation, low-income students or students of color especially believe that obtaining a college education will ensure their success and allow them to contribute to the welfare of their families and communities. Perhaps from a romanticized notion of individuals pulling themselves up by their own bootstraps, universities and colleges often do not take into account the importance of the familial, community, or ethnic group experiences of students of color and the importance of the communities from which they come. When I went to college, families were ushered out after they moved us onto the campus and attended the campus convocation.

The messages from speakers at the convocation announced that students, by themselves, would succeed or fail based on their individual merits and actions and that living in the residential college now meant letting go of where we were from and leaving it behind. For those who were poor or first-generation college students, the implicit—and sometimes not-so-implicit—message was that college was better than our former neighborhoods and that if we succeeded, we would, as individuals, be able to leave our neighborhoods to live in better communities.

W.E.B. Du Bois's (1903/1961) late 19th-century classic essay *The Souls of Black Folk* tells of a young Black man named John who was born and raised in the South during the era of Reconstruction. John took advantage of the opportunity to go away and attend college in the North. He was the only Black man from his community to go to college. When he returned home after years of being away, he seemed disconnected. He had changed greatly, while the community had not. His sister asked him, "John, does it make everyone unhappy when they study and learn lots of things?" And he responded, "I am afraid it does" (Du Bois, 1903/1961, p. 175).

The CCC and our students taught me that it was critical that resistance to dominant cultural norms be an integral part of their success at the university. One of the ways they practiced this resistance was to contest the characterization of their communities as bad, impoverished, or lacking. As such, many of the students I worked with at the CCC went back to their communities and their families or pursued work that contributed to helping people or rebuilding their neighborhoods. From these students, I learned a great deal about what transformative leadership meant. I learned from those who, like me, were the first in their families to attend college in the United States that colleges and universities do not have to take you away from your family and community; I learned that a truly transformative educational experience means creating positive impact in the communities and neighborhoods of our students.

Although I have had other leadership experiences, my work at the CCC will always be one of the most important places in my career development. My experiences there and the students I came to work with—and, indeed, love—gave me a sense of purpose that shaped me and the decisions I continue to make. The training I received at the CCC afforded me an appreciation not only for the concepts of diversity and multiculturalism but also for free speech, ally and community building, and grace in leadership. In thinking through my own development as a leader and my own transformative experience in higher education, I must go back full circle to my own understanding of power and the racialized experiences I had at schools.

BACK TO RACE

Race continues to be one of the most salient parts of my identity, regardless of whether I choose to make it so. While I proudly use the term *woman of color*, as an Asian American with a last name that was perceived to be "not Asian enough," I struggled about my own place in the discourse of race in higher education and beyond.

My first memory of racial discourse in America was an incident in fifth grade. During an activity, my teacher told me that I was an "Oriental" because I was Chinese. I told her that I was actually from the Philippines, and she said that it's all the same. As a college student, my encounters with race were similar to that experience. I realized then that not much was known about Asian Americans, and what was known was mostly incorrect. Asian Americans, even to my closest non-Asian American friends, are a racial anomaly. On the whole, we were not regarded as White and, therefore, experience racism similar to the ways other people of color do. And yet, we seemed to be "White enough" in the context of how race was understood and practiced in the framework of the Black–White paradigm that dominated—and continues to dominate—the racial landscape in the United States. With Blackness as the signifier for failure and Whiteness as signifier for success, the stereotype of Asian Americans as the "model minority" places us in the middle without any agency in the discourse of race (Lee, 2005).

Throughout my professional career, I have been witness to Asian Americans being "racially manipulated,"[1] depending on an institution's need to respond to calls for more diversity or to obscure the charges that it does not have enough of it. On the one hand, Asian Americans are not included—or are even deemed invisible—in discussions focused on programmatic support for people of color. On the other hand, when institutions want to showcase their commitment to diversity, Asian Americans are often counted in the demographics and seen in pictures on publications, websites, and panels. Nancy Abelmann (2009)

---

[1] Discourse or the act of placing Asian Americans in the category of either White or people of color depending on the particular situation. Such categorization—or mis-categorization, I argue— affects the psyche and the sociopolitical lives of both Asian Americans and non-Asian Americans (Gonzalez, 2011).

articulated in her book *Intimate University: Korean American Students and the Problems of Segregation,* "Asian Americans offer, by many counts, the one color that does not count" (p. 2). Navigating through the discourses of racial manipulation, my own work as a student affairs professional seeks to encapsulate the intrinsic complexity of the experiences of Asian Americans but even more so to argue that there is much at stake in getting right the "Asian American question," including the university's vision of diversity and its vision of a future in this globalized world.

Throughout college and later, as a student affairs professional, I had to navigate the Black–White racial paradigm. Depending on whom I was with and what issues I faced, I felt that I had to prove myself as a "true" person of color or as "Whitish." While the balancing act of being in a position judged either to be a "forever foreigner or honorary White" (Tuan, 1998) creates a psychological burden, it also gave me an unintended lesson on learning how to walk on a metaphorical tightrope between different worlds and groups. In my chosen profession, I must strike a careful balance: I am an administrator who is at the same time an advocate for both the students' and the institution's welfare. Like my racial identity, I have had to learn how to balance multiple situations and roles in describing and operationalizing my work. Back to my racial identity: I walk into different spaces, where I am initially judged by the body that I occupy. Some expect me to be an advocate for diversity; others assume that Asian Americans would not be interested in this subject at all. Depending on my actions, I am judged to be more like a geisha or a dragon lady.

ON ONE'S PURPOSE

I wrote this piece hoping to respond to the question I am asked often: "How did you become a senior student affairs officer?" I answer the question by sharing instead *why* I became a senior student affairs officer. The opportunity to respond to great societal questions, to solve problems, and to transform individuals and communities are the reasons why I continue to be invigorated by my job. I am driven to succeed by my hope that through my work with the future leaders of our society, there will be less injustice and suffering in our world.

References

Abelmann, N. (2009). *The intimate university: Korean American students and the problem of segregation.* Durham, NC: Duke University Press.

Bass, B. M. (1985). *Leadership and performance beyond expectations.* New York, NY: Free Press.

Bass, B. M. (1999). Two decades of research and development in transformational leadership. *European Journal of Work and Organizational Psychology, 8*(1), 9–32.

Burns, J. M. (1978). *Leadership.* New York, NY: Harper & Row.

Du Bois, W.E.B. (1961). *The souls of Black folk.* Greenwich, CT: Fawcett Publications. (Original work published 1903)

Gonzalez, A. (2011). *Sit down! You're rocking the boat: Asian Americans, racial manipulation, and the discourse of the denial of success* (Doctoral dissertation). Available from ProQuest Dissertations and Theses database. (UMI No. 3449919)

hooks, b. (2003). *Teaching community: A pedagogy of hope.* New York, NY: Routledge.

Lee, S. (2005). *Up against whiteness: Race, school, and immigrant youth.* New York, NY: Teachers College Press.

Lowe, K. B., Kroeck, K. G., & Sivasubramaniam, N. (1996). Effectiveness correlates of transformation and transactional leadership: A meta-analytic review of the MLQ literature. *Leadership Quarterly, 7*(3), 385–425.

Patton, L. B. (Ed.). (2010). *Culture centers in higher education: Perspectives on identity, theory and practice.* Sterling, VA: Stylus.

Rousseau, J. (1974). *The essential Rousseau* (L. Bair, Trans.). New York, NY: Meridian. (Original work published 1762)

Tuan, M. (1998). *Forever foreigners or honorary whites: The Asian ethnic experience today.* Piscataway, NJ: Rutgers University Press.

University of California. (2006). Regents policy 4400: Policy on University of California Diversity Statement. Retrieved from http://regents.universityofcalifornia.edu/governance/policies/4400.html

On Being Bold and Graceful

Leadership in Action

C. Renée Romano

When Anna Gonzalez interviewed for the position of associate vice chancellor of student affairs for intercultural relations at the University of Illinois at Urbana–Champaign, I was enthusiastic about her candidacy. She had the right combination of intelligence, charisma, and creativity that I believed could move us forward in creating a responsive and welcoming community at the university. Having just experienced a devastating racial incident involving a fraternity and sorority theme party, our campus needed help, and Anna was just the person to lead student affairs and the university.

But there was a problem. She had made a commitment to Semester at Sea—something that is very important to Anna as both a student and an educator of the world, someone who sees the values of all cultures toward an understanding of the human condition. She would not be

---

C. Renée Romano served as vice chancellor for student affairs at the University of Illinois at Urbana–Champaign for more than 10 years and retired in 2017. She previously worked at the University of Northern Iowa, the University of New Hampshire, and Hollins University in Roanoke, Virginia.

available to take the position until after the completion of Semester at Sea. When the search committee came to me with their decision, Anna was their first and only choice. I responded, "Find me someone else. I need help, and I need it now." The committee stuck to their conviction that Anna was the only choice, that she was the person we needed to help us rise again. So, with great trepidation, I followed the committee's advice and hired Anna, waiting a semester for her to travel the world while educating young people and gaining new insights.

It turned out to be the right decision; in fact, it was a phenomenal decision. Anna defined the position of associate vice chancellor of student affairs for intercultural relations and lifted the entire university's perception of culture centers and the role they can play at a Research 1 University. As her supervisor during her five years at the University of Illinois, I'm proud to say that I learned quite a lot from Anna.

I learned that culture centers are critical to having a coherent, strategic approach to creating a welcoming environment for students of color. Anna pulled a group of six culture centers—all operating on their own with separate missions and visions—into a coherent unit that identified their mission as recruiting and retaining students of color. She showed me that the culture centers were vital to our values of an inclusive university, and we couldn't get there without them. As a result of her leadership and vision for those centers, she made her staff feel critical and vital to the university as a whole.

With Anna at the helm, I learned how to respond quickly and intelligently to racial incidents and issues, a skill I have come to value greatly in the past few years of intense student activism and unrest. She pulled together a communications team to respond quickly and clearly to racial incidents and issues, whether they occur on campus, in the community, or in national arenas. She used the social media of the time and has continued to keep up with all the latest developments in terms of communicating quickly with students and the community.

Anna taught me how to work with activist students, to listen and try to understand their concerns and perspectives, and, in some cases, to challenge their ideas and their methods. She helped these students become more effective in pressing their ideas in a way that could create positive change at the university.

From Anna, I learned that free speech is critical to social justice. Sometimes students denounce racism in the name of free speech, but Anna knew the history of the civil rights, unions, and social justice movements and understood that free speech was the cornerstone of progressive change. She taught us all—students, faculty, and administrators—alike. It's a lesson we still struggle with, but in a historical context, I strive to maintain the delicate balance between free speech and community values

In many ways, Anna defined the associate vice chancellor of student affairs for inclusion position and framed the approach that student affairs took during her time at the University of Illinois and in the years since her departure. When she arrived at Illinois, the culture centers were a loose collection of houses and small buildings on the edge of campus and, in some ways, at the edge of our consciousness. She transformed them into a strong unit whose leaders spoke for inclusion, for the value of cultural competency, and for the role of culture centers in the recruitment and retention of students of color. Shortly after she assumed her leadership position, her staff knew and understood their roles as mentors and educators of students and student activists, not revolutionaries themselves.

Finally, I learned the value of relationships from Anna. She was very strategic about developing relationships with faculty, students, other student affairs staff, the athletics department, and anyone else who could be a partner in establishing a more just, equitable environment. I have never worked with anyone who was more skilled or more intelligent about developing relationships to create a shared commitment to diversity and inclusion.

In Anna's essay, she talks about transactional and transformational leadership. As a leader, she is extremely intuitive and has an innate ability to know the right approach and the right time in a changing landscape. At a time when higher education is experiencing a transformation, I see Anna as a transformational leader. She has the commitment, the passion, and the leadership skills to move her institution through the rocky waters of change. When I worked with her, I learned that one has to get on the boat or get out of the way. I am proud to say I got on the boat and am still hanging on.

Anna Gonzalez's narrative is especially relevant as college and university leaders, especially those in student affairs, seek to hear student activists and respond in a manner that addresses their immediate demands as well as the long-term educational and viability missions of the institution. As she reflects on her style of leadership and her motivation to become a professional in the area of student affairs, Gonzalez credits her own experience as a student activist around racial justice and a subsequent mentor relationship with her first dean of students, Barbara Avery.

Though she has held several leadership positions in higher education, Gonzalez attributes her most significant lessons on leadership to her experiences at the University of California, Irvine, where she had to work with a team to justify the existence of the institution's cross-cultural centers. This experience transformed her career and sharpened her understanding of the purpose of higher education. This awakening continues to serve as a motivating force in her work, because it was during this time that she discovered the complementarity of transactional and transformational leadership styles.

During her work regarding the cultural centers, as an immigrant herself, Gonzalez had little difficulty in understanding the importance of the centers to the retention and success of students who were, in many ways, also immigrants to higher education. More challenging for her was to prioritize her roles as an educator and professional considering her identities as an immigrant, a person of color, and an activist. She was able to address this challenge by emphasizing and aligning programs in the cultural centers with the mission of the institution.

The author is the first in her family to graduate from college, making her what we call a first-generation student. From her personal experience, she speaks to the internal conflict caused by the dual identity of first-generation college students—something that makes it difficult for them to, figuratively, ever go home again. Because she sees this dilemma among first-generation students, she encourages them and students of color to consider what positive impact they may be able to make on their home communities.

As an Asian American from the Philippines, Gonzalez has experienced the complexity of being in the middle and manipulated in the context of a society where race is seen through a Black–White lens. This racial position as Asian American among people of color and other experiences have helped her become an effective administrator who knows how to walk the fine line between being an administrator on behalf of the institution and being an advocate for students. Most of all, she sees the role of higher education as critical to transforming society in the most positive manner possible.

—Gwendolyn Jordan Dungy

Walter M. Kimbrough

A native of Atlanta, Georgia, Walter M. Kimbrough is the president of Dillard University. He is a graduate of the University of Georgia and Miami University in Oxford, Ohio, and holds a doctorate in higher education from Georgia State University. He has enjoyed a fulfilling career in student affairs, having served at Emory University, Georgia State University, Old Dominion University, and Albany State University, where he became the vice president for student affairs at the age of 32. Kimbrough is recognized for his research and writings on historically Black colleges and universities and African American men in college, and *The Chronicle of Higher Education, CASE Currents, and Arkansas Life* have noted his active use of social media to engage students.

Putting Me On

Providing Opportunities for Promising Professionals

Walter M. Kimbrough

As our nation continues to diversify, there is understandably a lag in proportionate representation in many fields, particularly at senior-level positions. From members of Congress (particularly the Senate) to governors of states and CEOs of Fortune 500 companies, a tremendous lack of diversity is evident. Even higher education lacks diversity, as those who hold the office of president are most often male and White.

Somewhere along the way I decided that I wanted to become a college president. Until entering college I had planned on becoming a veterinarian, but my experiences in college created a new idea. In order to fulfill this goal, I would need a series of development experiences that would enhance my chances at obtaining a presidency. A limited number of presidencies are available in higher education, fewer if you limit the scope to four-year institutions, and even fewer for historically

Black colleges and universities (HBCUs). This position lacks diversity, and the people I met on my journey played important roles in my development.

My narrative provides a personal account of the experiences that supervisors and mentors can provide to professionals of color to enable them to build a skill set that can ultimately propel their careers. Although no coordinated effort was made by these individuals, they all shared a desire to mentor and guide. In one instance, the opportunity was provided by a younger, new professional who used his ability to network to create an opportunity. The examples presented here will show that what may seem to be insignificant actions, when added together, can have a tremendous impact on professional development.

I've decided to use a phrase that is often associated with the hip-hop generation: *putting someone on*. In some instances, it means to tell someone about something they did not know of, but now that they do they are extremely pleased. It also can mean that a person provides an entrée into a certain field or opportunity, in essence to get a prospective president into the right place to showcase their skills and abilities. Over my career numerous people have put me on by providing education and information, as well as exposure. I will highlight six people who, at various points during my journey, put me on.

PUT ON TO MY CALLING

During my freshman year at the University of Georgia (UGA), I pledged the Alpha Phi Alpha fraternity. At that time all of the historically Black fraternities and sororities at UGA were members of a Black Greek Council, which functioned as a committee of the Interfraternity Council (IFC). The advisor for the IFC was Ron Binder. Ron, an Ohio native, was a member of Sigma Phi Epsilon fraternity and, based on his college experience, I doubt he had much interaction with Black fraternities and sororities. But his willingness to learn was very evident by those of us who were students during that time, and we readily sought to engage him in our activities. We found this to be a great alliance, as Ron not only supported our programs with his presence but was often helpful in acquiring resources. When the UGA Black Greek Council decided to create a perpetually funded scholarship using proceeds from our annual step show, Ron convinced the IFC and Panhellenic Councils to cover the cost of renting the University of Georgia Coliseum to ensure that ticket sales would go directly to the fund, virtually eliminating the overhead for the event.

During the spring of 1989, which was my second-to-last quarter in school, Ron proposed a presentation at the annual Association of Fraternity Advisors (AFA) conference, which would meet that December in Dearborn, Michigan. He indicated a desire to do a presentation on Black fraternities and sororities and discuss working with the groups as an advisor. He asked me to provide an overview of the groups from a historical perspective. I had done a presentation during our Greek series at Georgia where we tried to educate fraternity and sorority members on the history and traditions of White and Black groups. I was excited about the opportunity to present, and I readily agreed. Fortunately, the program was presented during the end of my undergraduate experience (I think I may have already completed finals), and I found myself in Michigan at this conference of professionals who work with fraternity and sorority members all across the country. To say that I was overwhelmed is quite an understatement.

When it was time for the presentation, we found ourselves in a full session. Not only were professionals and graduate students there, but also persons who worked in the national offices of the historically Black fraternities and sororities. I was definitely nervous as a graduating senior getting ready to talk about the history of these groups in front of people who work for these organizations every day. But the time I spent researching the history of the groups was well received, and this presentation, called "Black Greek 101," became a staple for me during the early part of my career, as colleagues often asked me to give historical presentations about Black fraternities and sororities.

After the presentation, I found myself hanging out with these professionals, developing some lifelong connections. Several of them provided opportunities later on (which I will discuss in greater detail later in this chapter). This opportunity to network with these professionals, most of them Black, came because of my White Greek life office advisor. The opportunity could only happen because of his commitment to first serve all of his students, not just those who looked like him.

Ron's willingness to expand his comfort zone created an opportunity for me. And it is this trait that many in higher education, be they campus advisors, professors, or administrators, should model so that more students benefit from these kinds of experiences. In fact, people who make their career in higher education have a duty to ensure they do not create artificial barriers that block students from great opportunities.

PROVIDING A FOUNDATION

Because of my involvement on campus and in my fraternity, I had a number of unique out-of-class learning experiences. During my senior year—while I was experimenting with veterinary school—I served as the regional assistant vice president for Alpha Phi Alpha fraternity. During the fall of 1988 I traveled to conventions across the South, representing undergraduate members of the fraternity. I was in veterinary school at the time and struggling mightily, so these trips were also a time to get away from tough situations.

But during that year I was also questioning if veterinary medicine was the right path for me, and I was really trying to figure out my next steps. Veterinary school was not fun like I had imagined. I was working extra hard to barely make C grades. At the same time, I was enjoying the work I was doing with my fraternity and being engaged in campus life. I began to think that after a career as a veterinarian, I could end up on a campus in some capacity.

My commitment to veterinary medicine waned. After the first quarter ended in December of 1988, I went into the veterinary school admissions office and announced my intentions to withdraw from the veterinary program and return to my undergraduate experience. The program advisors convinced me that I had not given it the old college try, so I returned for the winter quarter. My fate was sealed by a neuro-anatomy course where 75% of the grade was based on the final. I failed the final. But because it was a high-stakes test, the school allowed a retake. I went through the motions for the retake, but I had checked out by then.

So there I was, back as a regular undergraduate and really not sure what the next steps would be. It was the summer of 1989 when the path became clear. During the board meeting at the Alpha Phi Alpha national convention, I had a chance to meet with Walter Washington, who was the former president of Alcorn State University as well as the past national president of Alpha Phi Alpha Fraternity, Inc. I remem-ber telling him that I wanted to be a college president, and I had done enough study to know that most had hard science degrees, so I figured I would need to return to school for a master's degree or PhD. But Washington said I needed to understand students, and he suggested I get a degree in college student personnel services.

I had no idea what that was, but I researched the program and pos-sible schools to attend. I didn't question Washington. He was a long-serving college president, so I believed that he knew what he was talking about. I began seriously to consider graduate studies in college student personnel services while I finished up my last two quarters in school. As a December graduate, I found myself in an awkward position to start graduate school that January, with most programs starting new cohorts each fall. In October of 1989, I attended a large graduate school fair at the University of Georgia. I went from table to table to find out if schools had a college student personnel program, and if financial aid support would be available for a student to start in January.

I received a lot of interest, but the challenge was that I was encouraged to apply for fall of 1990. Table to table, I heard the same response. I was about to give up hope but made one last stop at Miami University's table, where a Black woman, Judy McConnell Jackson, was stationed. I felt I should at least stop and say hello to her, so I did and I asked the two questions. She said yes to both, and the next thing I knew I was interviewing for assistantships in Oxford, Ohio, a place I knew nothing about and where I had no family nearby. Yet that opportunity to go to Miami probably was the most important experience I had along my journey. Moving to a new region that provided new experiences was priceless, and the graduate program provided a tremendous foundation for my professional career. My graduate experience was defined by the work of two White women, Marcia Baxter Magolda and Judy Rodgers. As the major faculty for the program, they personally engaged and mentored all of their students.

This kind of engagement, which I believe is consistent with the values of student development, was extremely important to me in an environment that was very homogeneous. In one of my interviews, a staff member, making sure I was aware of the environment that I would be entering, asked why I wanted to come to "lily-white" Miami. And that turned out to be a very accurate characterization, as I could go days without seeing someone who looked like me. As it turned out, I was the only Black student in the entire program my first semester there.

But that never proved to be an issue. Marcia and Judy modeled inclusivity, and both in different ways became great mentors. Again, part of the ethos of student development theory is to understand students where they are and provide appropriate challenges and support as they matriculate through college. Both women were strong cheerleaders who were always able to ask the right questions to force me to consider multiple perspectives.

The real value of these relationships was not limited to the year and a half that I attended Miami University. Despite graduating in 1991, I never hesitated to contact them on a variety of issues throughout the course of my career. Sometimes it was for the latest research on particular topics. Marcia always led me in the right direction for developmental theories I might apply for the diversity of students I engaged, not just HBCUs but also urban institutions, which had largely commuter populations. Judy was a great resource when I sought to develop leadership programs at both Georgia State and Old Dominion Universities. I think she recommended the Phil Jackson book *Sacred Hoops*, which is still one of my favorites for leadership discussions.

I remember being told as a graduate student not to feel pressured to take the first job I was offered. For many of us, this is counterintuitive, for if you need a job and you're offered a job, you are inclined to take it. The adage "a bird in the hand beats two in the bush" fits nicely here. In many ways, I have followed this mantra. In fact, before I landed my first professional job at Emory University, I was offered a Greek life position at Iowa State University, a large system at a well-known university. However, there were too many signs that it probably wasn't the best fit for me, and when Emory became an option and then a reality, I was convinced I made the right decision.

Even as a president, I have followed this logic. After about five years as president of Philander Smith College, I began to receive information regularly about other presidencies. My team's work at Philander had received national attention, and because of our success my visibility increased. I was nominated as president of a much larger HBCU with a national reputation and decided to go through the process. After the semifinalists were interviewed in person, three of us were selected for the final stage. It was at that time that I withdrew my candidacy. Both the president of the system as well as the search consultant contacted me asking me to reconsider, but I didn't feel the right kind of energy at that time from the search committee, not related to my candidacy but to their level of confidence in the institution's stability. It was definitely the right decision for me and the university, as I believe the committee selected a leader who meshed well with that time in the school's history.

In fact, this lesson that I learned from my graduate professors is one of the main ones I pass along to young and aspiring presidents. Even more so now, I pay close attention to the fit of a president and an institution, and have been able to spot clear mismatches that resulted in failed presidencies, defined by Stephen Trachtenberg, Gerald Kauvar, and E. Grady Bogue (2013) as those that last only for one contract. Presidencies are few, so it becomes difficult to tell someone who really wants a presidential position to turn it down, but if the fit is not a good one, the institution suffers from a short-lived presidency, and the candidate has a mark on their record that they have to explain for the rest of their career. Anytime I see a short-term presidency, particularly fewer than three years, I believe that although the governing board may have misfired in its selection, ultimately it was up to the candidate to determine the best fit for them and, if applicable, their family.

Part of my own vetting process has been those calls to Judy or Marcia to discuss an opportunity and receive feedback. In fact, I have constantly utilized a wide network of diverse professionals when considering a new position. Even as I contemplated a move to Dillard University, which I knew almost immediately during my first interview would be a great fit, I sought honest feedback from several mentors and colleagues, which was invaluable.

Judy and Marcia model behavior that many of us should emulate. This is especially needed by people of color seeking to advance professionally.

Although time constraints prevent us from mentoring everyone who wants to be mentored (I get requests every other month), we should never be too busy to spend 30 minutes with someone trying to think through an opportunity. I often call these "mentoring moments," which are topic- or situation-specific and can be extremely helpful.

There is also a role for long-term mentoring relationships. For me to have access to two people who have known me now for more than 25 years is important, because they have watched my personal and professional growth and, therefore, have a fuller understanding of me as a person. To continue to diversify the ranks of senior administrators, more of these types of relationships are needed.

PROVIDING PLATFORMS

One of the people I met in 1989 at the AFA meeting was Michael Gordon. Michael made history after becoming the first Black dean of students at a Big Ten university, serving in this role at Indiana University Bloomington. Michael was active with AFA because he was instrumental in the National Pan-Hellenic Council (NPHC), the organization that represents the nine largest African American fraternities and sororities, gaining its first permanent headquarters, at Indiana University. In fact, the university subsidized much of the operations during the headquarters' early years.

I was off to graduate school and would not regularly engage with Michael until I began my first full-time job as coordinator of Greek life at Emory University. But part of that job meant attending the AFA meetings, which, for me, meant presenting at practically every one I attended. Because of the work I was beginning to do about Black fraternities and sororities, Michael began to provide opportunities for me to speak at NPHC-related events and conventions.

Although I tried to give strong presentations, I believe there was great value in being mentored and validated by Michael. Essentially, he helped to radically expand the platform for me to share my work, which helped not only to grow my vita for professional presentations, but to strengthen my speaking and research skills, both of which I use frequently as a president and have used throughout my administrative journey.

Although this may appear to be a simple act, the fact that these opportunities helped me to establish an area of professional expertise was critically important, especially because I would never serve as a full-time faculty member. New opportunities meant I had to continue to grow my research, as I could not simply conduct the same workshops over and over again. Therefore, knowing that I would be asked to present regularly, I began a serious research agenda, most of it consisting of visits to Black college archives across the nation, some 40 or more at that point, conducting detailed historical research on these groups and then sharing the findings at various conferences, meetings, and campuses.

I soon found myself at several events where both Michael and I were presenting. In 1998, we were part of a *Black Issues in Higher Education* (now known as *Diverse*) teleconference on hazing in Black fraternities and sororities. Although it was a thrill to be part of this event, which featured university presidents, national organization leaders, and an attorney, I was just as excited to be there with a person who helped make that opportunity possible.

The major lesson from this relationship is that those of us in key positions can impact professional growth by providing opportunities for upcoming professionals to showcase their ability. This is what Ron as a White man did for me as an undergraduate, and what Michael as a Black male continued. Both had the sole power to include me, which provided not only an opportunity at that instant, but additional opportunities for the future.

This can be more difficult than it appears. First, it is easy to go to the established people in a field to ensure quality of the product. My wife marvels that I am still occasionally asked to keynote Greek life–related events. Although I have cut back on those types of engagements tremendously, focusing more on HBCU-related events and discussions, I do like to engage in that space from time to time. The challenge is that we (myself included) have not done a good enough job of developing new voices. I generally have about five people I readily recommend if I am asked, but now I am so far removed from a new generation of speakers on that topic, I would not know where to begin.

Yet there are campus administrators, professors, and other leaders who should see potential every day and should then seek to provide platforms for these people to develop their skills. It really is about always being ready to spot talent and then finding ways to help that person grow.

Not long ago I wrote an article for *The Atlantic* about hazing in Black fraternities. In response, I received an e-mail from a young man named Michael Morton. I knew the name immediately—Michael was arrested for hazing and spent roughly two years in jail, the first case tried after the state of Florida made hazing a third-degree felony. Michael expressed support for my work and offered his services to address the issue.

Soon after, I was asked to lead a task force on hazing for the North-American Interfraternity Conference, where we would have monthly calls and an in-person meeting. During our in-person meeting in June of 2015, I wanted us to have Skype discussions with students who experienced hazing. I asked Michael if he would participate, and he agreed. In this meeting room, which contained campus professionals, professors, and staff members from fraternity headquarters, Michael engaged us in a compelling conversation that, at the end, left everyone mesmerized.

As I listened to the conversation, I wondered how I could get Michael Morton to speak on my campus. I quickly followed up and—three months later—he was at Dillard speaking in front of 600 students, captivating that audience as he did our small committee. I also connected him with national leaders in my fraternity to schedule a presentation at a regional conference, plus shared his information with several colleges.

My role had evolved. Now I had the platform and the ability to decide who could access it, and I provided Michael Morton the opportunity that Michael Gordon provided me. Incidentally, Michael Gordon and Michael Morton are fraternity brothers, so one of them mentored me, and I have been able to mentor the other. We shared an inter-fraternal connection, which in some ways made it easier to extend the mentoring; the real work comes when we as mentors have to provide platforms for people who may not be as closely linked.

Providing platforms is extremely important in ascending to the presidency. In my history of speaking at a variety of higher education functions, I have not known everyone in attendance, or their connections. A strong presentation may cause someone with influence to be curious to know more about a speaker. What, then, if that person is a board member for a school or a system, or a senior administrator looking for talent? That platform can, and often does, lead to another opportunity. A number of times in my career someone has heard me speak or read something I wrote and followed up to ask about a possible opportunity.

Although providing a platform for an up-and-coming professional has merit on its own, in some cases it can become an opportunity for you to find talent. I once met an admissions director after a speech I gave, and I was so impressed, I hired him. The energy and excitement he had for that role translated into the enrollment numbers we desired and, eventually, saw on that campus.

Michael Gordon provided a platform for me, but unknowingly he provided a blueprint for me to reach out to a new generation to provide the same kinds of opportunities. If we are to increase the pool and subsequently the number of senior administrators, we have to be intentional in providing opportunities.

FROM PLATFORM TO PLACE

While Michael Gordon was with NPHC, he often collaborated with other conferences, like the Black Greek Leadership Conference. Started in the mid-1980s by Robert Page, a student at Central Missouri, it grew to sometimes more than 500 attendees who met to discuss special issues related to Black fraternities and sororities. In the late 1990s, one of the conferences was held at Indiana University, and I was a presenter.

As I stated in the previous section, we never really know who is in an audience we are speaking to, or whom they know. This was one of those situations. Keep in mind the audience was primarily undergraduate students, with a few graduate students, campus personnel, and fraternity headquarters staff members. In fall 1999, I received a call from Shaun Harper, a graduate student at Indiana University Bloomington. He was a recent graduate of Albany State University in Georgia, where he served as student government president. I don't even remember meeting Shaun at the conference at Indiana. But he remembered the presentation. He called because Albany State was looking for a vice president for student affairs and he thought I would be a great candidate, and he indicated that he was going to contact the chair of the search committee, who was the vice president for academic affairs, and nominate me. This position was not unfamiliar to me. I saw it when it was first listed but decided not to apply, even though it put me closer to my hometown of Atlanta. At that time, I had been in Norfolk as director of student activities only for about two-and-a-half years. Soon after I saw the listing of the position, a colleague who also saw it called me and said he thought I should apply, but I still declined.

Shaun didn't ever ask me if I was interested in the position; he just indicated that he was going to nominate me. I guess I agreed but didn't think too much about it because I probably underestimated his relationship with the vice president handling the search. Yet the very next day, Mollie Brown from Albany State called me and instructed me to fax her my letter, résumé, and references. Within weeks, I found myself interviewing for this position in Albany, and by December, the president of the university was making a visit to Norfolk as her final screening to meet with people on the campus to ask them about me.

In essence, I made the leap from director of student activities to vice president for student affairs because of a first-semester graduate student. There are probably a great number of lessons to be learned here, but let me focus on a couple. First, it really is possible for virtually anyone to help advance a career, so when given any opportunity one should maximize that relationship. In the end, I think people ruin future opportunities if they take lightly any opportunity. If a platform (speech, job, etc.) is one that you can't fully embrace, it is clearly best not to do it at all. If in my mind I thought a presentation for some students at Indiana University was something I could half do, I might have missed out on an opportunity that in the end was probably the most important in advancing to a presidency.

There is no doubt: My Albany State experience is the reason I became a president quickly at age 37. That opportunity would not have happened if something about my work did not move Shaun. Incidentally, Shaun has gone on to earn a doctorate and is the nation's foremost expert on Black men in higher education. Because of the tremendous value of his work, he has spoken at both institutions where I have served as president.

The other major point I would like to make is that career advancement can be influenced greatly by students, even though they may never be in a position to vote for you as a president. No matter what topic I speak on, I love to engage students. This makes sense, of course, with my background in student affairs. One of the reasons I enjoy this engagement is that you can get honest, open feedback from students. More important, in this social media era, student voices have been democratized so that they can share their thoughts unfiltered by formal university communication channels, and those voices can affect change. The 2015 campus protests that led to the ouster of the president of the University of Missouri System and the chancellor of the flagship campus are great examples of the potential impact of student voices.

Likewise, I have seen students rally behind a leader they perceive is being targeted or challenged, as students at Florida A&M University did for their president in 2015 at a time when other students were pushing their leaders out. Strong student voices can influence searches, so engaging them is key. Depending on a search process, the students may not have much involvement; but in all cases, they will have a say as to whether a person stays and is successful.

I believe that success at achieving a senior position and ultimately keeping it depends on the ability to see everyone and engage everyone. This definitely must include the voices that are often on the margins, such as custodial staff. I believe those voices could open up opportunities because they would be able to speak with a power that no other could. So, for the person who aspires to senior leadership, it would be good to think about what those various voices would say if they were asked about you.

PUSHED TO THE PEAK

The final example is a continuation of my story at Albany State. As I indicated, the president, Portia Holmes Shields, visited Old Dominion to thoroughly check me out. She had me schedule groups for her to speak with during a half-day visit. That was an awkward situation to say the least, when you tell the vice president, the associate dean (my direct supervisor), my staff, and some student leaders that I am a finalist for a job and may be leaving. But everyone was a good sport about it and participated in the groups. During my lunch with Shields, she offered me the job (I almost choked, as I was not expecting it at that time). I later learned from the SGA (Student Government Association) president that, in the student meeting, Shields kept saying, ". . . when Walter Kimbrough comes to Albany State . . . ," which caused the SGA president to cry.

Shields did a couple of things at that lunch that I will never forget. But the main one was that she set an expectation for me. She said if you come with me, you will be a president in five years. There was no maybe about it; she said this definitely. As colleagues, when she gave me projects and assignments that stretched my job duties, she would remind me that they were things that would help me reach my goal. "You want to be a president, don't you?" she was quick to say.

So, at 32 years old, I joined her team as the vice president. Before I started I knew there was something different about her. During my interview, I met the school's chief financial officer. He reassured me that Shields valued young leadership—he was only 29. Soon after I arrived, I learned that she had a chief advancement officer also in his early 30s. So, while we had seasoned leaders all through the academic affairs division, young leaders also filled other roles, including chief of police, athletic director, and general counsel. It was a dynamic, intergenerational leadership team that functioned well under a dynamic president.

Shields created a style of mentoring that I have adopted. She was very hands-on, pushed people to expand their comfort zone, and provided great support and encouragement in her own way. In fact, I generally have few true mentees located across the country because I believe that the ability to frequently interact and discuss creates numerous learning experiences. These experiences with Shields took place in a one-on-one meeting, in a discussion during a football game, and even on a cabinet trip for a meeting in Atlanta where the van broke down. There were numerous opportunities to learn by watching, by questioning, and sometimes by doing.

Those in a position to mentor, by way of their being a supervisor, must communicate to potential employees a willingness to mentor them. There will continue to be a lack and a lag in diverse presidents if there aren't more sitting presidents who accept this role and explicitly talk about grooming their direct reports so that they can become presidents. I have even counseled people who are moving into a vice president position to ask the president whether she or he is willing to serve as a mentor. Having a supervisor who supports your ambitions is critical to maximizing the chances of landing a similar position.

Even in positions that are more removed from the presidency, I believe it is possible to learn a great deal from presidents. Watching Jim Laney at Emory, Carl Patton at Georgia State, and Jim Koch at Old Dominion all were important experiences. While at Old Dominion, I was able to have lunch with President Koch even though I was director of student activities. I had one of those mentoring moments to ask him about the presidency, and he gave some great advice—to consider the position seriously once you are close enough to see what it is like. Incidentally, I reached out to President Koch when I was offered and accepted the presidency at Philander Smith College, and he provided great insights for starting in that role.

Being a vice president for student affairs was a close fit with my ideas of what a presidency could and should look like, especially since it fit with the way Shields operated, especially her strong emphasis on students. Likewise, I have had staff who report directly to me say they never want to be a president after seeing some of the challenges one may face in this role. There is value in proximity, especially for mentoring relationships.

Shields did a lot of pushing. The method behind this approach was to provide experiences to help me prepare for the presidency. When

I arrived at Albany State, state laws had been passed that limited the number of underprepared students attending four-year institutions. State lawmakers justified that if students needed to repeat some parts of high school, it should be done at the less costly community colleges. Therefore, the four-year schools had to develop phase-in plans.

Many in the HBCU community doubted that the rules would be enforced because HBCUs enrolled a large number of students who needed remedial work. But, in time, the realization came that this plan was serious and had to be presented. I happened to start right when that realization took place; therefore, I was tasked with developing our phase-in plan.

This was a great experience on a number of levels. First, it forced me to dive in and understand all the metrics associated with the university. Second, it gave me an opportunity to showcase the skills I developed throughout my career of organizing and making presentations. But this experience also provided great access to key staff members in the University of Georgia System office. Being engaged at that level helped provide a larger context for our work, and for my understanding of the role of a president. My engagement with the phase-in plan led to opportunities to work on system-level projects.

Another experience that helped prepare me for a president role was serving as the point person when a football player died on the first day of practice. I was thrown into the fire not only to assist the family and provide support to the team, but to work with the coaching staff and the media. Because athletics did not report to me, I had a challenging time reigning in the coaching staff, who wanted to make comments on air without the administration knowing what happened. The experience of managing the institution's response to a student death helped prepare me for the responsibilities of a presidential position.

I spent just fewer than five years as vice president at Albany State, proving Shields right that I would become a president in that time.

That mentoring relationship continues today and has often been somewhat reciprocal in nature. Shields spoke at one of my opening convocations at Philander Smith College, thoroughly engaging everyone there. She asked (more accurately, *told*) me to do a workshop for her male students when she was interim president at Concordia College in Selma, Alabama, as well as when she became interim at Tennessee State University. I also gave a winter commencement speech there.

This relationship has lasted in part because she personally invested in my success and continued to do so even after I became a president. She has been a great model for me as I work to assist new presidents in similar ways, whether it is dealing with a current campus issue or considering a new job opportunity. Her spirit to mentor is needed by many more, especially targeted toward people of color who are underrepresented in higher education leadership.

PUTTING PEOPLE ON

Diverse people played and continue to play key roles in my professional development. Most of them saw talent in me enough that they decided to invest in my growth and development. They all have maintained an interest over the course of my career, as I have kept in touch with all of them, including Ron Binder, who has known me the longest of anyone in this group. As the relationships developed, I found myself in a position to have something to offer them in return, hopefully proof that their investments had paid off.

This diverse group played key roles in putting me on, in launching and fueling my professional career. Through a series of simple actions, each made a significant contribution. The goal for many in similar situations is to find ways to do as these exemplary role models do. An investment of time is extremely important in cultivating a diverse pipeline of candidates for senior-level positions. I am sure that all of them would agree that these relationships have been mutually rewarding, and I would guess that each shares a level of pride in what I have been able to accomplish because they were critical to the journey.

Reference

Trachtenberg, S. J., Kauvar, G. B., & Bogue, E. G. (Eds). (2013). *Presidencies derailed: Why university leaders fail and how to prevent it.* Baltimore, MD: Johns Hopkins University Press.

Making Diversity Live at a Historically Black University

Portia Holmes Shields

Despite the rise in wage earnings among all ethnic groups in America in 2015, an ever-widening wealth gap continues between people of color, whose population is increasing, and White Americans, whose population is decreasing. According to the latest census predictions, by 2050, one of every two individuals will be a person of color. Currently, twice the numbers of Whites attend and graduate from college as those in minority groups and, unassailably, college graduates command higher salaries than those without degrees or special technical college experience. Clearly, for the United States to remain the leader in this global economy, a well-prepared, multicultural workforce is required. Therefore, the concept of diversity at institutions of higher education must change from important to priority.

Since the end of the American Civil War, historically Black colleges and universities (HBCUs) have produced some of the nation's

Portia Holmes Shields served as president of Albany State University for eight years and was later named president of Tennessee State University in 2011. She was the first woman to serve as president in the history of both schools. A noted fundraiser, she was named as one of Georgia's 50 most influential women.

renowned leaders and most productive citizens. Today, though, some HBCUs are finding it difficult to compete financially with historically White institutions (HWIs) in hiring the best and brightest administrators, especially vice presidents for student affairs (VPSAs) who, regardless of ethnicity, have to be more than the sum of experience and degrees. To me, the person in this role is the catalyst for student success on campus, and to succeed at HBCUs, he or she must be knowledgeable, creative, and authentic.

When I began my tenure as president of Albany State University, I learned that most of the students were the first in their families to attend college and the majority of them were receiving financial aid. They had experienced little diversity in the schools they attended before enrolling at Albany State and, at the time, some had never traveled out of the state of Georgia.

Thus, in addition to high-quality academic preparation and noteworthy previous employment, the VPSA at Albany State needed to be able to create an environment that accepted and respected students without stereotyping them. He or she also had to present a certain level of sophistication, cultural confidence, awareness, and sensitivity. In addition, the individual selected had to demonstrate an understanding that, while they looked like all other college students, Albany State students were also individuals with special talents and interests to exploit to the fullest extent for them to be competitive upon graduation. Also, and most important, the VPSA had to understand that these students came to college, as they expressed so often, "to get a good job" after they graduated.

With these and other requirements in mind, I reviewed the application of VPSA finalist Walter Kimbrough. His credentials revealed exceptional qualifications and experiences. He was also an honors student and a talented pianist. Still, I wondered if he could identify with these promising students and support our Albany State mantra, "Students First." So I traveled to Old Dominion University to observe him in his professional milieu, interview his supervisor, and watch him engage students. As he conducted a "rap session" with a group of Old Dominion students, I was immediately impressed with the ease with which students shared their views among themselves as well as with him. He introduced me, and I asked the students about his qualities. They were effusive in their comments and praise. When I thanked them and said I was considering him for VPSA at Albany State, they all were dismayed; a few cried. I knew then that he had positively impacted the lives of these students, and I believed he could do the same at Albany State.

At the Albany State Forum where Walter was to make his first presentation, I spared no words in highlighting the qualifications, awards, and skills that he, at such a young age, had already amassed. When the applause died down, he strolled to the podium, and, to my dismay, his first three words were: "How y'all doing?" That, or the expression on my face, got everybody laughing. Then, with the entire university at rapt attention, excited, and eager to hear more, Walter went on to wow the audience with goals, plans, and timelines. Undoubtedly, he had done his homework on the southwest Georgia area, the students, and the university. From the very beginning, he exhibited, both in word and action, high expectations for all the students, which confirmed for me his leadership style. I believe that he reached the students through relevancy and not power play. He put them at ease, yet made sure they took the work seriously. He knew their heroes, music, and twists of word. He demonstrated clear understanding of the language and vocabulary students used with friends and, without criticism, helped them translate it into standard American language when required. He talked up, not down, to students. He made time for them and assumed responsibility for their progress. Was he a father or big brother figure? I don't know, but I am absolutely certain that Walter served as a living example of what they could become. In short, he made wearing a suit and tie, studying, working hard, and walking purposefully very, very cool.

Through his interactions with students at sister HBCUs and HWIs, in campus forums, during rap sessions, on travel, and at speaking engagements, Walter brought authentic multiculturalism to campus. Almost without recognizing it, students began to live, profit from, and contribute to diversity from a position of academic strength and pride. Our retention rate went from third from the bottom among Georgia state institutions to third from the top. Only the University of Georgia and Georgia Tech had higher retention rates. The school's graduation rates also rose substantially. Many students went on to graduate schools, academically and work prepared, comfortable with themselves, and comfortable with others. When asked about Walter's leadership style, one of the graduates he mentored, Ontario Wooden, who followed him into higher education administration, replied:

> I would characterize Walter as a transformational-inspirational leader who seeks change (at the institutional and individual level) for strong student outcomes. He genuinely wants what is best for students. I continue to be inspired and encouraged by his leadership, which is transforming the future of private HBCUs.

Another graduate, and now college professor, Regina Bradley, concurred.

> Dr. Kimbrough was frank and invested. One memory that stands out is from my freshman Honors Service to Leadership course. The first day, Dr. K gave us a quiz on state and national government, and many of us failed. As a result, he called a meeting with all of the Honors Program students, the president, and other professors to demand that we learn our civic duties as American citizens. He has always been bold, while encouraging . . . full of

tough love. I am appreciative of his candor and requirement for us, his students and future leaders, to 'step up our game.'

Disparity in earnings in America will continue without increasing the economic security of all its citizens. Yet upward mobility and higher pay are tied to higher education, not just in access but in completion and, more often, advanced training. Even so, classwork is no longer sufficient to guarantee success at work. For businesses to compete on a global scale, employers now seek individuals whose ability to communicate comfortably and collaborate across races and cultures not only adds value to the organization in productivity, but also raises the bottom line. Therefore, achieving diversity at all colleges and universities must become essential to each institution's mission and standard of success. Institutions—public and private, large and small—must now forge a clear path to inclusion through purposeful engagement and interaction from within, and not adjacent to, the institution's curriculum.

Wherever they matriculate, students must experience cultural comfort, which accrues from combining life experiences with classwork and opinions of peers and professors. For this to occur, genuine, proactive, ambitious, and measureable strategies must be in place to help students consider themselves valuable contributors not only in class but through various activities where they can test their mettle on local, national, and international levels.

VPSAs should create opportunities to make diversity integral to their own qualifications for leadership positions. This begins by first recognizing their own biases, then spending time working in multicultural environments and becoming champions for the change that is necessary.

Presidents and others who lead institutions of higher education must themselves participate in open dialogue about equity with students, faculty, and staff on their campuses. Through faculty exchanges, internships, cooperatives, conferences, and international travel, these conversations should extend to institutions that are more culturally and geographically isolated.

For college students to obtain a quality education and work-ready skills that will reduce disparity in both earnings and lifestyles, they will need to interact in a diverse university that is applying principles of otherness, naturally and honestly, throughout their college experience. VPSAs today are at the forefront of this movement, a seminal challenge to be sure; but one that can be met. Just ask Walter Kimbrough.

The Kimbrough chapter is chock-full of nuggets of knowledge about the power of mentoring both when one is being mentored and when one becomes a mentor. These nuggets of knowledge come with such interesting labels as "putting someone on," "model inclusivity," "wide network of diverse professionals," "expand my platform," "see everyone and engage everyone," "mentoring moments," and "gain the platform and decide who can access it."

Kimbrough uses the expression "putting someone on" to describe the activity and value of a mentor who might be the catalyst for one's self-discovery or the mentor who might link the aspirant with opportunities and experiences necessary to prepare one for a particular role or position. Although Kimbrough describes the value of being mentored by African Americans, his emphasis is not on their race but on the objective value they brought to the mentoring relationship.

One of Kimbrough's early mentors and other career-long mentors were not of the same race as him, and he continues to value them as resources and praises them for "modeling inclusivity." That is, they cared about the success of all of their students. Kimbrough describes how mentors who are White must move beyond their own comfort zone to provide opportunities for all of their students. Because of these experiences with a diversity of mentors, Kimbrough developed a "wide network of diverse professionals" who were instrumental in helping him to "expand his platform."

To Kimbrough, mentors who provided him opportunities to exhibit his skills and talents were expanding his platform. Opportunities to make presentations to groups about the history of Black fraternities provided the author an area in which he could grow in his research capabilities and presentation skills, eventually building his reputation as a national expert on the topic.

A poignant example to illustrate the importance of "seeing and engaging everyone" came when a student was so very impressed by Kimbrough's presentation, he recommended Kimbrough to hiring authorities for a position that became pivotal in Kimbrough's career path to the presidency. In this instance, it was a participant, not a mentor, who noticed the speaker. The lesson here is that students, custodial staff, and others who may appear to be on the margins in the academic hierarchy can be powerful allies as one aspires to leadership positions.

Many of us, including myself, avoid the title of mentor because we don't think we can give the time to fully support and help someone along their career journey. Kimbrough suggests that those who want to give back but feel they cannot commit sufficient time should not overlook the value of "mentoring moments." He encourages all in positions to help to be open to mentoring on specific topics or situations that do not require long-term commitments and suggests that, if there is to be increased diversity among college and university leadership, we can all find ways to mentor through long-term guidance or "mentoring moments." Having reached his goal of becoming a college president at a young age, Kimbrough sees that he has "gained the platform and now can decide who can access it."

—Gwendolyn Jordan Dungy

Thomas A. Parham

Thomas A. Parham is vice chancellor for student affairs and adjunct faculty at the University of California (UC), Irvine. He previously served as assistant vice chancellor for counseling and health services, director of the Counseling Center and director of the Career and Life Planning Center at UC Irvine, and faculty at the University of Pennsylvania. He received his bachelor's degree in social ecology from UC Irvine, his master's degree in counseling psychology from Washington University in St. Louis, and his PhD in counseling psychology from Southern Illinois University Carbondale. He has authored six books and numerous articles and book chapters on identity development, African psychology, and multicultural counseling.

Traversing the Landscape Between Academic and Student Affairs Leadership Opportunities

Thomas A. Parham

W hen you think about transformation, I suspect that you might envision a process whereby an individual, group, organization, or entity experiences some sort of change in its essence, nature, form, or character. Therefore, perhaps the best place to begin this narrative is by articulating the elements or factors that contributed to the transformative changes I have experienced throughout my life and my career.

A transformative experience could be working a high school summer job as an assistant to a contractor and recognizing that there were two ways I could earn a living: with my hands and back or with my mind. I started thinking about the latter rather than the former. Transformative could be attending a high school party one night where my brothers and I were confronted by some gang members who pointed a gun in my face as they robbed us. The next morning, I was not only grateful to be alive but cognizant of the fact that as a choice point, hustling in the classroom is a much more productive road than hustling on the streets. However, in thinking about my formative years, and the elements that set the stage for a truly transformative experience, I harken back to conversations with my mother about my academics and the effort, or lack thereof, I was putting forth. I remember her saying, "Tommy, if you get these kinds of grades by putting in little effort, imagine what you could produce if you tried a little harder and put in more effort." That was a seed planted in my head and heart that would lie dormant for a number of years through late high school and early college until a more formalized encounter with my first mentor at the University of California (UC), Irvine. There, Joseph White, as if he were channeling my mother's spirit, pulled me aside on campus one day and said, "Young brother, you have too much talent and you are too smart to be running around just playing basketball and chasing women." His voice was strong and affirming, as were the subsequent plans we worked out in his office to take me from where I was to where he thought I could go. That interaction, even as it echoed a voice from my adolescent past, was a transformative moment that is among my most memorable.

In retrospect, I can also see myself as a young academician and Ivy League assistant professor of psychology whose trajectory was pointed toward the domains of academic instruction and scholarly inquiry, mixed with a substantial portion of counseling and clinical work. Teaching and mentoring undergraduate and graduate students, engaging in research and scholarship, and providing individual and group counseling and therapy essentially defined my day-to-day professional activities. My identity was clearly defined by my role as a psychologist, and even as I traversed the landscape of professional associations in psychology and counseling, it never dawned on me that the legacy I sought to embrace would be any different. I remember, however, being mindful that the traditional lens framed with a Eurocentric worldview would not be able to represent my interests, ability, or character. For that, I would have to resurrect and recover vestiges of my own cultural tradition that would help illuminate my path. I think that I have been able to accomplish that with some help and support from individuals, professional organizations, and an immersion into the scholarly annals of African-centered Black life and culture.

So there I was, on the threshold of the professional world of psychology and academia, a 27-year-old newly minted doctor of philosophy in psychology, ready to embrace all that life had to offer. I arrived in Philadelphia eager to engage a new city, new job, and new adventure. I didn't know a soul. I had been to Philadelphia only twice in my life: once during my job interviews at the University of Pennsylvania (Penn) and a second time a month or so after accepting Penn's job offer, to look for housing and to get to know the city. Taking risks is important. While mine was a behavioral risk, there are also mental and verbal risks that you should consider embracing in your professional and personal life.

I arrived at Penn having been trained in my doctoral studies by the great Janet Helms, only to discover (via word of mouth) that I was the first African American academic psychologist the university had hired since its founding by Benjamin Franklin in 1751, some 25 years before the birth of the United States. I've never bothered to research that fact and verify that rumor, so I leave that to future generations of scholars to verify or dispute. The counseling program was housed in the Graduate School of Education, and while adjusting to the change from a core psychology department in which I was trained, I was impressed with the broad array of applications my psychological knowledge could be applied to across various fields in education. I connected well with my faculty colleagues in the department and across the university, and enjoyed tremendous support from the senior administration like the president (Sheldon Hackney) and provost (Tom Ehrlich) at the university. As I reiterate this lesson for future generations of leaders, I would invite them to consider becoming a consummate risk taker. Stepping out on faith proved to be a life-changing experience for me, and I have never regretted it.

Penn was a special place, not simply for its Ivy League history and tradition but for the celebrated academics, ambiance, and distinguished faculty that provided fertile ground for the academic and scholarly work my mind was set to do. The institution was steeped in tradition and blessed with tremendous resources to support faculty endeavors. It attracted some of the best and brightest students from across the country and around the world. To say that I enjoyed my time at Penn and in Philadelphia is an understatement. I considered myself blessed to have been hired, and subsequently to have passed my first three-year review toward tenure. However, just as I was celebrating my passage to the second tier of my two continuing three-year appointments, I was recruited to another position back home in California. So, several years after arriving at Penn, I accepted an opportunity to expand my horizons with a position as director of the Career Planning and Placement Center at UC Irvine.

That transition was not at all about giving up on academia; rather, it was an opportunity to fill out those categories of professional activity that were part of my broader interest areas. These included counseling and clinical work, research and scholarship, consulting and training, academic instruction, and, of course, administration. Consequently, if examining my career in aggregate, the categories of interest have not changed. What has changed is the proportion of time that I spend in each category. The transition was reinforced by a piece of advice I had received from White years ago when he reminded me and others he mentored that "the key to mental health, particularly for a young, Black male, is always having a broad range of choices and options." Thus, when he sent me off to graduate school in psychology and nurtured my growth and development in subsequent years, it was with the expectation and directive that I would master competencies in academic instruction, research and writing, and administration, and not just counseling and clinical work. It was that preparation that set the stage for the offers I was able to entertain and the decisions I was able to make, including my return to UC Irvine as the director of the career center.

The career center was an interesting opportunity, even though at first glance it seemed strange for a psychologist to be delving into the field of jobs, internships, and careers. People often forget, however, that counseling psychology training, in addition to the theoretical and applied counseling and clinical work, includes a good dose of vocational counseling and psychology. In fact, the roots of counseling extend back to the early years of the 20th century when severe unemployment, underemployment, and extreme poverty gripped the nation and communities needed the support, guidance, and expertise of professionals trained in the vocational guidance field. My insertion into the career planning and placement domain had an immediate impact, for it was clear to me that services in the center were severely skewed toward the placement end of the scale, and not as much on the planning or developmental end.

Thus, I suggested to my team and staff colleagues that we provide more services in the career development domain, intervening more intrusively into the lives of first-year and sophomore students who needed more focus on examining the interests, values, attitudes, and skills in their career exploration, and focusing less on placement services that they would not need until they were juniors looking for internships, or graduating seniors. If there is a lesson to be learned here for future leaders, it is to understand and evaluate how one's skills might be considered *transferable assets* when applied across a different occupational field.

After five years, my duties expanded to include directing a counseling center and, within another six years, I became an assistant vice chancellor, managing the counseling and health services at UC Irvine. Although my identity as a psychologist never changed, I found myself connecting with issues and colleagues that embraced an orientation tilted more toward student affairs. In short, changing jobs helped me to expand my perspective and gain a much better appreciation for the breadth of a student affairs professional. That breadth is clearly in focus in my current role as a senior student affairs officer, and over the course of the past 30-plus years, it has helped me broaden my identity as a student affairs professional, which I proudly claim.

While navigating the landscape of the professional world, my transformational encounters have influenced, and been influenced by, several themes that characterize my journey. These themes will be reflected in this narrative as I also speak to such topics as fulfilling a legacy, serving as a senior student affairs executive, clarifying the organization's mission, recognizing the values interspersed with cultural wisdom that drive my leadership style, surrounding myself with good people, and overcoming the challenges of balancing the professional with the personal. Finally, this essay will close with a few recommendations for future leaders.

FULFILLING A LEGACY

When thinking about the concept of legacy, one is immediately drawn to the past and thoughts of what has been handed or passed down to younger generations by the ancestors and elders. In a similar way, one of the conceptual anchors I have used to guide my career aspirations and activities is this notion of legacy and how that colors and shapes my reality. The great Algerian psychiatrist Frantz Fanon argued persuasively that each generation, out of relative obscurity, must reach out and seek to fulfill its legacy or betray it. My constant hope has been that my efforts and endeavors, whether administrative, instructional, scholarly, clinical, consultative, or service, would align with that side of the ledger that was judged as having fulfilled a legacy.

I recall in my early days as an academician at Penn challenging my colleagues to explore the question of whether it was right, professional, or ethical to be a part of a city like Philadelphia that was 44% Black, be engaged in training master's- and doctoral-level graduate students to deliver mental health services to that area's population, and have no course in African American psychology. While some thought the question interesting, others took offense, viewing my query as an indictment of the program. In some respects, it was. And yet, my true motive was less focused on critique and more focused on aligning our mission with the best practices available to us as a faculty and clinical staff. While some colleagues quietly whispered that raising such questions was not a way to make tenure in a Research 1 University, I knew that I owed a debt to the legacy that even allowed me to occupy that place and space in time.

Later in my career, while attending the annual convention of the American Psychological Association, I watched a presentation given by some of the most esteemed colleagues in our profession regarding working on therapeutic issues with a cross-cultural focus. During the question and answer exchange, I asked about the priority of focusing their study and inquiry on international populations while avoiding domestic cultural groups like African Americans, Latinx/a/os, Asian Americans, and American Indians, who were often neglected in the work my professional colleagues were engaged in, studying, and writing about. That query, which one panelist took as critique while others accepted as good feedback, was born from that need to give voice to those who had much to say but were rarely heard.

I have also delighted in attending and, in some years, serving as an instructor for the African American Male Summit in conjunction with the Annual Conference of NASPA–Student Affairs Administrators in Higher Education. The summit is a collection of young African American men (there is a summit for women as well) who are eager to learn and hungry for the lessons and wisdom older men like me have come to acquire through years of experience. It is a marvelous occasion to both instruct and find fellowship with other men in the NASPA organization, and a great opportunity to impact future generations of leaders in the student affairs field who desire to assume positions at higher levels of the organization.

In essence, each of these activities can be characterized as fulfilling a legacy, and that is a responsibility I have always taken seriously. Admittedly, there have been occasions in my life, whether attending professional conferences, conducting workshops, delivering keynote addresses, or writing manuscripts, when I have been vociferous in my tone and temperament. Indeed, I have learned to roar like a lion, particularly in matters of advocating for human decency or social justice. And while I am mindful of the feelings and sentiments of others, I carry with me in my mind a lesson from White. He said, "You cannot seek validation from your oppressor." Thus, I have been more persuaded by principle than personality, and I have been cautious of assigning too much value and power to organizations and their hierarchy that often seek to make others beholden to their validation and affirmation. Consequently, I like to remind myself and others that the wave of a movement that is built on truth and righteousness is bigger than any institutional policy or practice, and those of us who dedicate ourselves to operationalizing truth and justice do not need institutional permission slips in order to engage in any work that is aligned with a noble struggle.

SERVING THE CHIEF EXECUTIVE

As I mentioned earlier, my background in higher education began as a tenure-track faculty member at Penn. Thus, I am a core academic by training and mindset, and I have maintained a program of research, scholarship, and student mentorship that spans more than three decades. Currently, I serve as the vice chancellor for student affairs at UC Irvine. Between those two anchor points I have accrued 34 years in higher education and 31 years of progressively responsible experience in the administration, management, and strategic leadership of a key division within the university. In thinking about this segment of my life, I am mindful of the two people whose support, wise counsel, and role modeling have been instrumental in my growth and development, and ultimately my success as an administrator and senior executive. Horace Mitchell, now president at California State University, Bakersfield, and Dr. Michael Drake, former chancellor at UC Irvine and current president at The Ohio State University, individually and collectively have taught me much and I will be forever grateful for their intervention in my life.

The pride I feel in my accomplishments as a senior executive and leader is anchored in my belief (and the feedback I have received) that my contributions to the academic enterprise have been meaningful and substantial. I have sought to empower my leadership teams to create wholesome and collaborative work climates, and I encourage them to grasp for goals and outcomes that are beyond what is comfortable and convenient. I have brought together senior leaders at the university (mental health directors, deans of students, legal counsel, chiefs of police, university ombudsmen, human resources professionals, academic personnel managers, and others) over the past 20 years (even before behavioral intervention teams were common on campuses) to assess situational circumstances and consult on a broad range of intervention strategies to address urgent and crisis issues. I have advocated for and helped implement a successful student health insurance program. I have provided strategic leadership in the enrollment services cluster of units (e.g., admissions, financial aid, Center for Educational

Partnership) to recruit record numbers of applicants, while simultaneously increasing the diversity and excellence of the admitted class. In response to racially and religiously charged incidents on campus, I have created and employed a constructive engagement model to proactively address student groups and their issues, and manage protests and demonstrations on campus. I have also developed an award-winning "New Narrative" series that invites students, staff, and faculty to engage and interrogate issues of bias, oppression, and privilege.

My team and I have successfully cultivated what we hope will be the largest philanthropic gift in the history of the student affairs division, and have created, developed, and implemented a strategic vision for the student affairs division that has changed the culture and dissipated silos that existed prior to my leadership. I have also worked across divisional boundaries within UC Irvine to collaborate with deans and senior administrator colleagues in planning and budget, business and administrative services, strategic communications, university advancement, and other departments to achieve campuswide goals and objectives.

CLARIFYING THE ORGANIZATIONAL MISSION

Collaboration has always been an important value for me in the context of my managerial responsibilities. Because student affairs is so interconnected with the rest of the campus, it would be difficult to imagine being as effective as possible without collaborating across the divisional boundaries erected by the organizational structures and reporting lines we all work within. And yet, I try to never become confused about the weight institutions give to certain functions within the organization and where priorities lie.

I have spent my professional life in research-oriented academic institutions, so, at some level, the answer to the question of what is priority becomes rather obvious. The answer of course is academics and all that is associated with that side of the institution. This point is critical for younger administrators, who sometimes confuse the importance of some units within the domain of student affairs versus what the culture of the institution is organized around. No matter how important student affairs professionals believe units like housing, counseling, student organizations, health education, career centers, student health, and even disability services and recreation are, all will take a back seat to promoting and sustaining excellence within the academic enterprise of the university.

Even with that recognition, I have always understood the importance of student affairs to the academic enterprise. In fact, I have previously argued that student affairs and academic affairs exert a profoundly reciprocal relationship to one another such that success in one domain of the university should facilitate success in the other. Clearly, the intellectual pursuit of knowledge and the advancement of scholarly research drive the university. Student affairs has a role to play in contributing to that educational mission by providing cocurricular experiences and other programs through such units as residential life, career and counseling centers, cross-cultural and international student centers, and student activities. Regardless of which division within a university provides the learning experience that students receive, academic endeavors are potentially compromised if students who avail themselves of program offerings are themselves consumed by concerns over mental health issues, career dilemmas, physical disabilities, medical ailments, residential accommodations, financial aid problems, and quality of campus life issues. Indeed, student affairs facilitates the academic mission of any college or university by assisting students in successfully confronting the logistical, social, and developmental tasks that characterize their undergraduate and graduate school years, and by contributing to the cocurricular aspects of the academic and learning experience. Students must have a robust and quality campus experience that allows them to fully engage the resources of the institution.

VALUES THAT DRIVE MY LEADERSHIP STYLE

Leadership has always been an important attribute to me and something I have prided myself on. The salience I place on the principle, however, has less to do with the positions or the titles one holds, and more to do with the behaviors one engages in that frame and characterize one's style and influence those with whom we work. In my professional life, I learned that there are many styles of leadership (e.g., autocratic vs. collaborative vs. laissez faire), but just a couple of basic types. Those types can be categorized into *paper pushers* and *people pushers*. I have always been more of the latter.

I believe that people are important to any enterprise and often an organization's most important assets. I am most comfortable being a people-oriented individual who believes in open, honest, and direct communication with others. In my roles, I find it essential to listen as much as I speak, involving individuals at every level of the institutional hierarchy. I have come to recognize that whatever effectiveness I demonstrate as a manager is greatly impacted by the performance of individuals who work with and for me. Consequently, I strive to create a team-oriented organizational climate and working environment that allows my colleagues to maximize their efforts and potential. I am also a strong believer in and proponent of diversity and multiculturalism. This commitment has allowed me to endorse and advocate for issues and concerns in a manner where respect for diversity is operationalized into specific behaviors and programmatic initiatives for my staff and me as well as the entire institution.

In operationalizing this people-oriented philosophy, I have come to embrace a set of values that characterize my style of relating to my colleagues. These values are discussed in the following sections.

WHO IS IMPORTANT?

Early in my tenure as vice chancellor at UC Irvine, I held an assembly for the entire division. My goal was to bring the staff together, share my vision, update them on news from across the university that would affect our work, and challenge them to be at their best in serving our students and the broader university community. During that assembly, I asked the audience who they thought was the most important person in the division. Predictably, someone yelled out, "You are as vice chancellor." I quickly corrected the person, explaining that I was not the most important person, and shared a hypothetical example. I deliberately picked a unit in the division like the student health center to illustrate my point because it has a very established hierarchy. I told the audience to imagine a student who went to the health center to address some type of medical ailment. The student checks in with the front desk and then takes a seat in the lobby. Before the nurse can come to room this patient, the student realizes she needs to use the restroom. When the student walks into the restroom, she finds a facility that is smelly, unsanitary, and not well kept. I then ask, "Who is the most important person to that patient in that moment?" The answer becomes clear as several people shout, "The janitor/facilities person." They are correct. My position is always that the most important individual in the division or organization is not the boss but whoever is the first point of contact for our customer base. In this regard, everyone in the organization is important, and whatever their role and responsibility is, they have to believe that what they do is significant and worthwhile, and makes a difference.

AFFIRMATION RATIOS

Another of my exhortations is anchored in the notion of stretching oneself and the organization to serve our customer base, rather than

finding and hiding behind reasons and rationales about why something cannot be done. I have always encouraged my teams to vigorously engage those elements that we control and can do something
about. Having said that, I am cognizant that in any given circumstance,
numerous factors may be beyond the control of the people engaged
in the activity. However, although an individual may not control 8
out of 10 factors in a given situation, he or she can control maybe 2 of
them. Those are the elements that I try to have my people engage with
and influence. Consequently, my teams will attest that I am not interested in hearing about the reasons why something cannot be done;
I'm interested and focused on the reasons why it can be done.

LEADERSHIP BASED ON STRENGTH AND LOVE

Years ago, I had the opportunity to read the books *Strengths Based
Leadership* (Rath & Conchie, 2008) and *Love Leadership: A New
Way to Lead in a Fear-Based World* (Bryant, 2009). Both books spoke
to me in persuasive and meaningful ways. Their theses were simple,
and yet each made a very compelling argument that was difficult to
ignore. Rath and Conchie (2008) asserted that the most effective
leaders invested in the strengths of their people. They introduced the
reader to four domains around which people's strengths tended to
congregate. These included *executing, influencing, relationship building,* and *strategic thinking.* They walked the reader through anecdotes
from some of the most influential business leaders and how their
embrace of and reliance on the strengths of their people facilitated
their organization's growth. In a similar way, Bryant (2009) con-
trasted leadership styles anchored in the constructs of love versus
fear. He asserted that too much of the business climate in the world is
ruled by fear and that, ultimately, fear fails. He argued for the importance of employees and organizations to assess what each has to give
to the world, and then to care enough about humankind to engage

that world with an ethic based on love and a passion for doing good by others. Bryant's text takes a very different slant on defining success in business, even as it tries and succeeds at illustrating how *loss creates leaders*, how *fear fails*, how *love makes money*, how *vulnerability is power*, and how *giving is getting*. Bryant concluded by reminding the reader that with hope, anything is possible, and that part of the role of effective leaders is to instill hope in their teams.

Translating these books into strategies for my student affairs organization reminded me of the importance of finding and affirming the good in people. Believing that people really do value their jobs and the roles they play, my obligation as the leader was to help create—and encourage others in the organization to help create—a climate where strength and goodness could thrive. In addition, these texts resonated with principles and beliefs I had long embraced that sought to help people find hope in the face of despair, courage in the face of fear, sensitivity in the face of indifference, and optimism in the face of cynicism.

CREATIVELY SYNTHESIZING OPPOSITES

Within the context of my scholarly endeavors, I have come to understand and embrace certain ideas and beliefs that have guided my work. One of those conceptions I have stylized over time is: Life at its best is a creative synthesis of opposites in fruitful harmony. Although a variety of conclusions can be drawn from this pearl of wisdom, it reminds me that in life, sometimes one's best strength can also be one's greatest weakness, and one's greatest weakness can be transformed into a strength, depending on the context in which it is applied. There are a number of circumstances in which this axiom has proven to be absolutely true. Perhaps nowhere is this piece of wisdom more true than with budget challenges that test the viability of any student affairs enterprise on college and university campuses.

Earlier I talked about organizational mission and how that drove and influenced institutional priorities. The new reality in higher education is that officials in states across the country, while dealing with severe budget shortfalls and deficits, have been saying they value the necessity of colleges and universities but have been acting to disinvest their state systems of education. Consequently, university executives have had to make some difficult choices where funding is concerned, and out of necessity, student affairs has experienced a greater share of budget reductions in deference to its academic affairs counterparts. One might conclude that "being student affairs" becomes more of a challenge than an asset in this regard. However, a constant refrain I have sounded to my division is that while we have taken severe cuts and have had to rely more heavily on auxiliary enterprise to support units in the division, we actually have income-generating capacity that other academic units do not have.

If a school of humanities or social sciences is assessed a million dollar cut in its budget, it has little capacity to generate resources to fill the funding gaps beyond engaging in development activity to raise money from donors. Conversely, student affairs units have income-generating capability and, if managed properly, those units' resources can be used to support broader divisional priorities. Indeed, the "weakness" (i.e., less permanent funding for student affairs units) of the enterprise can be turned into a strength by viewing this circumstance through a different frame or lens.

DISSIPATING SILOS WITHIN THE STUDENT AFFAIRS DIVISION

Among the challenges that have been the most provocative to manage is changing the internal culture of the organization. In some organizations, the tendency for some individual units to operate with a high degree of autonomy impacts the ability of those units to collaborate and cooperate with other units, even within their own division. Although the desire to plan and execute programmatic initiatives in a collaborative fashion has been more evident over the past several decades, the willingness to share financial resources has been met with much more resistance. Here, I refer to the "silo mentality" where particular directors and their unit management teams adopt a perspective that indicates that human and financial resources belong to them, and they develop a level of resentment when asked to share resources in support of the organization's greater good. My bias has always been that the resources generated by any unit, while necessary to support and sustain its operations, belong to the broader collective and not just that unit.

SURROUNDING MYSELF WITH STRONG MUSICIANS IN THE ORCHESTRA

Philosophically, I have always believed that a manager or supervisor is only as good as the work produced by the people who work with and for her or him. The role of leadership then is much less about being in charge and much more about creating a positive work environment where talented, innovative, energetic, and dedicated professionals can find a place to work, contribute to something bigger than themselves, and engage in a reciprocal relationship with that entity or organization. The role of the senior executive then is to know his organization; provide a strategic vision for that organization's aspirational future; assess the human, fiscal, and space capacity to deliver on that promise and possibility; address whatever gaps appear in the plan; and seek to fill those disparities with talented people, resources, and space. But to produce a harmonious sound and create the grandest organizational symphony, the senior student affairs officer, much like the orchestra leader, needs at least two things: the right musicians with the expertise to play their instruments with a standard of excellence, and an orchestra culture where all work together for the benefit of the collective. The leader must be sure that the right musicians are in the ensemble. Their talent and experience are important, and their ability to listen as well as play their instruments is key. Beyond that, the orchestra leader must somehow get this collection of talented individuals to play in sync with one another such that the sound they produce is sweet music to those listening to the performance.

In a similar way, senior student affairs executives are wise to attract and cultivate the most talented people they can find. Experience, academic training, and performance excellence are all attributes that one looks for. However, talent alone, in my opinion, is insufficient to make a successful organization. The staff, directors, and assistant vice president-level or president-level personnel must also have a value system that aligns with the organizational culture. Without that, conflicts may develop, organizational inefficiencies will be enhanced, and the students and campus community we seek to impact will not be as well served as they might otherwise be. Throughout my career in administration as a director, assistant vice chancellor, and now vice chancellor, I have worked with some very talented people, said goodbye to others whose skills or values were a mismatch for the organization, and attracted others who both fit the mold and whose experience and values were just what the organization needed. I have preferred to work with people who could collaborate as well as compete; managers who could listen as much as they spoke; colleagues who, like me, sought to be people pushers and not simply paper pushers; leaders who were thoughtful and deliberate, rather than arbitrary in their decision making; staff who were committed to serving others and not just themselves; and professionals who approached situations with a perspective that the glass is half full as opposed to half empty.

For my part, unlike many people who go to work every day in this country, I have always loved what I do. Consequently, I assumed that staff, directors, and senior managers would likewise come to love their work if the proper organizational climate and work environment could be created. In that environment, I have always preferred to bring a positive work attitude to the office, to affirm rather than critique people and their performance, to collaborate and consult rather than rule, to affirm rather than assault people's humanity, to insist on communicating with one another and managing conflicts at the least intrusive level, to join staff in project endeavors and not simply direct that they be done, to proclaim diversity and operationalize inclusive excellence as a strength and not a liability, and to help my teams realize the difference between their reach and their grasp and never being afraid to seek the latter rather than rely on the former.

THE CHALLENGES OF BALANCING THE PROFESSIONAL WITH THE PERSONAL

Despite the degrees and certifications I acquired, or the awards and recognition I received in my professional life, nothing prepared me as a senior leader for the challenges of negotiating the balance between the personal and the professional. As I look back at my own journey thus far, I suspect that this may be one of my greatest downsides, as managing the challenges of professional life and personal life is rarely congruent. Several variables contribute to this circumstance. One factor is anchored in a value system that thrives on producing excellence in all that I do. Whether as a family man, an academician, a researcher and scholar, a clinician, a senior administrator, or a strong man in my community, my goal is always focused on managing my affairs with a standard of excellence. Looking at that mindset in isolation, it would seem to be an attribute that would serve me well, and I can say for certain that it has been a tremendous asset to me. However, excellence is not a standard I conjure out of thin air; rather, excellence takes commitment, planning, and executing that plan. In short, it takes time.

If you are successful in producing excellence in handling personal and professional endeavors, then you are likely to enjoy a fair amount of satisfaction. Earlier I shared the axiom, "Life at its best is a creative syn-thesis of opposites in fruitful harmony." In essence, your best strength can also be your greatest weakness, and your greatest weakness can be a strength, depending on the context. Being successful at produc-ing excellence has created many more requests and demands on both my professional and personal time, and this is the second factor about which senior student affairs officers will want to be cognizant. People who admire or even love your work performance will now want you involved in more and bigger things. All will acknowledge how busy you are, and then finish the sentence with a "however" or "but" in front of a request for more of your time. Administrative colleagues will invite you to manage more tasks or serve on more committees. Journal editors and publishers will invite you to submit more manuscripts and articles if they like what you write. Clients who are well served by your thera-peutic interventions will desire or need more of your time. Participants of training you conduct will want more of it and, consequently, more of you. People who hear you talk and speak at local, regional, and national events and conferences, or even at a church pulpit on Sunday, will extend more and more invitations to speak at other places. The result is now a schedule packed with many more requests and obliga-tions than you can possibly accommodate, and this in turn contributes to a desperate search for the one commodity each of us has too little of—*time*. That time is then taken from the personal side of the ledger, where decreasing minutes and hours are replaced with requests for con-sideration and empathy from family and loved ones who you hope and expect will understand.

On the other side of the coin, I have always embraced and defined myself in terms of family. Beyond my relationship with the Creator, there is nothing more important than my immediate and extended family and friends. Yet as I look back over my career, I wonder whether those who are most important to me will judge my efforts as a husband, father, sibling, son, social advocate, involved professional, and friend to be worthy of their praise or critique. I'm certainly hoping for the former but am prepared to accept their judgment in the latter, for there is no question that I have been very involved professionally and have struggled to find a proper balance in these two domains.

RECOMMENDATIONS AND ADVICE FOR FUTURE LEADERS

In thinking about what I'd like to share with colleagues, less experienced managers, or emerging professionals, I want to close with some simple suggestions. Perhaps now is also an opportune time to pass on the lessons my chief executive mentors have shared with me. These teachable moments have come through conversations, advice giving, and just paying attention to what each does and how each interacts with the environment of executive leadership in higher education. I'll share one lesson from each of them, and follow those with three of my own.

Lesson One: Recognize the Degrees of Excellence

One of the more profound lessons I have learned in my career was taught to me by Dr. Michael Drake, the individual who selected me to be vice chancellor at UC Irvine. His lesson to me and other members of his cabinet was "there is a big difference between A and A+." As chief executive, Drake valued excellence and was particular about always looking for that little something extra that might allow you to become a little wiser, sharper, and more compassionate and committed in whatever endeavor with which you are engaged. Whether it was a campus policy; an engagement with a student group; a press release from strategic communications; a staff, faculty, or administrator hire; a research conclusion that highlighted an innovation; or an engagement with a key stakeholder, he was often focused on excellence-plus. I now pass this advice along to you as you think about ways to exceed your own standard of excellence and do things that truly distinguish you.

Lesson Two: Remember Who Is In Charge

Twenty-five years ago, prior to becoming an assistant vice chancellor, I was serving as the director of both the career center and the counseling center at UC Irvine. During that time, I recall making an appointment with Horace Mitchell, then vice chancellor of student affairs at UC Irvine and my boss. In that meeting, I consulted with him about a dilemma I was having with a few employees and strategized some alternatives to manage the situation. After providing me with a listening ear and offering probing questions to ensure that I had thought through the range of factors involved in the issues, he shared a perspective I have never forgotten. Not only was the lesson wise counsel, it also served as a kind of administrator/manager's permission slip to deal with a situation when other strategies were less successful: "You have no business having things any way other than the way you want them to be when you are in charge." Part of being a good leader and manager is about collaborating, motivating employees, engaging your people, modeling what you expect from your team, and building consensus. However, there will be times when even your best strengths become your worst nightmare when the people you are working with are committed to being difficult, disruptive, myopic in their views, and less cooperative, but you are still dedicated to a collaborative management style. I now sit in the seat that provides counsel and asks probing questions of my managers when they come to me with challenges. Not surprisingly, I pass along this advice to them and I now share it with you.

Lesson 3: Build a Great Team

One of the constants in my professional life as a manager and senior administrator has been the importance of people. Surrounding yourself with staff who are competent, capable, and committed is a must. Yet, even with the challenges of recruiting, hiring, and then managing personnel, senior leaders are wise to remember a very important lesson:

Managers, senior or otherwise, are only as good as the people who work with and for them, and the outcomes they produce. Even as each manager strives to be proficient, expert, savvy, politically astute, and leader-like in their daily posture, they literally cannot do every job no matter how competent they think they are. The divisions they manage are too large and the range of issues they must manage is too broad a spectrum for anyone to assume that they can produce the outcomes they want by themselves. Learn to create the right environment where your people will want to work with and for you, and empower your staff to reach their full potential.

Lesson 4: Focus on What You Can Control

The social scientist in me understands that there is never a single factor or variable that accounts for 100% of the variance in explaining any equation. Usually, multiple factors both explain a phenomenon and must be managed in addressing a solution for the challenges one may be facing. Such is certainly true of university life whether inside or outside the student affairs division. In recognizing that fact, management can often be a frustrating experience because so many of the variables that impact a situational outcome are outside the control of a single individual.

Yet that recognition often does not reduce the amount of worry one engages in or the frustration one feels in not being able to totally guarantee outcomes. The lesson to be learned here? Focus on what you can control and worry less about factors over which you have little or no influence. That will provide for a much higher degree of satisfaction in your work, and much less frustration and anxiety in your professional and personal life.

Lesson 5: Maintain a Reciprocal Connection

The division of student affairs on college and university campuses is sometimes seen as a service delivery domain, and, to some extent, that is true. The fact that the units in this division directly connect with students on a range of issues is a posture we take a great deal of pride in. However, it is imperative that senior student affairs officers not forget that the service delivery we provide should take place within a broader context of a university's mission. In my opinion, the lesson here is: Student affairs exists to support the academic mission of the institution. This mindset will serve you well. Having said that, I am equally clear, as I argued earlier, that student affairs and academic affairs exert a profoundly reciprocal relationship to each other. Students will have a difficult time taking maximum advantage of the academic resources in any institution if they have concerns about how they can afford school, where they will live, how they will better crystallize their career direction, what they should do if they get stressed out, what happens if they get sick or physically injured, how they can have a disability accommodated, and what resources are available to help them connect with different clubs, organizations, and activities on campus. When student affairs staff and managers assist students in addressing these issues and more, then students can be free to focus their energies and efforts on engaging the academic and cocurricular learning aspects of university life.

A PATHWAY TO PRODUCTIVITY

In surveying the landscape of the world of work, I am cognizant that a great percentage of people in the United States, and maybe even the world, go to their jobs each and every day disliking or even hating what they do. Fortunately, and I say this as a true blessing, I get up every day going to work loving what I do. I love the place; the mission; the people I work with; the students I teach, train, mentor, develop, and nurture; and the satisfaction I derive from making a true difference in people's lives. That is a true blessing and one that I hope you can experience in your life.

The challenges we face are both simplistic and complex; they are life affirming and occasionally even life threatening. Yet our commitment to cultivate the possibilities and potential in students is what drives us to stay committed to this noble profession. Negotiating and navigating the pathways to productivity and success will not be easy, but it can and will be very rewarding. You must be careful, however, that you do not get into the habit of reacting differently to people, incidents, and situational circumstances. That will likely frustrate you to no end. You do have an option to remember that ideas are the substance of behavior. In essence, you should consider developing what I call a *conceptual template* that serves as a guiding force for your activities and behaviors. That template is composed of the assumptions and biases you make, the vision you aspire to, the values you embrace, and the legacy you recognize and carry with you. The more crystallized you can be with your conceptual template, the better able you will be to base your actions and behaviors as a senior manager on principle and not just personality and situations. That will be a true test of character and integrity and a doorway to discover your truest self within the context of your roles and responsibilities within student affairs.

References

Bryant, J. H. (2009). *Love leadership: A new way to lead in a fear-based world.* San Francisco, CA: Jossey-Bass.

Rath, T., & Conchie, B. (2008). *Strengths based leadership*: *Great leaders, teams, and why people follow.* New York, NY: Gallup.

In the Service for the Greater Good

Michael Drake

Universities are among the most enduring and complex institutions. Enduring, historically, because universities outlast businesses, governments, and even nations over the long arc of time. A 30-, 40-, or 50-year-old university is still referred to as *new*. Many American universities are well into their second century and growing. Europe's oldest institutions were established at a time when many national borders and most governments were distinctly different. Universities are complex because of the ever-changing nature of knowledge, transmitted through teaching or created through discovery, and resulting from the expanding diversity of community, thought, folkways, and mores represented by students, faculty, and staff. They are complex because we are complex. They endure because they adapt through the political and social changes that create the story of our civilization. They must reflect our diversity because we are diverse, and if they remain too firmly mired in a fading past they forfeit their position

Michael Vincent Drake, MD, became the current and 15th president of The Ohio State University in June 2014. From 2005 to 2014, he was the fifth chancellor of the University of California, Irvine.

as bastions of thought leadership, lose relevance, and silently slip from existence. Our diversity is reflected most clearly in our students, who look most like the "now" that they are. Annually, they refresh to some degree. They tend to see the world less as it was and more as it is, or as—in their dreams of the future—they think it should be.

The interface between students and the practical, external, administrative world of university leadership is one of the most intense in academia. The leaders who sit in these seats must embody the wisdom, values, and perspective of the institution, the needs and desires of an amorphous and changing student body, and the flexibility to connect the two. Students are extraordinarily sensitive to authenticity and are quick to reject anything that smacks of packaged programming meant to herd them submissively toward an externally determined endpoint. Student affairs leaders live at this interface. They must nurture and guide, listen and support, and acknowledge and champion students through the personal, political, and social maturation that is the college experience. Conversely, they must act as change agents within the institutional hierarchy, helping the institution itself adapt to the evolutionary progress of society. A diverse perspective is crucial, one of several necessary requirements of these leaders.

Among the host of characteristics Thomas Parham brings to his leadership style, the combination of love, humor, and courage set him apart and formed the basis of his appointment and subsequent exemplary success. His obvious love of his students, the university and what it offers, and the broader community were clear from the outset. He is earnest and honest, committed and dedicated, and it shows. He is a great communicator in venues ranging from one-on-one discussions to speeches in auditoriums filled with thousands. He sees the joy in life and allows it to animate his message. And finally, importantly, he is a soldier, willing to put himself on the line in service of the greater good. At the end of the day, through the most challenging and confusing engagements, he is steadfast and true.

He is able to be a mensch, a scholar, a professor, a psychologist, a colleague, and a "down brother" essentially simultaneously. He is an institutional treasure who has illuminated the path forward for a generation, channeling the guidance of his mentors to build a foundation for the leaders of our collective future.

One might surmise—correctly—that a successful leadership role that lasts more than 30 years is more likely to occur if the senior student affairs executive brings a wealth of talent and experience to the position, such as Parham did. Having identified early in his career as a psychologist, Parham obtained a tenure-track position as an academic psychologist at the University of Pennsylvania, then proceeded to take on successively more responsible roles as a leader in student affairs at the University of California, Irvine. The author exemplifies the use of important "transferable assets," which are skills that can be transferred from one occupation or role to another.

A strong advocate of collaboration between academic and student affairs, Parham sees the relationship between the two areas as reciprocal in that the success of one area contributes to the success of the other, and they both support the success of students. He emphasizes, however, that student affairs professionals should understand and accept the fact that "student affairs exists to support the academic mission of the institution."

Parham characterizes his leadership style as "people oriented." He compares the senior student affairs officer to the leader of an orchestra of talented musicians—someone who promotes a positive work environment and respects the talent of each person by seeing their roles as significant to the success of the endeavor. Although he does not describe himself this way, Parham is surely an exceptional leader in any situation in which he finds himself. We can see this when he talks about his desire to leave a legacy—one in which he is remembered as advocating for human decency and social justice in all areas.

The author succinctly summarizes lessons for the reader. However, lessons are given throughout the narrative, such as the value of risk taking in all its forms. The author says that when he took his first professional position in a state where he knew no one, he was "stepping out on faith." Another lesson that comes to the surface is his ability to find the strength in perceived weakness. So often, student affairs will think of itself as low on the totem pole because its budget is often the first to be cut in budget reductions. The author shares how this perception can be altered to see the strength of student affairs even under these circumstances.

I find especially touching the author's description of the difficulty of balancing one's personal and professional life, especially when excellence is a value. There is only so much time, and how one allocates that time can be a difficult choice. Although Parham knows he strived to put family first and strived to include the community as a top priority, he humbly accepts the judgment of those who may not see his efforts to give sufficient time the same way he sees them.

The author tells us, and it is obvious, that he loves all aspects of his work. He attributes his success and his sense of fulfillment in his work to having developed a conceptual framework to guide his actions and behaviors regardless of the situation and circumstances. This is another lesson that he did not enumerate in his list of lessons. There are many lessons and words of wisdom to be gleaned from Parham's essay.

—Gwendolyn Jordan Dungy

Doris M. Ching

Doris M. Ching is emeritus vice president for student affairs and acting director of the Academy for Creative Media of the University of Hawai`i (UH) System. She also served as interim chancellor and interim vice chancellor for academic affairs at UH–West O`ahu, and vice president for student affairs at UH–Mānoa and the UH System. She received her BEd and MEd from the University of Hawai`i and her EdD from Arizona State University. She was the first woman of color and first Asian American Pacific Islander (AAPI) to be elected president of NASPA–Student Affairs Administrators in Higher Education and the NASPA Foundation. She is author of various articles and coeditor of books on AAPI and student affairs executives of color in higher education.

An Unimagined Pathway to Leadership

Doris M. Ching

I have come to realize that my passion has always been to help others succeed. At the age of 7, my heart was already set on becoming a teacher as a means of helping students achieve in education and flourish as individuals. Years later, into adulthood, the desire of a career in secondary education never waned. This context did not include a professorial or administrative role in higher education. Yet just five years after I was assigned my first middle-school teaching position, I was offered an unsolicited position as a supervisor of student teaching in higher education. Firmly committed to secondary teaching and equally excited by the challenge the supervisory position might offer, I chose the latter. My anticipated lifelong teaching career in secondary education was suddenly short-lived. However, although it seemed at the time that I was compromising my passion and departing from the lifework of my childhood dream, I was delighted to discover that administrators do nurture and promote the success of students and others, albeit in different and often more extensive ways from those of the classroom teacher.

With no expectation of moving beyond the supervisory position and without applying for any position, I was invited to serve in several administrative positions over the next four decades. While I did not feel fully prepared as I entered each new position, I was gratified threefold in each post. First, I was elated that I handily accomplished the work of each office. Second, I was invigorated to make substantial institutional changes to enhance the lives of students, faculty, and staff through curricular reforms, program initiatives, policy changes, affirmative actions, and personal interactions. Third, I personally experienced profound transformational growth as a professional, as each appointment seemed to have prepared me for a future role that broadened my impact on higher education.

In my story, I relate a humble childhood and family life that shaped my values. I disclose my initial career goal of a lifelong profession as a secondary teacher. I describe the sequence of unexpected events and offers of administrative posts that are the building blocks that formed a pathway of leadership and fulfilling career I had not foreseen or imagined. I convey relevant national landmark events that occurred parallel to my leadership pathway to provide a historical context to my experiences and to underscore that the broad scope of student affairs work often extends beyond the campus and even the state. Embedded in the narratives are implications, personal insights, and analyses of my executive pathway in higher education. The underlying premise that persuades me to tell my story and share my interpretations of the events and invitations of executive offices is my hope that the experiences can—and will—be replicated by younger professionals who may face similar opportunities, chance encounters, and position offers.

MY STORY

Lee Bolman breathed inspiration into student affairs administration for me in his presentation at a leadership institute in Kona, Hawai`i. The theme of the institute, "Leading With Soul: An Uncommon

Journey of Spirit," was also the title of the book Bolman coauthored with Terrance Deal (1995). Author, scholar, consultant, and professor of leadership at Harvard, Carnegie Mellon, and Yale Universities, Bolman also coauthored with Deal *Reframing Organizations: Artistry, Choice and Leadership* (2003) and *How Great Leaders Think: The Art of Reframing* (2014). I begin my story of leadership with Bolman and Deal's (1995) simple yet profoundly enlightening observation that "past experiences provide a platform for the present and a launching pad for the future" (p. 145) because it describes my own professional experience across four decades. My career trajectory was an array of building blocks, with each block reflecting a past experience leading to an unknown step into a future leadership role, and resulting in a journey in higher education leadership that was uncommon for an Asian American woman of my generation.

A HUMBLE BACKGROUND

My journey is especially unexpected of one with so humble a background. I am the fifth of seven children. My father arrived in Hawai`i at the age of 12 with his parents, immigrants from the island of Okinawa, the poorest of all prefectures of Japan. After completing the seventh grade in Hawai`i , he worked as a truck driver for a food distribution company and was later promoted to assistant manager.

My maternal grandparents immigrated to Hawai`i as sugar plantation laborers. My mother was the eldest of eight children, all of whom were born and raised in Hawai`i . After my mother completed the third grade, she stayed out of school to care for her siblings at home while her parents labored in the sugar cane fields—a relatively routine expectation of the oldest daughter of sugar plantation families at the time. After she had her own family of seven children, my mother worked as a housecleaner for the families of military officers who were stationed at the Pearl Harbor U.S. naval base, five miles from our home.

A hard-working woman with a positive attitude and cheerful dispo-
sition, my mother was beloved by the Caucasian officers and their
families. I am indebted to the U.S. Navy admirals, captains, com-
manders and their spouses and children who regarded my mother—
an Okinawan American housekeeper with limited education—with
deep, genuine love and respect. Due to discriminations based on racial
prejudice, the Japanese attack on the United States and Europe that
escalated to World War II, and class consciousness of the time, not all
Caucasians treated Japanese Americans and service workers with the
level of respect these families afforded my mother.

Okinawans and Okinawan Americans have been portrayed as hard-
working people by historians and writers, as in *The History of an Island
People* by U.S. diplomat George H. Kerr (1958) and *The Teahouse of the
August Moon* by author Vern Sneider (1951). The trait describes my
parents well. With limited education and low-paying jobs, they worked
hard to raise seven children.

FINANCIALLY POOR BUT NOT DISADVANTAGED OR UNDERPRIVILEGED

As a child, I knew our family was financially poor. Still, I was startled
to learn in my freshman Sociology 100 class that families like ours
were defined in textbooks as *disadvantaged* and *underprivileged*. If
my family was culturally disadvantaged and economically underprivileged, neither status appeared to have an effect of deprivation
in our home. Although our household did not subscribe to monthly
magazines and journals, which was one of the criteria of a privileged
family according to the sociology course, culture was expressed in different ways.

My grandfather's mastery of the *sanshin*, a three-string Okinawan
instrument resembling a banjo, earned him a prestigious certificate and
a coveted license from Japan to teach the art of sanshin. Other music

often heard in our home was my grandmother playing the *koto*—an Okinawan long and narrow floor string instrument, my brother playing the four-string Hawaiian ukulele, and my sisters playing the piano. We had other cultural experiences. On my grandfather's chicken farm, I could slip my hand under the hens and pick up warm eggs. I had bunnies, dogs, and even a cow as pets. Our father took us fishing and overnight camping on the beach. Because of these memorable experiences, I refused to use either term to describe myself or my family. With rich experiences and an intact and supportive family, the labels of *disadvantaged* and *underprivileged* were not relevant to our household.

LOVE OF LEARNING

Although my three sisters and three brothers were academically capable of pursuing college degrees, their vocational interests led them to choose jobs without this prerequisite, and they all succeeded in their chosen fields of work. I have often wondered why I was the only one and the first of all generations in my family to complete a college education. I respect my siblings for what they accomplished in their chosen vocations, and I am forever grateful for their unwavering support and encouragement of my pursuits. My sisters read books to me daily and taught me to read and write before I entered the first grade. I looked forward to Saturdays, when they took me to the public library. Their gifts of *Golden Books* were germane to my love of books and learning. I was elated that they allowed me to share in their high school homework of memorizing Henry Wadsworth Longfellow's long narrative poems of *Hiawatha*, *The Children's Hour*, and *Evangeline*, some of which I can still recite now after six decades.

I was 4 years old when I begged and nagged my sister to take me to school with her. My persistence overwhelmed my mother into relenting and allowing me to join my sister for one day. I was ecstatic to sit in the back row of the fifth grade classroom absorbing everything the teacher,

Mrs. Lau, taught the class. The euphoria ended when the school principal informed my sister that a 4-year-old was not welcome in the school and she was never again allowed to take me to class. However, the incident did not deter my love of school, learning, and education. Now, decades later, I can still recall the euphoria I felt that day in school.

TEACHING AS A CAREER CHOICE

At age 7, I decided that I would become a teacher, an interest that persisted through my elementary, high school, and college years. Scholarships were scarce when I attended college, and college financial aid was nonexistent. Throughout my high school years, I worked summers at the Dole pineapple cannery to earn and save for my college tuition. After I entered college, I was fortunate to be hired as a live-in babysitter for a family in an affluent neighborhood five miles from the university campus. This position allowed me to attend classes during the day and fulfill my babysitting responsibilities in the evening, sparing me the daily 20-mile commute from our family home to the university campus. College tuition was affordable then, and the wages of $1.05 per hour from my summer work of packing pineapples and allowance of $35 per month I earned as a babysitter sufficiently covered the expenses of my tuition and other educational costs.

Teaching continued to be my passion. I was excited when I completed my bachelor of education degree and was hired as a middle school English teacher at a time when there was a surplus of English teachers. I looked forward to beginning my first teaching assignment and launching my lifelong teaching career. Helping seventh and eighth grade students learn and grow academically, psychologically, and socially stimulated me. Seeing my students every day was a joy. I loved their sense of humor. I was amused by the playful pranks that they played on me. Their gleeful giggles and hearty laughter after knowing

I was duped by their jokes were delightful moments. My childhood dream of becoming a teacher had come true.

AN UNIMAGINED CAREER IN HIGHER EDUCATION

I envisioned that I would be a teacher for life. It had never entered my mind that I would someday be a college professor. Yet, five years after I started my teaching career, the University of Hawai'i College of Education offered me a faculty position as a supervisor of student teaching. Although I neither applied nor felt fully qualified for the job without a graduate degree, the opportunity to share successful methods of development of student teachers with colleagues in the field prompted me to accept the position. I immersed myself in the faculty role, and the revelation that I could succeed in academia impelled me to enroll in the master of education program albeit with some trepidation. While I had previously lacked confidence in my ability to achieve a graduate degree, any uncertainty dissipated after I discovered that I enjoyed the challenge of the master's program and could succeed in it after all. I was then further emboldened to apply for tenure in the College of Education, which I was subsequently granted.

I view tenure as an enormously major responsibility to students and the institution. My high regard for tenure and my commitment to provide the best possible education for students motivated me to pursue a doctoral degree immediately after my tenure award. The pursuit of a doctoral degree required studying at a university in another state across the Pacific Ocean, as no relevant program was available at that time in the state of Hawai'i. This situation required my spouse, whose employment allowed me to be a full-time student, to be the sole parent at home in Hawai'i to our 9- and 11-year-old sons during my absence.

After a wrenching and soul-searching deliberation, and with the blessing of our pediatrician and the unequivocal support and encouragement of my spouse, sons, mother-in-law, and sister-in-law, I fully immersed myself in a doctoral program at Arizona State University. Incited by the urgency to return to my family at the earliest possible time, I imposed an accelerated degree schedule upon myself, and within 14 months I fulfilled the requisite coursework, internship, comprehensive examination, and defense of my dissertation prospectus, and I returned to Hawai`i to conduct my research for the dissertation. Two years later, I was awarded a doctor of education degree in educational administration and supervision.

Even with the doctoral degree, thoughts of serving as associate dean, vice president for student affairs, vice chancellor for academic affairs, or chancellor never entered my mind. For an Asian American woman of my generation to hold any of these positions was not commonplace, even in Hawai`i where Asian Americans, Native Hawaiians, and Pacific Islanders compose two-thirds of the state population. Still, these unexpected offers and appointments persisted throughout my career.

FROM TEACHER TO ADMINISTRATOR

The first unanticipated administrative work was a request by the associate dean of education of the University of Hawai`i to write the proposal for a federal Teacher Corps Project grant to develop a pilot field-based teacher education program in a low-income community. As a junior faculty member with no track record in external grants, I was astounded to be tasked with the critical assignment to advance teacher education in our college and state, as were many of the senior faculty. However, the intense responsibility I felt to the university, students, and the state overpowered any thought of failure. To not write the proposal was not an option. I had to rise to the challenge of the request, and I had to succeed.

I consulted daily with a cadre of inspired teachers of the middle school designated as the site for the pilot project and met daily with them for a month to develop the proposal. At each meeting, the teachers expressed their desires to meet the needs of the students, families, school, and community, and I translated their aspirations into a narrative of project goals and strategies. The teachers related the training they required to increase student success and self-esteem, and I expanded the narrative to include their every insight. Our request for $338,000 for two years was nearly tripled by the federal agency. The actual award of $1.2 million for five years was a far greater grant than we had originally proposed.

The overwhelming demands and unrelenting administrative tasks of implementing the project within intense timelines left no time for rest. I learned the painful consequences of sleep deprivation. Nonetheless, I was energized by the development of collaborative decision making, a school–community council, the newly enacted Elementary and Secondary Education Act (which would later become the No Child Left Behind Act), proactive field-based pre-service and in-service teacher education, and—especially—the opportunity to raise the levels of achievement and student self-esteem in a low-income population. My greatest fulfillment came from the resoundingly successful transformation of the pilot school. After two years, it became a model school, a source of pride for its students, and a vibrant center of learning and community engagement.

DEVELOPING A LEADERSHIP STYLE

Although collaborative decision making was a new concept in education formally introduced in 1976 by the National Teacher Corps as the intended administrative procedure, it fit naturally into the leadership style I had already formed as a way to exercise participatory decision making and consultation with individuals and groups who would be affected by the outcomes. While collaborative decision making and consultative administration may appear as an inability to make decisions, as a core theme of Teacher Corps, they validated and characterized a clear mark of managerial strength. Though consensus building and shared governance can be painstakingly time consuming, the participant buy-in and ownership of the results are proof of their efficacy.

In *Leading with Soul,* Bolman and Deal (1995) stated that leaders must take the spiritual journey and inspire others to take it with us. That's what leadership is to me—influencing public policy, impacting behaviors in positive ways, and involving all constituents and stakeholders in planning and decision making on matters that directly affect them.

The focus of Teacher Corps on diversity, nondiscrimination, and collaboration made it inclusive for persons of all races, ethnicities, and characteristics to be fully engaged. Despite being aware of this focus, as the sole Asian American among scores of Teacher Corps directors across the nation, I did not expect and was awed that my fellow directors unequivocally accepted me as a full partner in collaboration and deliberations.

I did not foresee the significant impact of Teacher Corps on my career until it actually became a launch pad for my future work in higher education administration. As Teacher Corps came to a close after five years, I was nominated for the office of associate dean of education at the University of Hawai`i . The job description portrayed a mundane role, unappealing to me following the dynamic, innovative, and progressive Teacher Corps directorship I was leaving. Regardless, I accepted the nomination and, when I was appointed, I tailored the work of the associate dean of education to reflect the vibrant, proactive, and dynamic place of learning for future teachers the College of Education needed to become. The 1983 report *A Nation at Risk: The Imperative for Educational Reform* from President Ronald Reagan's National Commission on Excellence in Education fueled the ongoing complaint that American schools were failing. This landmark report in modern American educational history placed enormous pressures for reform on colleges of education across the country, including our college.

The governor of the state of Hawaiʻi formed the inaugural statewide Board of Education–University of Hawaiʻi Board of Regents joint committee to address the issues raised in *A Nation at Risk*. To my surprise, the governor asked that I chair the statewide committee. Although I was a new associate dean, I accepted the responsibility. With full faculty engagement in collegewide curricular reform and active dialogue with students on their educational experience, we created a vitalizing education program with stronger relationships with public and private K–12 schools and greater opportunities for faculty and student engagement and leadership. The College of Education transformed into an energetic, dynamic, student-centered hub for innovative programs with a robust teacher education program to develop stronger and more effective teachers.

When the dean of education announced his intent to retire, the college faculty members were adamant that the candidates for the next dean would be external to the college. This was logical, as the previous deans over three decades rose from the local internal faculty. I also personally believe that the predominantly White male faculty was not ready for an Asian American woman dean. Clearly, I would not be a candidate for the office. I had two options. I could serve as associate dean under a new dean, or I could seek other positions. I chose the latter. I pondered the uncertainty of my next job, as I had done five years before when I left the directorship of Teacher Corps prior to being appointed associate dean of education. Such lulls between jobs are disconcerting and discomforting, analogous to a "time of the parenthesis," a phrase coined by John Naisbitt (1982), author of *Megatrends*:

> It was the time between eras . . . as though we have bracketed off the present from both the past and the future, for we are neither

here nor there . . . we are clinging to the known past in fear of the unknown future. Those who are willing to handle the ambiguity of this in-between period and to anticipate the new era will be a quantum leap ahead of those who hold on to the past. The time of the parenthesis is a time of change and questioning. (p. 249)

Although Naisbitt (1982) was writing of global directions and transformation of lives in an international context, I found relevance and logic in applying his global concept to a personal context. Naisbitt (1982) provided valuable lessons in patience through his philosophical writing:

Although . . . the time of parenthesis . . . is a time of challenges and possibilities . . . and a time of uncertainty, it is also a great and yeasty time, filled with opportunity. If we can learn to make uncertainty our friend, we can achieve much more than in stable eras. (p. 252)

UNFORESEEN CAREER OPPORTUNITIES IN EXECUTIVE LEADERSHIP

In my critical *time of parenthesis*, the University of Hawai`i president, Albert J. Simone, offered me the position of assistant to the president. Naisbitt's (1982) advice proved true for me. My bonding with *uncertainty* became a benefit to me.

I was honored to serve as assistant to a president as brilliant, innovative, and visionary as Simone. His bold and enterprising plans to thrust the university into greater heights of world renown and academic and research excellence in astronomy, ocean and earth science, Native Hawaiian studies, Pacific Island studies, Asian studies, and other areas in which the University of Hawai`i could make major global contributions in knowledge were exciting and ambitious. I cherished the privilege to be a part of an executive administration of a large, complex university system of a flagship research-intensive institution, two liberal arts campuses, and seven community colleges on four islands across the Hawaiian Islands chain. I was excited to work with a president so physically and intellectually energetic, creative in problem solving, and committed to the local community, with a vision of world-class programs that would compete—even surpass—reputable universities and research institutions across the nation. To witness a vigorous effort to transform the University of Hawai`i to be both contender and contributor to a global and universal context was most stimulating and memorable. Today, three decades later, I am ecstatic to observe the actual realization of Simone's ambitious initiatives of 30 years ago.

The front-row seat to the stage of a dynamic, formative new direction of the university evoked a sensation of power and excitement. The vision of elevating the respect of the university, nationally and internationally, would benefit students as well as the people of the state of Hawai`i. Simone's extremely strategic mind and energy also generated an exorbitant amount of work on my office. I was again reminded of the serious effects of sleep deprivation, which this time manifested as an extreme case of vertigo resulting from only two hours of sleep each night and overconsumption of coffee to keep myself awake over extended periods of weeks and months. In spite of the pain and discomfort, I loved every moment of the experience, vertigo and all.

One year after my appointment as assistant to the president, Simone presented another new and unanticipated opportunity that would further extend my administrative experience in higher education. "You learned the work of assistant to the president too quickly," he said. "You will be bored with it within a year, and I want to keep you on the president's team, so I would like you to consider accepting another position." He suggested, "You could be vice president for student affairs and still be a member of my administrative team." He then confessed, "You were nominated for vice president for student affairs last year, but I didn't think you were tough enough to handle the work. But, I was wrong. You're as tough as they come." He admitted he misjudged me because of my relatively quiet demeanor and later realized—after observing me as his assistant for a year—that an externally calm demeanor did not denote administrative weakness and may not reveal the competencies and inner strength of an executive.

In my simplistic mind at that time, I did not see a negative connotation in Simone's confession. In fact, perhaps naïvely, I accepted it as a compliment. I also believe he intended it to be a compliment. However, I now recognize it as a frequent misinterpretation of capable Asian American leaders whose administrative styles are misunderstood, whose managerial effectiveness is unrecognized, and whose inner strength is underestimated. Often, people who misperceive a situation in this way are unaware of the misconception, so it was refreshing that Simone admitted the discovery of his incorrect thinking and his intent to correct his misperception. In retrospect, I now understand that for the sake of justice to Asian Americans and for the benefit of institutions of higher education, it is essential that such mistaken beliefs are not accepted or condoned.

From the vantage point of the president's office, the system of 10 University of Hawai`i campuses was exciting and invigorating. Education is ever-uplifting. Observing the myriad programs and avenues of access to a college degree by thousands of students was a daily inspiration. Although the work of the president's office was intellectually stimulating in every possible way, my passion for improving opportunities to help students succeed in their educational pursuits continued to surge. My yearning to enhance the campus climate for students became evident to Simone, which may have led to his creating an opportunity for me to serve as vice president for student affairs while continuing to be a member of his administrative team.

BECOMING A CHAMPION OF STUDENT AFFAIRS

The Office of Student Affairs had previously been led by the dean of students, who, organizationally, reported to the vice chancellor for academic affairs. The proverbial neglect that results in a university when a student affairs officer reports to an academic affairs executive was evident. The support services that students need to succeed in college were sorely and embarrassingly overlooked. Programs to serve students were scattered across the campus in cramped, nondescript quarters. Student affairs programs were understaffed and extremely underfunded. The existing staff were caring, spirited, and proficient in their work, yet received little recognition and had no voice in decision making for the institution. Much needed to be done to create meaningful campus experiences for students, promote student success, and elevate the importance of the work of student affairs professionals.

Simone's intent was to improve both assistance and status to student affairs. With staunch backing and support of the president and the board of regents, higher focus and greater importance were placed on the needs of students within the institution. As vice president for student affairs, I ensured that student affairs had voice and visibility at the table of the president's executive team. New programs were established to support the educational success of students by addressing issues of student diversity and equity, students with disabilities, school and college relations, scholarships and financial aid, student leadership development, gender equity, child care, and women's issues. Campus-based child care and resource centers for women, LGBT (lesbian, gay, bisexual, and transgender), and nontraditional students were developed. Collaboration between student affairs and academic affairs increased.

In 1987, Ernest Boyer, a fellow with the Carnegie Foundation for the Advancement of Teaching, wrote the milestone book *College: The Undergraduate Experience in America*, calling for reform in U.S.

undergraduate education and greater focus on educational excellence. Boyer criticized the "confusion" in American higher education and ticked off critical components of a *college of quality*, including success in transition from high school to college, curricular and educational goals, faculty priorities, condition of teaching and learning, quality of campus life, college governance, outcomes assessment, and connection between the campus and the outside world. He referenced needs-based student support and recruiting underrepresented populations. He stated that the structure of colleges needed reforms to support the undergraduate experience and student success. Boyer's book gave a boost to the importance of student affairs.

With these assurances and the tenacious support of Simone, the primacy of students peaked, student affairs burgeoned, and I thrived in the role of vice president for student affairs, a position from which I retired after 36 years in higher education administration.

ASIAN AMERICANS AND PACIFIC ISLANDERS AS ACADEMIC LEADERS

For an Asian American woman of my generation, it was unthinkable that I would be viewed as a leader or prospect for any administrative position. In "Asian American and Pacific Islanders in Leadership: Pipeline or Pipe Dream?," Audrey Yamagata-Noji and Henry Gee (2012) related how non-Asian Americans frequently characterize the working administrative styles of Asian Americans and Pacific Islanders (AAPIs). Some are complimentary descriptors, such as AAPIs are perfect team players who take direction well, work hard, work for the good of the cause, remain loyal and humble; they listen and observe before speaking, do not boast of their accomplishments, and work diligently until a job is done; they wait to be recognized and believe that hard work and dedication will be duly recognized. On the other hand, many of the descriptors are inaccurate: AAPIs are neither risk takers nor willing to stand up or speak out; they are not leadership material; they are quiet, nice, hard workers, but are not seen as leaders; they do great work, but are not very assertive; they are not very communicative; they don't stand out as leadership material; they blend in with the group. Such inaccurate perceptions clearly indicate the underestimation of the strength of AAPI leaders. These misperceptions demand correction. Hence, both locally and nationally, I am gratified to have demonstrated the credibility of successful Asian American leaders.

D. Quinn Mills (2005), the Albert J. Weatherhead Jr. Professor of Business Administration (emeritus) at Harvard Business School, presented the nine key qualities sought in a successful leader, as found in research studies: passion, decisiveness, conviction, integrity, adaptability, emotional toughness, emotional resonance, self-knowledge, and humility. Mills further saw five leadership styles among American executives, in general: directive, participative, empowering, charismatic, and superstar celebrity. Mills claimed that self-knowledge and humility are less common among American executives and may be a strength of the Asian American executive.

CONFRONTATION WITH DISCRIMINATION

Mistaken beliefs of AAPI leadership qualities can be detrimental to the career advancement of Asian Americans and Pacific Islanders. As an administrator in higher education who faced discriminatory situations, I credit the late U.S. Congresswoman Patsy Matsu Takemoto Mink (1927–2002) for the opportunities I have had in higher education administrative roles. As the first Asian American woman and first woman of color to serve in Congress, trailblazer Mink battled racism and gender discrimination from the start of her elected seat representing the state of Hawai`i . Discrimination was not new to Mink, who had not been accepted at any medical school to which she had applied despite her impeccable academic credentials and undisputed eligibility for meeting the admission criteria. She eventually chose to study law and was admitted to the University of Chicago School of Law and became an attorney. In Congress, Mink championed women's rights and civil rights and served as assistant secretary of state for oceans and international environmental and scientific affairs. Mink was a dear personal friend for whom I had immense gratitude and admiration. She is most noted as coauthor of the landmark Title IX of the Education Amendments of 1972, which led to the transformation of all aspects of gender equality in American education institutions. As a tribute to Mink's momentous achievements for equal rights for all in the nation, the act was named the Patsy T. Mink Equal Opportunity in Education Act.

I relate to Mink, for I was disadvantaged threefold as a woman, as a person of color, and as a professional in student affairs as opposed to academic affairs. Professional women—both White women and women of color—in higher education executive positions in the 1980s were scarce, and student affairs professionals were regarded as lower in rank than faculty in academic positions. The principles of administration on which my style of leadership is based are consistent with those of AAPIs and include the following: (a) integrity is uppermost in every action I take; (b) hard work is essential to achieve the goals of the institution; (c) sacrifice of personal needs is expected at times when I must give higher focus and greater importance to the needs of students and the institution; (d) doing the right thing for the right reason is my daily guide; (e) it is requisite to gather courage, negate fear, and persevere even under the most difficult circumstances; and (f) hubris is neither acceptable nor defensible at all times. These principles contributed to my leadership effectiveness and success, as evident in the executive positions I had not sought but to which I was appointed and in which I succeeded.

Despite any disadvantage and discrimination I may have faced in my career, it was, nonetheless, fortuitous for me to be a professional in higher education at a time when the U.S. Supreme Court ruled that Title IX bars sex discrimination against students and employees of educational institutions. Women were coming into their own. The American Council on Education released *The New Agenda of Women for Higher Education,* coauthored by Donna Shavlik, Judith G. Touchton, and Carol R. Pearson (1988), calling for institutions to educate women systematically for leadership in society. The report could have been a direct response to my situation, for I did not feel fully prepared to take on any of the leadership positions to which I was unexpectedly appointed. Indeed, I would have benefited from leadership education and training.

STUDENT AFFAIRS TRANSFORMATIONS

Perhaps my personally most rewarding and unique contributions to the strength and stature of student affairs educators at the University of Hawai`i are three major initiatives that I advocated and was influential in establishing. First, NASPA–Student Affairs Administrators in Higher Education, the leading voice for student affairs administration, policy, and practice, grew in Hawai`i from a single member in 1987 to the current and steady 50-plus memberships among higher education institutions within the state of Hawai`i . The increased NASPA membership brought national recognition to the work of student affairs professionals in Hawai`i and resulted in professional and leadership opportunities for local student affairs educators. Second, the University of Hawai`i 's tenure track structure, normally unique to academic faculty appointments, was expanded to student services specialists. This structure allows student affairs faculty to engage in academic endeavors related to their student affairs work; to earn tenure and sabbatical leaves; and to be promoted to assistant, associate, and full specialists. Third, a state-of-the-art student services center was constructed in a prime spot on the flagship University of Hawai`i at Mānoa campus. The center houses most student programs in one convenient location. This establishment reassured me that programs to ensure student success would endure and continue to advance.

My guiding principles as I strived to improve the educational environment for women, students, persons of color, and student affairs professionals were, always, to look at the higher purpose and cause in everything I chose to undertake, to vow to leave each place I served better than I found it, to turn negatives to positives, and to turn things around where transformation was clearly needed.

As I reflect on the approach I have cultivated to execute my leadership of an organization, it occurs to me that there are differences between the way I address my work and the administrative styles of my colleagues, both in Hawai`i and in other states and countries. Although I am not clear that the differences are related to Asian or any other ways of management, my personal observation is that my managerial philosophy and style is an aggregation and embodiment of all parts of my mind, passion, and spirit. It is an integration of who I am, what I have observed, what others have taught me, and what I have internalized over the decades of my career.

Without doubt, the post-retirement urgent request to serve as interim vice chancellor for academic affairs of a baccalaureate campus was my most unanticipated career experience, and the timing of the offer—amid my nearly 10-year happy retirement—was extraordinary. The second post-retirement appointment as interim chancellor of the institution was both unanticipated as well as astonishing. Today, in this age of digital arts entertainment, collaborative scientific visualization environments, video game development, film and digital media, and other media technology, my third and current post-retirement position as acting director of the Academy for Creative Media of the University of Hawai`i System is the most amazing, exciting, and innovative position in which I have served. As I previously stated, there are times, such as these, when the needs of students and the institution outweigh one's personal preferences. How could I not accept the urgent calls to serve?

AN UNIMAGINED CAREER PATH

My career trajectory included being the first woman vice president of the University of Hawai`i and the first Asian American and first woman of color to be elected president of a leading professional organization, NASPA. It was uncommon, especially three decades ago, for an Asian American woman to serve as the vice president for student affairs of a research-intensive institution or be elected president of a major national professional association. Even today, to be appointed interim vice chancellor for academic affairs and interim chancellor of a baccalaureate university after a retirement of nearly 10 years is highly improbable, especially as each position was neither sought nor imagined by me.

The Japanese writer Haruki Murakami (2006) noted, "A series of coincidences took me somewhere I never expected to be" (p. 253). However, I believe my pathway was not the result of coincidences. In retrospect, it was the outcome of making decisions based on what was best for the institution, students, state, and profession. It was leading with integrity and caring deeply and genuinely about the success of everyone to whom I was responsible and every organization and entity that depended on my work. Most importantly, it was giving total focus and commitment and achieving the best possible outcome in the current work at hand and not constantly looking ahead to a future aspired position.

It has been four decades since I spent 14 months away from my home, spouse, and two sons in a doctoral degree program more than

3,000 miles away across the Pacific Ocean. Our family stayed intact over the years. Each of us gained and grew from the challenge in positive and transformational ways. Our two sons, who were then 9 and 11 years old, later pursued their doctoral degrees and are currently tenured professors at prestigious universities in the continental United States. My spouse of 56 years and I are heartened that both of our sons have encouraged their respective spouses to pursue their graduate degrees and careers at distinguished universities.

If my career were an unimagined journey of spirit, it presented an unanticipated event or surprise at every turn and continues to do so. Moreover, every event proved to be an opportunity to help more students and colleagues on my campus and across the nation succeed than I would have been able to effect as a classroom teacher. The role of executive in higher education became and continues to be an unanticipated means to fulfill my passion of helping others succeed.

References

Bolman, L. G., & Deal, T. E. (1995). *Leading with soul: An uncommon journey of spirit.* San Francisco, CA: Jossey-Bass.

Bolman, L. G. & Deal, T. E. (2003). *Reframing organizations: Artistry, choice, and leadership* (3rd ed.) San Francisco, CA: Jossey-Bass.

Bolman, L. G., & Deal, T. E. (2014). *How great leaders think: The art of reframing.* San Francisco, CA: Jossey-Bass.

Boyer, E. L. (1987). *College: The undergraduate experience in America.* New York, NY: Harper & Row.

Kerr, G. H. (1958). *The history of an island people.* Boston, MA: Tuttle.

Mills, D. Q. (2005, June). *Asian and American leadership styles: How are they unique? Harvard Business School Working Knowledge.* Retrieved from http://hbswk.hbs.edu/item/asian-and-american-leadership-styles-how-are-they-unique

Murakami, H. (2006). *Blind willow, sleeping woman.* New York, NY: Vintage Books.

Naisbitt, J. (1982). *Megatrends: Ten new directions transforming our lives.* New York, NY: Warner Books.

National Commission on Excellence in Education. (1983). *A nation at risk: The imperative for educational reform: A report to the nation and the secretary of education, United States Department of Education.* Washington, DC: Author.

Shavlik, D., Touchton, J. G., & Pearson, C. R. (1988). *The new agenda of women for higher education.* Washington, DC: American Council on Education.

Sneider, V. (1951). *The teahouse of the August moon.* New York, NY: G. P. Putnam's Sons.

Yamagata-Noji, A., & Gee, H. (2012). "Asian American and Pacific Islanders in leadership: Pipeline or pipe dream?" In D. Ching & A. Agbayani (Eds.), *Asian Americans and Pacific Islanders in higher education: Research and perspectives on identity, leadership, and success.* Washington, DC: NASPA–Student Affairs Administrators in Higher Education.

How I Came to Know and Partner With Doris Ching

Albert J. Simone

There I was, very early in my term as president of the University of Hawai`i system and chancellor of the University of Hawai`i at Mānoa, the system's research university, and I already had to seek a replacement for the assistant to the president. Because this was a particularly important and sensitive position, I realized it would be difficult to find the right person.

This seemingly straightforward position would be difficult to fill for many reasons. The factors affecting the ultimate decision were complex and not necessarily easy to assess, and included

- personal attributes;
- academic experience;
- entrée to the state legislature and congressional delegation;
- comfort and rapport with the Hawai`i community at large;
- earned respect from students, faculty, staff administration, and regents; and

Albert J. Simone served as president emeritus at the University of Hawai`i at Mānoa from 1984 to 1992, and as president emeritus at Rochester Institute of Technology from 1992 to 2007.

◆ thorough understanding of teaching, curricula development, research, and community service.

One could rightfully say that this was quite a tall order—perhaps too tall and unrealistic for any single individual to attempt to fill. I realized at the time that this was probably "Mission Impossible." But I decided to aim high and work hard to identify such an individual, hoping to come as close as possible to the ideal candidate.

I was lucky. I discovered Doris Ching and persuaded her to join the President's Office.

How did Doris match up with the selection factors summarized above? With regard to personal attributes, I needed someone who would be loyal to me personally, to the Office of the President, to the University of Hawai`i, and to the state of Hawai`i. That person had to be of the highest ethical and moral fiber, someone who could be trusted completely in all matters and who knew how to be discreet and keep confidences when necessary. I was looking for someone who would be selfless and able to place the responsibilities of the job above personal and professional goals and ambitions. That person would need to have an extremely strong work ethic—the fortitude to get the job done right and on time, regardless of the stress or number of hours required. Finally, it would be highly desirable if this person could also have a reasonable family–work–extracurricular balance. Where could I begin to find such a person? A typical job search process would not likely be able to ascertain such personal characteristics.

Here is where my luck began. At that time, I played golf regularly on Saturday mornings with Paul Yuen, dean of the College of Engineering, and Pat Takahashi, director of the Hawai`i Natural Energy Institute. One morning, we started discussing my search dilemma. They immediately brought up the name of Doris Ching, then associate dean of the College of Education. Doris had been collaborating with them on grant proposals regarding the Pacific International Center for High

Technology Research. They could not say enough good things about her, particularly with regard to the personal attributes criterion. Here were two good friends, one with a PhD in electrical engineering and the other with a PhD in biochemical engineering, vouching vigorously for a colleague with an EdD in educational administration. Typically, these disciplines do not coalesce. My friends' enthusiasm caught my attention. I thought that Doris may, indeed, be someone special.

She was no stranger to me. I had seen her at various gatherings and spoken casually with her. She was always wearing a smile, impeccably dressed, and readily approachable by everyone. I thought I should attempt to get to know her better.

With regard to personal style, I found that in dealing with others in a professional capacity, Doris was humble and respectful. She listened intently, processed information well, and was always fully prepared to discuss the issue at hand. She knew how to compromise when that was required to move forward. She knew her territory and understood and acknowledged the territory (i.e., responsibility, expertise) of others. She could communicate well and work effectively within a team environment. She could take on leadership roles when appropriate. She had shown the ability to delegate responsibility and be held accountable for her own actions. So far, so good.

Regarding the second criterion, academic experience, I hit a home run. Doris started out as a middle school English teacher, moved on to a university faculty position, worked as a team leader with K–12 and university faculty, published, received research grants, revised course curricula, served as an officer in the University Faculty Senate, and on and on.

Investigating the third criterion, entrée to the state legislature and congressional delegation, I learned that Doris knew the governor and numerous key legislators. She had ready access to them and, from time to time, they would contact her regarding issues of mutual interest.

With regard to comfort and rapport with the Hawai`i community at large, again I struck gold. Doris was well known in the greater Hawai`i community, especially in organizations relating to Okinawan heritage and culture. She often collaborated with the state department of education and related programs.

Because of her initiative, selfless effort, caring nature, and record of accomplishment, Doris easily met the criterion of earned respect from students, faculty, staff, administration, and regents.

As I turned to the final criterion, thorough understanding of teaching, curricula development, research, and community service, I found that one of Doris's exemplary achievements—in fact the one that impressed me the most—brought together and integrated all of the preceding criteria: her ability to obtain a federal grant of more than a million dollars to create and implement a five-year program, the Teacher Corps Project. This project, which was completed a few years prior to my considering her for the assistant to the president position, involved collaboration among middle school and university faculty, parents of students, students themselves, and community members, and resulted in major curriculum reform and the creation of innovative student support programs.

I was not alone in my assessment of this endeavor as quite impressive. The Hawai`i State Legislature officially commended Doris for her work on the Teacher Corps Project. Moreover, the governor, in large part because of her accomplishment on the project, subsequently asked her to chair a joint committee of the top administrators from the University of Hawai`i and the state department of education to address the issues raised in two landmark 1983 publications—the National Commission on Excellence in Education's *A Nation at Risk: The Imperative for Educational Reform*, and Ernest Boyer's paper *High School: A Report on Secondary Education in America*, which was released prior to his 1987 book *College: The Undergraduate Experience in America*. Under Doris's leadership, the committee produced outstanding results that had positive repercussions throughout the Hawai`i State Department of Education and the University of Hawai`i .

I could go on, but suffice it to say that I concluded that Doris was actually too good for the job of assistant to the president. Then again, nothing ventured, nothing gained, so I decided to give it my best shot. Much to my delight, Doris accepted the offer.

During her first year as the assistant to the president, Doris totally lived up to my expectations—in fact, not surprisingly, she surpassed them. One dimension of her professional personality, a dimension about which I was previously unsure came to the fore. I knew Doris could lead through collaboration; that was her style and strength. But sometimes, a leader must be forceful and tough in dealing with certain individuals and certain segments of an organizational structure. In other words, "Get on board or get out of the way." I'll be darned if she didn't come through in that regard as well.

After Doris had been on the job for about a year, it became evident that she could contribute so much more to the university in a different and much more challenging position. It was to be a newly created position, one of critical importance that would correct important weaknesses in the university system as a whole—vice president of student affairs for the university system and the research campus at Mānoa.

The university system then served 65,000 students spread across 10 campuses (one research university, two baccalaureate colleges, and seven community colleges) distributed among four islands. From a system perspective, a critical problem (both academically and politically) was the very difficult, if not impossible, curricula articulation process among the 10 campuses. For example, course work completed at a community college often was not recognized at the Mānoa campus.

A second critical problem, from the perspective of the Mānoa campus of approximately 20,000 students, was making student services readily available. At the time, student services were distributed all over the campus, some in nondescript locations. Among other issues, students could travel around the campus all day long attempting to get a problem resolved, and student affairs personnel, because of the geographical distribution, had difficulty communicating and working together on behalf of students.

The university had to recognize the primacy of students and do a better and more comprehensive job of serving them. I asked Doris if she wanted to take this on. She could hardly wait. It was as if she had lived her entire life to prepare for this challenge. She took the bit in her teeth and took off.

But it wasn't that easy, at least at the outset. Before the decision was announced, some folks questioned the wisdom of a systemwide female vice president—there had never been one at the university. And others, as it turned out, were misled by Doris's humble, respectful, and collaborative demeanor and relatively small physical stature. They wondered whether she could "command and control" those "big men." These voices were few. They brought a smile to my lips as I thought, "Just you wait and see." Later, these same voices were singing her praise.

And what did Doris accomplish as the first vice president for student affairs? Regarding the two issues I mentioned, she worked with others to establish a process in which students could now readily transfer from the community colleges to the baccalaureate colleges and the research campus, and from the baccalaureate colleges to the research campus. On the Mānoa campus, she led the charge for the establishment of a student services building in the center of the campus, which brought together almost all of the many student services programs.

Along the way and over the years, Doris has brought to fruition a multitude of significant programs that have enriched the student experience in so many ways. Student government, student scholarships, sexual harassment awareness and prevention, diversity and inclusion, college opportunities, the children's center (child care), health services, the student regent position, intercollegiate athletics, the women's center, and residence halls are just a few of the programs in which she took an active and major leadership role to make things happen, sometimes through undertaking the initiative, obtaining funding, and then handing it off, and other times by providing continuing oversight and management.

Doris's distinguished work—in the local, national, and international communities and within academia on the local, national, and international levels—is too voluminous for me to fully comment on here. Her presidency of NASPA–Student Affairs Administrators in Higher Education (she was the first woman of color and first Asian American to hold this position), her service as chair of the Hawai`i Judicial Selection Commission, and her recognition with the Hawai`i United Okinawan Association Legacy Award provide only a flavor of her accomplishments.

Of the many leadership appointments I have made during my career as a university department head, dean, vice president, and president, I have never made one of which I am more proud. In the beginning, I had high expectations for Doris. I set lofty goals for her. She has exceeded every one of them, and added accomplishments beyond my imagination. She is a role model for every student who embarks on a collegiate experience and for every faculty member who seeks to contribute to the fullest of her or his ability.

I thank her for her friendship. I thank her also for her significant contributions to my University of Hawai`i presidency, to the University of Hawai`i over the many years, to the State of Hawai`i, and to academia as a whole.

References

Boyer, E. L. (1983). *High school: A report on secondary education in America*. New York, NY: Harper and Row.

Boyer, E. L. (1987). *College: The undergraduate experience in America*. New York, NY: Harper and Row.

National Commission on Excellence in Education. (1983). *A nation at risk: The imperative for educational reform: A report to the nation and the secretary of education, United States Department of Education*. Washington, DC: Author.

n her narrative, Doris Ching gives a biographical sketch that serves as a background for her incredible career path. While she would never promote herself, there is no question that she is an exceptional leader, role model, and mentor who has had a profound impact on higher education through her various administrative and volunteer positions. Because she has a proven record of enhancing the quality of programs, institutions, and operations, she continues to be asked to serve in interim leadership positions even into her official retirement.

Ching notes that her parents lacked formal education, and she was the "first of all generations in my family to complete a college education." Today in higher education, there is a special focus on *first-generation students*. When Ching completed college, there was no financial aid or other supports for students who were the first in their family to attend college. Completing college without institutional support took grit, hard work, and a belief that she could accomplish her dream of being a teacher. There was no question about whether she would achieve her dream.

In addition to an unwavering optimism about her abilities to achieve, other patterns that track through Ching's career journey are being rewarded for creativity and hard work with new opportunities, employing collaborative decision making as a leadership strategy, seeing the possibilities for enhancing programs and giving staff a voice, and staying abreast of developments in higher education and the world and using what she learned to support needed change.

Though her accomplishments have been recognized and rewarded with honors, as an Asian American woman, Ching has faced double discrimination regarding her ability to be an effective administrator because of stereotypes and misunderstandings about the qualities of successful leaders. Because of these experiences she is a strong advocate for not accepting and condoning stereotypes about Asian Americans as strong leaders.

Ching has made history not only as an Asian American, but as a woman and a woman of color. She has been a pioneer in her various career roles. As Albert Simone, former president of the University of Hawai`i, noted about Ching in a 2015 commencement address, "Both men and women, alike, could not have a better role model or guiding light."

—Gwendolyn Jordan Dungy

Index

A

Abelmann, Nancy, 182–183
Accapadi, Mamta M., 113–138
  ambition and, 130
  authenticity and, 113, 121
  background of, 113, 116, 128
  Black-Latinx/a/o-White racial paradigm
      and, 121
  cisnormativity and, 119, 123
  classism and, 119, 123
  cultural humility and, 125–126, 137–138
  diversity and, 121, 131–135, 138
  doubt and, 115–116
  Dungy on, 137–138
  identity and, 119–125, 137–138
  institutional missions and, 127, 129, 134
  leadership and, 117–120, 122, 124, 127–
      128, 133–134, 138
  LGBT students and, 121–122, 124
  liberation and, 120, 122, 127–128, 130
  mentors and, 116–119, 122, 137
  multicultural affairs and, 121, 125, 132–
      133, 138
  narratives and, 115–116, 121, 129–130
  oppression and, 119–120, 123
  power and, 121, 126
  privilege and, 120–121, 125
  racism and, 118–119, 123–125
  Roper and, 122, 129, 131–136, 138
  Rumi and, 120
  sexism and, 119, 123
  skills of, 133–135, 138
  social justice and, 120, 125–128, 131, 137
  sororities and, 118–119
  student affairs and, 116, 120, 127
  transformation and, 116, 132
  values and, 126–127, 135
  yoga sutras (Patanjali) and, 128–130
Activism. *See also* Social justice

diversity and, x
Gonzalez and, 171–174, 177, 186–187,
    189
identity and, x
Jackson and, 69–70, 87
Kimbrough and, 207
Parham and, 232
privilege and, x
racism and, x
social justice and, ix–x
University of Missouri protests (2015) and,
    ix, 207
ADHD (attention deficit hyperactivity
    disorder), 69
Adichie, Chimamanda Ngozi, xiii
Administrators. *See also* Higher education;
    Multicultural affairs; Student affairs
  diversity and, x, xiv–xv, xvii, 60, 193, 201
  higher education and, 60–61
  priorities of, 233
  student success and, 257
African Americans. *See also* Historically Black
    colleges and universities
  fraternities and, 194–197, 201–205,
      219–220
  Jackson and, 67, 73, 82, 88
  Kelly and, 102
  Kimbrough and, 194–197, 201–205,
      219–220
  Parham and, 225, 229–230
  Roper and, 154
  stereotypes about, 43–44, 182
  White and, 43–45, 49, 51, 63
Albany State University, 191, 205–208, 210,
    213–215
Ambition
  Accapadi and, 130
  Carvajal and, 6, 9, 24–25, 35
  Ching and, 257–258, 262, 275, 289
  Gonzalez and, 180, 184